# Impact Investing at a Crossroads

There is no questioning the enthusiasm that welcomed impact investing as an alternative approach to making investments: Take account of both financial returns and the social and environmental impacts. But there is no denying that the approach has fallen well short of expectations

Impact investing has shown great promise as a major transformational investment paradigm, but in practice under-performing woefully and its prospects are dimming: It comprises less than 1% of the world's equity investments, and too many claims of success are more about marketing and reputational value than hard evidence of positive social impacts. Drawing on over a decade of hands-on experience, this book presents a unique combination of a how-to guide and a reimagining – new models, frameworks, techniques, and tools – of what impact investing could be and could accomplish. It points to a new direction for future impact investments: achieve higher financial returns, more positive social and environmental impacts, and lower risks than conventional investments. Readers will learn what actions should be taken at each stage of impact investing, and which models, analytic frameworks, and techniques to use – and how to use them – for optimal results.

This book offers a step-by-step guide to how impact investing can achieve its promise of transforming global investments into a powerful positive force for change. It is an inspiring and comprehensive resource for anyone who wants to understand how impact investing works and how it can be done better, from professionals at foundations, international NGOs, consulting firms, and government agencies, to students of finance, public policy, ESG, sustainability and international development.

**John J. Forrer,** Director, Institute for Corporate Responsibility; Research Professor, Strategic Management and Public Policy; and Associate Faculty, School of Public Policy and Public Administration at George Washington University. He leads the activities of the ICR and teaches and conducts research on corporate social responsibility, economic sanctions, sustainable supply chains, public-private partnerships, business and peace, ESG, and impact investing.

**Terry R. Gray** has been working internationally in the field of impact investing for the past fifteen years. He is currently the Executive Director at Impact Bridges Group, a professional service social enterprise, that specialize in investment appraisal, risk analysis, impact measurement, and management of social and economic development projects and small and growing business.

# Impact Investing at a Crossroads

A Pathway Forward

John J. Forrer and Terry R. Gray

Routledge
Taylor & Francis Group

NEW YORK AND LONDON

Designed cover image: Faye Mao

First published 2025
by Routledge
605 Third Avenue, New York, NY 10158

and by Routledge
4 Park Square, Milton Park, Abingdon, Oxon, OX14 4RN

*Routledge is an imprint of the Taylor & Francis Group, an informa business*

ISBN: 9781032233659 (hbk)
ISBN: 9781032233642 (pbk)
ISBN: 9781003276920 (ebk)

DOI: 10.4324/9781003276920

Typeset in Sabon
by Deanta Global Publishing Services, Chennai, India

# Contents

# Acknowledgements

We have been thinking about the ideas we discuss and the arguments we make in this book for a long time. Years of research on, and practical experience with, impact investing have shaped our ideas and informed the new slant we present in this book. But we would not have had success developing and formalizing many of our claims and observations without the substantial and enduring contributions of numerous colleagues, partners, and research assistants.

Thomas Niemann, Ford Motor Co., Cheryl Self, World Vision, and Meaghan Chappell, George Washington University were great partners and co-collaborators in building and developing the Better World Learning Community (BWLC) from which many of our ideas about impact investing originated. Angela McConnell, Northern Virginia Veterans Association, Peggy Tadej, Norther Virginia Regional Commission, and Thomas Niemann were the 'brain trust' that developed the VetsDriveVets project to support more wholistic mobility solutions to problems faced by Veterans and advanced our thinking on the role impact investing could play. Prof. Pathmanathan Umaharan, University of West Indies, John Brittell, SideB Group, Scott Sklar, The Stella Group, and Mark Christian guided the creation of the Cocoa, Carbon and Community project for Trinidad and Tobago cocoa farms—which incorporated into the project many of the suggestions, and spurred many new ones, included in this book.

We also want to mention the many inspiring discussions and debates we have had over many years on the challenges and opportunities faced by impact investing with Steven Livingston, Grameen Foundation, Beris Gwynne, Incitare, Prof. Jeffrey Lenn, George Washington University, Amir Dossal, Global Partnership Forum, Seth Miller Gabriel, DBO, Jeremey Ebie, Phoenix Infrastructure, Peter Lazou and Maria Maloub, OtherDots Foundation, Bahman Kashi, Limestone Analytics, and Rodney Schmidt, Intellexys International.

Many George Washington students worked as research assistants on the above projects or assisted in research on impact investing: Andrea Cook, James Daley, Kathleen Harrington, Chase Johnson, Roxanne Kaplan, Ridhima Kapur, Megan Kavanaugh, Gabriela Malek, Jesus Marcial, Ryan Nasser, Gareth Norris, Puja Patel, Emily Pearson, Liam Perry, Anna Pelesh, Maria Alejandro Porras, Reagan Putnam, Priyadarshini Rakh, Daniel Reisch, Chandler Sease, Aditi Seth, Caroline Sroka, Camila Rueda Torres, Vincent Villenueve, and Jacob Willis.

A special thanks goes to the Impact Bridges Group members of the Advisory Group who provided input and assistance and to the IBG board members and work colleagues who provided support and insights. Recognition is given to Christian Ferraro, an Impact

Bridges Group colleague, who was instrumental in providing insightful comments and for his encouragement, especially during the final months of writing the book.

We owe Bruce Baron an immeasurable debt of gratitude as he proved himself to be an invaluable and patient advisor and copy editor as the book chapters took shape and eventually found their rightful form.

John would like to thank his wife Sharon for the patience, kindness, and love she provided during the many months of researching and writing this book.

Terry would like to express his deepest gratitude to his wife Susan who has stood by him during the writing of this book and during a career that often involved frequent travel. She provided support and help, along with his daughters Annet, Miriam, and Liana.

# Introduction

This book provides a fresh perspective on impact investing. Impact investing is a powerful idea and it has the potential to bring about radical improvements in the prosperity, health, security, and well-being of communities worldwide who otherwise face bleak prospects for their futures. In fact, it is a near certainty that the United Nations Sustainable Development Goals will not be achieved without a robust contribution from impact investors. But despite all the enthusiasm for, discourse on, exhortations made, and experience with impact investing—the very idea of impact investing is at risk of falling out of favor and languishing as a once interesting movement that ultimately lost its way.

First, it is underperforming woefully. Even when documented through self-reporting surveys, impact investments comprise less than one percent of all global investments. And that level of impact investments is no doubt overly optimistic. The United Nations estimates that $5 trillion to $7 trillion per year between 2015 and 2030 is needed to achieve the SDGs globally. And there is a current funding gap of around an estimated $4 trillion (World Economic Forum 2023). Yet recent estimates project that impact investments (i.e. from the pool of assets under management) could only cover—at best—12% of that need; and that is putting a positive spin on the situation to say the least. It is true that many impact investments focus on SDG topics. And while reports on which SDGs are the most popular targets of impact investors (e.g. Goal #2 (Hunger), Goal #7 (Energy), Goal #13 (Climate Action)) may vary, they concur that impact investors in SDGs are heavily weighted to only a few of the SDGs. Finally, impact investments have been found to be typically concentrated in a limited number of countries. In short, impact investing as currently practiced is too small, too narrowly focused to produce the transformational effects advocates hope for. If we are being honest, at this point, impact investing is much more about the 'gung-ho' than the 'know how'.

Second, without a doubt, there are many, many impact investors that are using innovative financing to deploy capital to funds, firms, and projects that strive to make major positive social impacts while offering financial returns acceptable to their investors. There are plenty of lists that toast the best impact investors. But there are even more firms touting their impact investments whose actual results are suspect at best and whose impact investments are indistinguishable from conventional investing after you scrape away the marketing. Our point is that it is difficult for investors to distinguish truly impactful investing opportunities amongst all those claiming to be making impact investments. The prevalence of the 'greenwashing', boosterism, and marketing that favor investments that are not so

DOI: 10.4324/9781003276920-1

impactful—or their actual impact is not in fact known—is crowding the genuine impact investors and stifling the future growth of impact investing.

Third, the current practice of impact investing is way too difficult, takes too long, and costs too much. There are numerous barriers to mobilizing capital for impact investments, especially in low- and middle-income countries. There are little to no market incentives for making impact investments ever more impactful. Data to measure social benefits is typically expensive to collect and often unreliable. The cost of an appraisal on potential investments takes up too much time and money. For innovators with new impact investment ideas there is little funding available to conduct the feasibility study that impact investors typically require in order to make an investment decision.

The good news is there are many lessons learned that have been harvested from both successes and disappointments. And there are the experiences of innovative financing models and techniques—such as public-private partnerships—that have been successful in mobilizing private capital to invest in public infrastructure. These insights and experiences lay the foundation for repositioning—and thereby revitalizing—impact investing in the future. Our vision for impact investing is founded on what was once referenced as the 'Holy Grail' of impact investing: investment opportunities that offer greater financial returns, more social benefits, and lower risks than alternative investment opportunities. Our idea for impact investing is not to presume that financial gains must be sacrificed and used to create positive impacts; we argue that investments that solve some environmental or social problems can be structured to be synergistic and expand both financial and social ROIs. What we offer in this book is a way to achieve that vision and a new way to think about and conduct impact investing in the future.

Impact investing may appear to be a modest re-orientation of conventional investing. Start with the traditions, norms, assumptions, and practices of investing where financial return—mediated by risk—is the standard of success, add in some positive social outcomes, shake well, and there you are. But after nearly 15 years of efforts selling impact investments to investors, many barriers to making a smooth transition from investing to impact investing have presented themselves:

- A constant complaint among impact investors is the difficulties in finding 'good deals'
- Standard financing instruments often have few applications in emerging markets
- The pricing of risks often puts financing out of reach for small and growing businesses, even if they are creating positive impacts
- 'Greenwashing' undermines the authenticity of what are otherwise promoted as impact investments
- The branding of investments as 'impact investing' has greater value in the market than the demonstration of accomplishing the actual impact itself

Boosters of impact investing continue to hold conferences and webinars and write books and reports touting its advantages. The financial sector is flooded with investment funds, financial advisors, deal makers, and consultants that promote and sell 'impact investments'. And we share their enthusiasm for impact investing as a potential force for change in the world and linking the trillions of dollars of investments made every year to providing social benefits along with prospects for financial return that meet investors' expectations. But impact investing will remain a 'boutique' business unless we recognize that impact investing needs a fresh start and a new outlook.

If impact investing is to reach its full potential, we need to change our approach to deciding in what to invest in and our expectations about the results of those investments—and not just on the margins. We are not suggesting tweaks to the conventional approach to investing, but rather a wholesale reconceptualization of the idea of impact investing, the decision-making process employed to select impact investments, and the toolkit used to design, finance and manage impact investments—in short, we are proposing a new 'paradigm' for impact investing.

We detail the essential elements of such a new impact investing paradigm in extensive detail and scope in the book. We clarify the basic notion of 'impact investing' and offer an alternative conceptual model. We describe the impact investing process that would be used to identify, vet, and finance impact investment opportunities using this new approach. We offer a toolkit of how to design, finance, and operate future impact investments. And we describe new roles that governments, NGOs, and development finance institutions would play to support the new approach.

To be clear, we are not suggesting that the conventional practice of impact investing be abandoned. But a much clearer distinction needs to be articulated on what separates conventional investing from impact investing—right now it is a very fuzzy line. As we envision it, impact investing should be thought of as a profound and radical departure from the conventional investment norms—you cannot successfully just add the consideration of social impact as an add-on to investing and accomplish the full potential that the originators of the impact investing concepts sought. Recognizing impact investing as a radical departure from conventional investing is the first step to developing the new impact investing 'paradigm'.

## Why Is It Important?

Convincing investors to consider the social impacts of their investments is a powerful concept. It creates opportunities for (literally) billions of people to gain access to capital that could be applied to advance their health, security, and prosperity. Foundations, development agencies, corporations, and government agencies provide support for underserved communities, but the amount of funding available is eclipsed by the amount required. But engaging investors to think about how they might address and reduce social and environmental problems—locally and globally—opens up massive reserves in sovereign wealth funds, investment firms, banks, mutual funds, exchange-traded funds, and pension funds to be directed at solving the world's biggest needs as described by the UN's Sustainable Development Goals (SDGs).

A new impact investing paradigm can shift the discussion of impact from being about 'intentionality' to being about 'purposefulness'. Investments can be made in problem-solving activities—both efforts that have proven to be effective and new, innovative efforts that show great promise. Using such an approach would turn impact investing on its head. Rather than determining what makes for a good impact investment by assessing their financial returns and then documenting what positive social impacts could be achieved, we start with identifying investment opportunities in business, programs, and projects that help solve problems that are priority to the investor, such as:

- Climate change
- Migration and refugees
- World hunger

- Affordable housing
- Sustainable supply chains
- Global education
- Peace
- (There is no limit)

And then we apply the tools and techniques that can identify opportunities to generate revenue streams and lower risks to provide impact investors a financial return. This new approach means rethinking what we mean by impact investing, what we expect from impact investing, what impact investors invest in, and how we design, finance, and operate the activities financed by impact investments. To distinguish our proposed 'reboot' of impact investing from how impact investing is conceived and conducted today, we have branded it as I3: investing in innovation for impact.

It is important to say it plainly: The prospects for millions of communities around the world today are bleak. For most of them the chances of gaining access to the resources needed are slim to none. The way impact investing is conducted today, investors will understandably seek out those investment opportunities where the risks regarding an achievable social outcome are low-risk—the low-hanging fruit. But a re-imagined impact investing approach can open up the poorest communities for investments—reaching the 'high-hanging fruit' should be one of the goals of impact investing.

Finally, impact investments that are successful in achieving social impacts can in turn be leveraged to generate 'blended financing' arrangements. Foundations, development agencies, and corporations all struggle mightily to find and validate high-quality projects that are well-managed and offer high confidence in success. Impact investors can be the ones to source such projects and then other funds can be used to add program enhancements, add risk-mitigation investments, and expand the social impact side of the equation. If we continue to conduct impact investing the way we do now, none of these futures is possible to imagine. Adopting a new impact investing paradigm makes the impossible possible.

## Why Has Impact Investing Been so Misunderstood?

There are several reasons why impact investing in practice has yet to achieve its full potential for driving investments towards accomplishing positive social impacts. First, the idea of impact investing is elegant in its simplicity—adding social impacts to the investment decision-making process—but it contains some unintended ambiguities that open up the door for various interpretations of what type of investments qualify as impact investments. Second, many entities promote and advocate it for the potential benefits it can provide. But also, that enthusiasm has an understandable bias toward broadening the concept to include a wide range of investments that could be considered impact investments to build an ever-larger community of supporters. Third, selling impact investing is a growing industry, and the easier it is to sell an impact investment, the bigger the market, so there is a natural inclination to dilute the required significance of social impacts from investments so more investments can qualify as impact investments. The result of the boosterism on behalf of the idea of impact investing, and the growing market for selling impact investments, has resulted in impact investing being considered more of a brand than a specific undertaking. Fourth, as we have already mentioned, there are a limited number of real impact investors in the market. Interest in impact investing by investors may be growing, but the willingness to trade financial returns—being realistic—for social impacts has its limits. Fifth, if an investment is labeled as green, sustainable, or environmental, social, and governance (ESG) there is only so much interest in looking in detail behind the labeling. As long as the buyer and seller of an impact investment are content, the transaction self-defines what is considered an impact investment—at least for them. Sixth, the actual documentation of social and environmental impacts from investments can be expensive and unreliable despite best efforts. The cost of reporting and documenting the actual results adds to the cost of the investment, and since the actual social impacts may in and of themselves affect the financial returns of the investment, there is limited motivation on the part of all parties to be overly precise about quantifying the actual impacts.

The unfortunate experience of impact investing going through a transition from a commanding concept to a diluted brand is not unique. Other concepts that address the interests of business and society such as corporate social responsibility and sustainability have suffered a similar fate. And early warning signs are pointing to ESG heading down a similar path. Unless impact investing practices are changed in significant ways, it will suffer from a loss of credibility due to a widening gap between what is seen in practice of the claims of the potential for the concept. Expanding the level of impact investing by lowering the bar on what type of investments qualify may seem like a good strategy in an effort to grow and expand the practice, but once its reputation as a credible label becomes suspect, and people begin to make accusations of 'impact investing-wash' (and this is already occurring), the value of the idea to bring about change is undermined forever.

We present our new impact investing paradigm in thirteen chapters that speak to four broad topics. Chapters 1, 2, and 3 provide background on the concept of impact investing, the opportunities and challenges impact investing presents to investors, and lessons learned for the practice of impact investing respectively. Chapters 4, 5, and 6 combined provide a description of our new impact investing paradigm. Chapter 4 describes our reconceptualization of impact investing. Chapter 5 provides a comprehensive model of our proposed approach and its five key features. Chapter 6 details tools and techniques that are invaluable for designing impact investments that help discover investable projects that achieve the Holy Grail of impact investing.

Chapters 6 through 12 provide a detailed description of the stages of the impact investing appraisal process and the appropriate assessments and analyses employed to identify, select, and finance an impact investment. Finally, Chapter 13 identifies the different roles institutions will need to consider playing in order to support the new impact investing paradigm.

## Reference

Zhan, J. X., Casella, B., Wambui, R., & Vine, R. (2023, September 18). 'See why trillions are needed to bridge the SDG financing gap #sdim23'. *World Economic Forum*. https://www.weforum.org/agenda/2023/09/why-trillions-more-are-needed-to-bridge-the-sdg-financing-gap/.

# Chapter 1

# Impact Investing
## What's the Big Idea?

The basic idea behind impact investing is pretty straightforward—investors invest in assets that generate social benefits in addition to the traditional expectation of financial returns. Impact investors seek both positive social and financial return on investment (ROI). Impact investing is a powerful concept and a relatively new approach. The idea has been warmly received by academics and practitioners alike. From the early days of introducing the idea of impact investing to recent discussions, the enthusiasm for the idea has been very strong. We have identified a few examples of champions of impact investing in Box 1.1 for readers who may want to explore the topic in greater detail than provided here.

---

**BOX 1.1   ADVOCATES FOR IMPACT INVESTING**

Bugg-Levine, Antony and Jed Emerson. *Impact Investing: Transforming How We Make Money While Making a Difference.* 1st ed. Jossey-Bass 2011.

Rodin, Judith and Margot Brandenburg. *The Power of Impact Investing: Putting Markets to Work for Profit and Global Good.* Wharton Digital Press 2014.

Simon, Morgan *Real Impact: The New Economics of Social Change.* Nation Books 2017.

Cohen Ronald. *Impact: Reshaping Capitalism to Drive Real Change.* Ebury Press 2020.

---

Impact investing has been identified as 'a turning point in the evolution of global finance'. Some have suggested that enormous profits are waiting for investors savvy enough to embrace this new approach. And some have labeled impact investing as a transformational investment vehicle and a positive disruptive force, while others have noted that impact investing could help us take on the greatest challenges we face—climate change and lack of access to health care, water, and affordable housing for billions of people—with better prospects for success than philanthropy and government programs. And some even see in impact investing a means to reshape capitalism itself no less and bring about greater equality and shared prosperity in the world.

The enthusiasm for impact investing has been embraced by development finance institutions as well. The U.S. International Development Finance Corporation (IDFC) promotes its

DOI: 10.4324/9781003276920-2

commitment to 'supporting projects that deliver a significant and sustained positive impact in the developing world' and how it has 'developed an impact strategy that identifies priority sectors and strategic priorities and includes impact targets across each' (IDFC, n.d.). USAID's Center for Innovation and Impact argues that now investors are more 'focused on measuring the social impact of investments' and that they 'represent a shift away from the rigid dichotomy of once-perceived tradeoffs between social and financial returns toward a more dynamic and nuanced development finance architecture comprised of diverse sources of capital' (USAID, n.d.).

A report in 2020 by the International Finance Corporation identified USD $349 billion of impact investments (when intent, contribution, and impact measurement are identified) managed by 36 different development finance institutions (DFIs). The same report also identified 11 multilateral development banks (MDBs) cumulatively managing $18 billion in intended impact assets, and 67 other national development banks (NDBs) and regional development banks managing $1.32 trillion in intended impact assets (Volk 2021).

One of the great opportunities created by impact investments is expanded investment in communities that are 'investment deserts' with limited prospects for attracting attention from conventional investors. This opportunity is particularly important with regard to the United Nations (UN) Sustainable Development Goals (SDGs). The UN has set a target date of 2030 for achieving the SDGs. But it estimates that $5 trillion to $7 trillion per year between 2015 and 2030 would be needed to achieve the SDGs globally. Those projected levels of required investments translate into an estimated annual investment shortfall at current levels of funding of $2.5 trillion. Impact investing is the perfect approach to filling that gap.

For example, Lizz Welch, CEO of iDE, argues for the importance of investing in female entrepreneurs as the best way to reduce poverty (SDG 1). Women are more likely than men to invest in the health and education of their children. And compared to businesses led by men, those led by women are more likely to hire women as employees. Welch uses the experience of Salima Lungu Nosiku to illustrate her point: Salima is an entrepreneur in Zambia with an agro-supply business who has been able to grow it dramatically, resulting in positive social impacts such as job creation, higher living standards, and inclusive growth. Welch urges the global community to invest in women as a means to help achieve the SDGs and reduce poverty (Welch 2023).

> "Impact investments are investments made with the intention to generate positive, measurable social and environmental impact alongside a financial return."
> Global Impact Investment Network https://thegiin.org/impact-investing/ (last visited April 6, 2024)

The idea of, and the merits underlying, impact investing may be so obvious and intuitive that it does not seem worthwhile to spend much time scrutinizing the concept. Conventional investments seek the greatest financial return in the least amount of time with the least amount of risk. Impact investing adds positive social impacts to the list of expectations—simple enough. But we understand the concept of impact investing as being more complex and nuanced than it may appear at first, with unintentional ambiguities and loopholes embedded into the overall idea. And these uncertainties explain in large measure the failure of impact investing to achieve in practice what is so hopeful in theory.

## What Is Different about Impact Investing?

Before we dive deeper into what constitutes impact investing compared to traditional approaches to investing, it will be helpful to explain how the idea differs from other types of investments that also claim to be making the world a better place. Here are some other alternative investment strategies that have gained popularity in recent years:

- Socially responsible investments
- Green investing
- Sustainable finance
- Environmental, social, and governance (ESG)

Like impact investing, these terms also have some ambiguity around what types of investments would qualify, and different people use the terms in different ways. But each term is connected to a specific idea about investing and there are distinctions worth noting between these strategies. Here, we present what we find to be the distinguishing feature(s) unique to each concept. Our ultimate goal is to help provide some clarification on what the rationale is for having different terms for these similar or related approaches.

*Socially responsible investing* involves choosing or disqualifying investments based on specific ethical criteria. Choosing socially responsible investments is often based on the nature of the business of the company. Investment decisions can be made regarding an individual firm or an ETF (exchange-traded fund) or mutual fund that itself invests only in responsible companies. One common approach for investors is to employ 'screens' to identify business sectors or Individual firms whose operations or products or services cause significant societal harm. Alcohol, gambling, and tobacco are commonly targeted sectors, but the potential list of perceived harmful sectors and firms is unbounded: firearms, sugar-sweetened beverages, pornography, human rights abuses, fossil fuels, and private prisons get their share of attention as well. The concept is to avoid investing in firms that use the money to make a profit at the expense of ecological and/or human suffering.

*Green investing* involves investments aligned with advancing eco-friendly business practices and the conservation of natural resources. It can have more specific targets and restrictions, but the environment is such a dominant phenomenon in day-to-day life that there are endless possibilities for investments that would qualify as green investing. The focus can be on a wide array of environmental issues, such as carbon, waste, water, pollutants, biodiversity, harmful chemicals, microplastics, and deforestation. Any investment that reduces environmental degradation and helps to restore ecological health by eliminating externalities qualifies.

*Sustainable finance* takes a broader view of the challenge of how to invest in steady, long-term growth while taking environmental and social factors into account. Investors are seeking alternatives to the 'unsustainable' approach of disregarding the impact that global and local business operations can have on the planet and people. The aim is to minimize harm to the planet— and today particularly on easing the damage caused by climate change—and to improve the health, prosperity, and security of vulnerable communities while supporting long-term growth. This approach recognizes the interdependencies of a company's prospects for growth and the social and environmental conditions in which it does business. Sustainable finance looks for the long-term benefits that mitigating and/or avoiding environmental crises and poor social conditions can generate back to the firm. Sustainability bonds are one financial instrument commonly used for sustainable financing. Alphabet (the parent company of Google) completed in 2022 the allocation of the proceeds of its 2020 $5.7 billion sustainability bond to these ends.

*ESG* is the newest approach used to select investments that aim for more than just financial returns. ESG investing highlights the fact that environmental, social, and governance issues can have powerful effects on investment risks and financial returns for some firms. Numerous competing ESG frameworks and standards are promoted by third-party certifiers, consulting firms, advocates, development finance institutions, and governments. Climate change and how firms are adapting their business strategies to accommodate future changes in the environment (e.g. warmer temperatures and their impact on cities, agriculture, and diseases; more violent and more frequent storms; rising water levels, etc.) have been the lead topics for ESG. But other ESG topics include ending deforestation and promoting conservation; diversity, equity, and inclusion (DEI) in the workplace; social justice; corruption; and corporate board diversity.

All four approaches summarized above describe an approach to investing that aims self-consciously at improving society through investments, whether the sought-after outcomes are grounded in avoiding negative impacts or advancing positive impacts. Why, then, do we need such a concept as impact investing? Given the extensive choices available to investors who consider matters other than financial returns, what added value does impact investing approach provide?

## Impact Investing: Theory versus Practice

We believe that the concept of impact investing deserves to be considered as different and separate from other approaches to investing that take account of non-financial consequences. What distinguishes impact investing is its attempt to create something positive (rather than avoiding something negative), the obligation to measure impacts, and the fact that those impacts must be intentional. These three traits require an investment process, data analyses, decision-making criteria, and monitoring that differ from what is required to achieve the goals of the other alternative investment approaches.

And yet, after more than a decade of practice, even those people who are enthusiastic about impact investing, make their living advising on or making impact investments, or teach about impact investing, still have some fundamental, unresolved concerns about putting the idea into practice. What set of investments actually qualify as an impact investment? How precisely and reliably does the impact need to be measured? What if the positive impacts are only temporary—do they qualify as an impact investment? What is to be done about the problem of 'impact-washing'?[1] If an impact investment produces a similar financial ROI and similar results as a conventional investment, does it still qualify as an impact investment? What if an investment accomplishes the intended social impact but also causes harm in other ways—is it still an impact investment? We believe that those and other lingering questions are not hair-splitting but important issues that deserve to be addressed. The accepted definition of impact investing has a common-sense appeal, but attempts to operationalize it have revealed several shortcomings in the basic conceptualization. We argue that the uncertainty over how impact investing distinguishes itself from other investment approaches in practice is the consequence of the less-than-robust definition used to explain which investments are 'impact investments' and which ones are not.

First, you don't have to think about impact investing for very long to realize that all investments could be classified as 'impact investments' in some way shape or form. That is, all investments have some type of positive impact, even if small or unnoticed. For example, an investment in establishing a chain of Kentucky Fried Chicken restaurants in Uganda will generate positive social impacts. It will create jobs and expand business operations through the supply chains associated with the restaurants. In low- and medium-income countries, the creation of jobs and the expansion or creation of new businesses can have very positive social impacts. However, although investing in Kentucky Fried Chicken stores generates positive impacts, no one who is serious about impact investing would label a KFC franchise as an 'impact investment'—or should they? Or what if a Coca-Cola bottling plant in India invests in technologies that require less water to sterilize their bottles? Why isn't that impact investing? It would draw less water from communities where water shortages and droughts have devastating effects on local populations. Or is such an investment really an example of conventional investing—basically, ways to lower operating costs, reduce operating risks, improve stakeholder relations, and enhance the company's reputation among their customers who care about sustainability?

Since impact investing and conventional investing both achieve positive social benefits, it is easy to understand the ongoing uncertainty over which investments deserve to be labeled as impact investments and which ones do not. This ambiguity has created both an opportunity and a dilemma for the impact investing industry. The opportunity is for investment firms and advisors to compete for investors' capital based on the scale and scope of their projected (and subsequently reported) social impacts. The dilemma lies in the advertising of conventional investments as if they were impact investments, because it is so difficult to discern one type from the other.

Second, the Global Impact Investment Network's (GIIN) definition of impact investing anticipates just such a definitional muddle by clarifying that impact investments are also distinguished from other investments by their 'intention to generate positive, measurable … impacts'. Adding intentionality and metrics into the equation offers a more specific idea of what qualifies as impact investing, but it doesn't blunt the problems regarding the difficulty of translating the theory of impact investing into practice. Investments in restaurant franchises could be made with the goal of creating jobs intentionally. And quantifying the number of jobs created does encounter many methodological challenges, but measuring the number of jobs created is a commonplace metric. The GIIN definition's requirements of intentionality and quantification don't fully close the unintended loophole embedded in their definition.

Take the example of an investment in a new drying shed and related equipment for a coffee farm in Kenya. Harvested coffee beans are subject to mold growth. Under-drying the coffee beans results in damage and a reduction in how much can be sold and a loss of revenue. But over-drying the beans results in weight loss, and the accompanying loss of color also translates directly into lower coffee quality. When moisture drops below 10%, aroma, acidity, and freshness begin to fade away, and at 8% or below, these features have completely disappeared.

An investment in upgraded drying sheds and related equipment would lead to better quality control and would be projected to produce higher-quality beans that command higher market prices while creating less waste and yielding more beans to sell. The resulting positive impacts generated—all quantifiable—would include more money for the farm owner and workers, as well as more jobs associated with the expanded commercial activity for the community. And an impact investor might decide to invest in just such an opportunity because of the economic benefits it would bring to communities in emerging markets. But the positive effects that come from upgraded drying processes will produce the same outcomes irrespective of whether an investor intended those community-sustaining results or not. Under that scenario, how can anyone differentiate impact investments from conventional investments? The intentionality of a conventional investor and an impact investor may differ, but the actual positive impacts of their investments could well be identical.

Third, discussions of impact investing do not tease out how the effort to achieve both financial ROI and social benefits affects either of the two goals themselves. For many investors, an impact investment carries the underlying presumption that financial returns must be sacrificed to achieve the social benefits. The logic is as follows: for any given investment, any costs incurred that are directed at generating social benefits mean that those funds cannot be directed toward activities that could produce higher financial returns. This argument implies an unavoidable trade-off between financial returns and social benefits. But does that really make sense? Is that how it actually works? Must there always be a sacrifice of financial gains to achieve social impacts? Is that trade-off built into the DNA of impact investing?

That question is tough to answer. It can be difficult to compare the financial returns of impact versus conventional investing when—as we have argued—it is difficult to distinguish one type of investment from the other. But a study by the Royal Bank of Canada (RBC) examined over 40 major studies and found no evidence that socially responsible investing resulted in lower investment returns (RBC 2012). This finding is consistent with the GIIN's 2017 Annual Impact Investor Survey (Mudaliar et al. 2017), which found that the majority of respondents achieved market-rate returns, with 91% claiming their returns met or exceeded their professional expectations (CNote 2020).

The conventional definition of impact investing does not address the mechanics of precisely how impact investments accomplish their two goals simultaneously. Does it happen when the investment is made into the firm (input)? Or is it achieved through the operations of the business? Or is it associated with products and services sold and their use by customers? The haziness about how impact investments accomplish their dual goals leaves unresolved the key question for potential investors: is a lower financial return an unavoidable feature of impact investments?

Fourth, how does the joint goal of achieving financial returns and social impacts affect the risk profile of the entire investment? Are impact investments implicitly more risky than conventional ones? One standard joke at a large investment firm was that it would assign potential investments to the 'impact investment fund' whenever the investment risks were considered too great for conventional investing. The logic behind assuming that impact investment risks are higher than conventional investment is drawn from the same logic as assuming that financial returns are lower: funds spent to achieve social impacts could have been used otherwise to take risk mitigation actions.

An example that contradicts that assumption is the growing interest in Peace Bonds. Peace Bonds are modeled after Green Bonds. which are financing instruments that raise capital to invest exclusively in environmentally friendly projects. Similarly, Peace Bonds raise capital to invest in projects that reduce violence and conflict. Investments in a conflict or post-conflict zone face high-risks due to the potential disruptions to construction and operations. But a Peace Bond could be used to develop an investment in a solar farm in that same conflict zone that would ensure access to electricity for all local communities. Regardless of ethnic or political affiliations, the investment would reduce energy inequities in the region, lessen political risks, and thereby reduce the cost of the project (GWICR n.d.).

Of course, Peace Bonds will reduce risks only when they are designed to lower existing conflict, which means each investment needs to be tailored to local conditions. If we do not have thoughtful ideas about the interactions involved in attempting to achieve the two goals simultaneously—financial returns and social benefits—how could we predict with any certainty what the effects of an impact investing approach would be on overall project risk? For example, when the goal of impact investing is to generate financial returns and social benefits, it only makes sense to structure the investment and address the risks in such a way as to optimize both values. But is that what is accomplished in practice? And what techniques would we use to design and finance projects to accomplish that goal?

Fifth, the definition of impact investing does not account for other negative impacts that occur beyond the positive ones that could result from an investment. An impact investment may provide positive and measurable impacts, but what if it also causes social and/or environmental damage at the same time? The damage caused by the rapid growth of Fast Fashion in the apparel industry is gaining greater attention. The increased use of polyesters as material for apparel and the introduction of 'new seasons' every month—or more often—results in the production of low-cost clothing, worn only a few times and then discarded to make way for a new outfit. The trend has overwhelmed landfills and created a global business for shipping waste around the world, typically to emerging markets. A robust new market for buying and selling clothing—including luxury brands—has emerged, led by firms such as The RealReal or Poshmark. Expanding the market for used clothing could be viewed as an impact investment by keeping clothing out of landfills and extending its usable life. But the shipping of the items by sellers and then to buyers expands the sector's carbon footprint in the face of deep concerns over climate change. Does creating one positive impact count as impact investing if the activity also generates new harms? This issue could be addressed by adding in a requirement of *net* positive impact, but the methodological challenges of assessing the benefits and the costs comprehensively would be an evaluation nightmare.

All five of the issues discussed above detail the insufficient ability of the accepted definition of impact investing to help investors translate the inspiration of impact investing into practice. On one hand, the loose definition has helped to grow the sector. The broader the definition of impact investing, the larger the number of investments and investors are eligible. And a broad definition helps to attract new players to the impact investment space: investors, advisors, consultants, analysts. But it also limits the possibility of describing and promoting impact investing as a distinctive approach—not only distinctive from the other four approaches we discussed previously, but even from conventional investing. Such a situation helps explain why the whole field of impact investing has underperformed. If there is no consensus on what constitutes impact investing in practice, how can success be documented and promoted? How can best practices be identified and adopted? How can the results of impact investing be anticipated and the positive aspects accentuated or the negative ones reduced? How can investors discern the difference between conventional and impact investments?

## Investment First or Impact First?

In response to ambiguity over what constitutes an impact investment, some have turned away from thinking about the approach and instead have looked for guidance by describing the preferences of the impact investors themselves. A familiar distinction has been drawn between 'investment-first' and 'impact-first' investments. The idea is that some impact investors are more committed to the cause than others. Investors may be attracted to the idea of producing social benefits while reaping financial returns, but they may have significant limits as to how much of the financial return they want to forgo. They may not be in a financial position where they can afford to sacrifice much financial return in exchange for the social benefits, or they may just want more money back from their investments. Under such circumstances, investment-first investors might look at the potential social benefits with greater scrutiny and skepticism. If an investment-first investor is going to consider sacrificing some financial ROI for positive social benefits, those outcomes had better be certain. After all, such an investor is unlikely to give away some financial return without good assurances that it went to a good cause.

An impact-first investor takes an opposing view. For those investors, the main purpose of the investment is to bring about positive social benefits. But impact-first investors also want some return on their investment, even if it is below market rates. People may be motivated by the opportunity to use their money to bring about positive social change in the world (or their neighborhood), but they are typically not independently wealthy and need to think about their own future savings as well. For these investors, impact investing is not charity. Some family philanthropy offices, which might have provided grants to support program activities addressing social problems, can be frustrated with the lack of impact they achieve, and have turned to impact investments instead. And some impact-first investors may not actually be interested in receiving a financial ROI from their investment, but they may call for a validated theory of change, a rigorous business case, and well-established metrics and reporting requirements—typical prerequisites for impact investments—in the hope that these processes will improve the prospects for successful positive outcomes in the activities they are financing.

Using these alternative categories as shorthand provides one way to distinguish between different types of impact investors, but the dichotomy does not in fact help to clarify what constitutes an impact investment. There will always be uncertainty as to where to draw the line between the two types of investors and how to know when the financial return is insufficient to attract an investment-first investor, even if the projected social impacts are sufficient to attract impact-first investors. Moreover, the two labels are applicable only *ex post facto*—after the investment is made and the preferences of the impact investor can be assessed. They cannot give us any insights *ex ante*—before an investor invests—because there are no means to clearly distinguish how to categorize the two types of investors prior to an actual investment decision.

Rather than providing a useful way to distinguish two types of impact investments, shifting the focus from the investment and its consequences to the investor's expectations does not help to clarify what constitutes an impact investment; it only muddies the waters further. Relying on the investor's expectations as a guideline only reinforces the proposition that impact investing is in the eye of the investor, which makes any defined conception of impact investing meaningless—because now it is an impact investment whenever an impact investor decides to invest in it. This perspective is rooted in conventional financing. No matter what anyone thinks about the attractiveness of an investment opportunity, in the end, it is the investors who decide, according to their investment goals, mandates, risk tolerance and best judgement. An investment isn't 'good' or 'bad' in advance; it is simply an opportunity to be evaluated. Investment decisions are all transactional.

Supporters of impact investing have a stake in promoting the idea and the results that have been achieved thus far. But the absence of a rigorous definition or a robust model of, impact investing has caused impact investing to be dragging its anchor. It cannot achieve its full potential without a clearer, easily demonstrable concept of what distinguishes impact investing from conventional investing. Sharpening the robustness of the definition of impact investing may appear to be only an academic exercise, but this is not the case. One unflagging (and justified) complaint about impact investing analysis cites the challenges involved in finding data to measure the social impacts. Poor data—along with expensive and unreliable data collection solutions—plague those attempting to attract or retain investors in funds, firms, or projects that produce positive social benefits. The absence of good data is one matter, but poor data availability is also the result of ambiguous and fuzzy definitions of impact investing. If you do not know with precision what you should be trying to achieve, there is no way to measure it! The weakness of the operational definition of impact investing is itself a major impediment to measuring social impacts that would qualify as impact investing, and thereby a major impediment to the acceptance and popularity of impact investments themselves.

If the idea of impact investing is to realize its potential and create a powerful approach to using investments, it will need a new operating definition. The basic concept needs to be revitalized by considering carefully the challenges and opportunities impact investors face when attempting to discover and make investments that provide reasonable financial rewards and also make the world a better place.

## Note

1  Impact-washing is analogous to the more familiar idea of 'green-washing' where claims that investments produce environmentally friendly impacts are exaggerated or misrepresented.

## References

'Does impact investing equate to lower returns?'. (2020, April 30). *CNote*. https://www.mycnote.com /blog/does-impact-investing-have-lower-returns/.

GWICR. (n.d.). 'Investing in business and peace project | GW school of business | The George Washington University'. *GW School of Business*. Accessed 9 November 2023. https://business .gwu.edu/investing-business-and-peace-project.

Mudaliar, A., Dithrich, H., Schiff, H., & Bass, R. (2017, May 17). 'Annual impact investor survey 2017'. *The GIIN*. https://thegiin.org/research/publication/annualsurvey2017/.

RBC Global Asset Management. (2012, September). 'Does socially responsible investing hurt investment returns?'. *RBC Global Asset Management*. https://funds.rbcgam.com/_assets-custom /pdf/RBC-GAM-does-SRI-hurt-investment-returns.pdf?source=content_type%3Areact%7Cfirst _level_url%3Aarticle%7Csection%3Amain_content%7Cbutton%3Abody_link.

USIDFC. (n.d.). '"Approach to impact | DFC." U.S. International development finance corporation'. Accessed 9 November 2023. https://www.dfc.gov/our-impact/approach-to-impact.

Volk, A. (2021, July). 'Investing for impact | The global impact investing market 2020'. *Open Knowledge World Bank*. https://openknowledge.worldbank.org.

Welch, L. (2023, August 10). 'Why investing in female entrepreneurs is the best way to eliminate poverty: Impact entrepreneur'. *Impact Entrepreneur*. https://impactentrepreneur.com/why-investing-in-female-entrepreneurs-is-the-best-way-to-eliminate-poverty/?mc_cid=f222295dc1&mc_eid=aeb59b41cd.

Wilson, J., Sharma, P., & Fowler, R. (n.d.). *Capitalizing on the Emerging Landscape for Global Health Financing*. USAID Center for Innovation and Impact. https://www.usaid.gov/sites/default/files/2022-05/investing-for-impact-may2019-updated.pdf.

# Chapter 2

# Opportunities and Challenges for Impact Investors

Impact investing has an important role to play: filling in the gaps where government and private investing are currently inadequate or ineffective in addressing the often-desperate needs of underserved communities. The fundamental notion that investors could look to leverage their investments in ways that produce a positive social is very powerful, the significant conceptual laxness of the popular definition of impact investing notwithstanding.

Many investors have embraced the idea and put it into practice and have financed projects that have accomplished significant successes. There are a range of opportunities for impact investors to experience this success. These opportunities can be put into four investment capital categories.

## Social Enterprises

Social enterprises will be discussed later in the book, but for now it is important to know that a social enterprise is financially sustainable and has an intentional social mandate. It is argued that social enterprises are often the focus of impact investing. Social enterprises come in various forms and sizes and are located in low, medium, and high-income countries. The source of investment capital is often diverse and can range from individual loans through to institutional investors.

Social enterprises primarily create social value through their products and services; whereas, a for-profit company would ordinarily achieve their impact through their operations and how they source and produce products. Most social enterprises are very selective in their products and services as they are focused on their primary area of influence. As with all businesses, social enterprises will have secondary impacts that result from their supply chain, employee selection process, procedures and policies, and byproducts they might produce.

Social enterprises are focused on providing products or services that improve the lives of a targeted population. In delivering these products and services the environment will be given close attention both in their direct operations and in their supply-chain. Another common characteristic is the creation of high-quality jobs.

## Social Impact Funds

As mentioned above, the social enterprise can receive financing from a number of sources, directly from an individual, a family foundation, or from a more formal institutional lender such as an impact fund. In these cases, there will not be a direct relationship between the

DOI: 10.4324/9781003276920-3

entrepreneur and the investor. In these cases, investors have chosen to work with a social impact fund. There are many advantages for investors to work with a social impact fund. The most notable is the due diligence and managing the investment process. Potential investors should expect that a complete investment appraisal will have been conducted by the fund.

Christian Super is an Australian-based superannuation fund that serves over 28,000 members. Since its founding in 1984, Christian Super has pursued investments ethically aligned with Christian values. Of its $1.1 billion USD portfolio, 10% has been allocated to impact investments, managed by a dedicated team seeking environmental and social impact in tandem with risk-adjusted, market-rate return management fee. In selecting a social impact fund, a potential investor will initially want to align themselves with an investment fund that matches their sector, geographic location, or other interests and priorities. Another consideration for some investors is whether they want to invest through a specific type of fund. For instance, faith-based funds have become very popular. The Global Impact Investing Network (GIIN) has a faith-based repository that includes research, case studies, and other resources including webinars and books to align theology with impact investing. There are large and small funds. Christian Super has over 28,000 members with impact investments of over $110 million of its $1.1 billion portfolio. There are a growing number of small faith-based funds. As an example, Talanton invests in values-driven, growth-stage enterprises in E. Africa. These enterprises have an annual revenue of $500k to $5 million and are providing jobs for people living in poverty. Many investors are attracted to Talanton because of its investment appraisal process, but also because of the meaningful relationships that are formed with the social enterprise leaders and management team.

Other consideration that need to be considered by a potential investor are the stage of investment and the type of capital they provide--such as debt or equity. In the case of Talanton, investments are made in growth-stage social enterprises that have a proven track record and achieved annual revenue of at least $500k. Talanton provides debt financing and allows investors to use their existing Donor Advised Fund to transfer funds (Calvert Impact, n.d.).

Calvert Impact (formerly Calvert Impact Capital) hosts the Community Investment Note®. It has a 25-year history of providing positive social and environmental impact and financial returns on more than $2.5 billion of investor capital. Community Investment Note® proceeds are invested in support of mission-driven organizations that advance social, economic, and environmental justice. It invests across nine impact sectors based on the needs and opportunities in communities, as well as investor interest. Rigorous credit and impact risk management has contributed to a less than 1% loss rate in this portfolio since 1995. Calvert Impact is known for its low minimum requirement of $20 for investors to invest in their Notes.

In addition to knowing the investment stage, investors will also need to know what level of financial return is considered acceptable for their investments. Is a below-market rate of return acceptable if there are significant social impacts? A potential investor will need to know their willingness to have tradeoffs between financial returns and social impact. Some funds are designed to be impact-first which means there will often be a financial return, but it might not be a risk-adjusted return on the type of investment. In other words, emphasis is being given to achieving the highest level of social impact while still maintaining an acceptable financial return. LeapFrog uses private equity investments in high-growth enterprises in fast-growing markets. This investment strategy allows them to provide investors with a competitive market return on a similar risk profile. In contrast, Root Capital does not offer competitive financial returns, but uses strategic initiatives to reduce the risk with their investments. Blue Orchard, another impact-first investment fund, is known for its microfinance debt investments in small businesses and entrepreneurs.

## Real (Hard) Asset Impact

Very often tangible or physical assets such as farmland, affordable housing, and natural resources can lend themselves to impact investing when they are intentionally developed to improve environmental outcomes, such as improved livelihoods. Real assets, also sometimes referred to as hard assets, are physical assets that have a calculated and objective value. Their intrinsic value can be calculated because of the asset's substance and properties.

GIIN partnered with Cambridge Associates, a global investment firm, to develop performance benchmarks for hard or real assets. In their report, *The Financial Performance of Real Assets Impact Investments*, they present an analysis of the financial performance of hard/real assets in impact investing funds for the forestry, real estate, and infrastructure sectors.

Quantified Ventures developed the Soil and Water Outcomes Fund. It provides financial incentives directly to farmers who transition to on-farm conservation practices that yield positive environmental outcomes like carbon sequestration and water quality improvement. They provide new market opportunities and revenue streams for farmers by selling these environmental outcomes to public and private beneficiaries to meet regulatory and voluntary sustainability goals, such as scope 3 greenhouse gas emission insets. By stacking the many positive environmental outcomes of on-farm conservation practices, they deliver substantial per-acre payments to partner farmers partners and extremely competitive environmental outcome pricing to their customers. (Soil and Water Outcomes Fund, n.d.)

It should be noted that real assets are often not included in impact investing conferences and discussions because they are often limited to accredited investors. As with the many impact investing innovations, there are financial instruments being developed that allow retail investors to invest modest amounts in conservation, infrastructure, and other real assets that are contributing towards improving communities.

## Results-Based Financing (Impact Bonds)

Results-based financing (RBF) is also referred to as performance-based financing (PBF), payment by results (PBR), and in some cases as pay-for-performance (P4P). The two most common instruments in impact investing are social impact bonds (SIB) and development impact bonds (DIB). Both SIBs and DIBs are financing instruments that are premised on payment being made subject to certain outputs or outcomes being achieved. A conditional contract will provide the details of the payment terms. The payment metrics are the results that are being paid for is the central focus of an RBF agreement. SIBs and DIBs are discussed in detail later in the book.

Social Finance UK developed the first SIB that addressed the reduction of recidivism among prisoners released from the Peterborough prison in the UK. The first DIB was in Rajasthan, India where Instiglio worked with a nonprofit, Educate Girls, to improve their education programming impact. Instiglio has continued to do groundbreaking work using results-based approaches.

The use of RBF has provided government with a valuable tool for improving social outcomes. The Government Outcomes Lab based in the Blavatnik School of Government, University of Oxford has been a leading research and policy center that is examining the use of SIB and other instruments as effective and efficient means of improving social outcomes.

The number of impact investing opportunities has grown over the past fifteen years, but the pressing question is whether the supply of investment opportunities will allow the sector to grow and achieve its potential. The supply of investment opportunities is clearly insufficient, but the rationale for this is not always clear. In our experience, most of the fund managers are highly professional and are managing their portfolio of impact investments as well as any other investment manager. Still, there are a disturbing number of social impact funds that have never undertaken a proper investment appraisal of social enterprises or projects. Similarly, there are many social enterprises that are making claims of social impact, but without any verifiable evidence.

The pervasiveness of poor due diligence, greenwashing, and social washing presents a significant risk to the impact investing sector. There are several risks associated with a lack of quality investments that will inevitably lead to a lack of confidence in investors that will limit the potential of impact investing and achieving SDGs.

RepRisk is a Zurich-based leader in data science and ESG and business research. In their October 2023 report (RepRisk 2023) they mention

that a growing number of both public and private companies have been linked to misleading communication around environmental issues. Greenwashing risk has accelerated in Europe and the Americas, with the Banking and Financial Services sectors particularly exposed.

- In the past year (September 2022–September 2023), one in every four climate-related ESG risk incidents was tied to greenwashing, an increase from one in five in our last report
- The Banks and Financial Services sectors saw a 70% increase in the number of climate-related greenwashing incidents in the past year, compared to the year prior
- For many, the practices go hand-in-hand, with nearly one in three public companies linked to greenwashing also associated with social washing

## The Impact of Impact Investing

Unfortunately, despite all the enthusiasm for impact investing, the idea has underperformed thus far. According to GIIN's Annual Impact investor Survey, they estimate the size of the worldwide impact investing market to be $1.164 trillion (as of December 2021). The International Finance Corporation (IFC) has an even more bullish estimate: $2.3 trillion in global impact investments. But even considering the high-end of those estimates, that is still only around 2% of all global assets under management. Currently, impact investing is very much a 'niche practice'.

The underperformance of impact investing is also found in the types of impact investments being made. Research on impact investing reveals some common assets into which the money is invested. Many impact investing firms explicitly state that they link their investments to the SDGs.

Quantifying accurately the extent to which impact investors are targeting SDGs is a challenge. A 2018 survey by GIIN reported that Financial Services (including microfinancing) and Energy were the target of 28% and 14% of assets under management (AUM) respectively. Those numbers mean that two areas comprise nearly half of all the SDGs combined. By far the most popular SDG target for impact investors are SDG #7 and SDG #13. These two SDGs are linked to renewable energy and carbon financing. The contemporary, high-profile concerns about climate change have motivated impact investors to look for investments that will mitigate or reduce carbon emissions. Renewable energy technologies and carbon financing both respond to that interest while producing competitive financial returns for investors. But the enthusiasm for investing in SDGs #7 and #13 reveals the limited effect impact investing has had on the other SDGs. Impact investments in renewable energy and carbon emission reductions across global supply chains are not a bad thing. But impact investing cannot be considered significant when it takes a narrow view of what social impacts it is willing to address.

In a recent study it was found, 'Our analysis shows that most investment deals are directly or indirectly linked to only four SDGs: SDG 1 (no poverty), SDG 2 (zero hunger), SDG 3 (good health and well-being), and SDG 8 (decent work and economic growth)', 'As a result, many other SDGs are relatively underrepresented in the available impact investment deals'.

> Furthermore, most investment deals directly or indirectly contributing to the SDGs are highly concentrated in two regions—US and Canada, and Sub-Saharan Africa. Also, many emerging regions (e.g. Southeast Asia, the Middle East and North Africa) have a severe shortage of impact investment dealflow.
>
> (Islam and Rahman 2023)

Overall, the expressed excitement for impact investing has far exceeded its actual results, and the idea has not achieved the transformational sea change its originators sought—or at least not yet. The many great anecdotes that validate the benefits of trying to combine positive social impact and competitive returns do not mask the fact that making impact investments faces many challenges.

## Challenges to Impact Investing

Despite the enthusiasm for impact investing's potential to mobilize commercial financing in support of solving communities' problems, and especially achieving the SDGs, important questions persist about the effectiveness and scalability of current approaches to impact investing. The challenges are extensive and imposing:

1. 'Deal flow' is not flowing
   a. The cost of preparing impact investments, including the costs of measuring impact, is too high
   b. High project-level risks exist in low-income countries
   c. Detailed knowledge of local markets and investment opportunities is limited and expensive to acquire
2. Local capacity has significant gaps
   a. Entrepreneurial and project management capacities are limited
   b. Most participants have limited experience with innovative financing tools

   c. A major barrier is market risk arising from poor market governance and a weak enabling environment; this is the main barrier addressed by blended finance
3. Metrics on social impacts are tough
   a. Data collection can be expensive and unreliable
   b. Multiple social outcome metrics are available, making comparisons across different investments difficult
   c. Little is known about actual social returns on investment; typically, projects do not measure the social rate of return
4. Aligning goals across the impact investing ecosystem is difficult
   a. It is difficult to match impact investors with the right combination of investment platforms, project structures, and financial instruments through which impact investments are made
   b. Donor preferences may not align with local priorities, and assumptions about the SDG services people need and how to address them cannot always anticipate local conditions and preferences
   c. Non-profit organizations are not always receptive to an entrepreneurial approach and innovative techniques that seek to fund SDG services by mobilizing commercial financing
5. Greenwashing
   a. The cost of preparing impact investments, including the costs of measuring impact, is too high
   b. High project-level risks exist in low-income countries
   c. Detailed knowledge of local markets and investment opportunities is limited and expensive to acquire
6. Assessing success
   a. The cost of preparing impact investments, including the costs of measuring impact, is too high
   b. High project-level risks exist in low-income countries
   c. Detailed knowledge of local markets and investment opportunities is limited and expensive to acquire.[1]

The challenges faced by impact investors that are summarized above are well-recognized. But to provide a more detailed understanding of how these challenges slow down and inhibit impact investments, we need to take a closer look at them in context. First, we take a geographic focus and zero in on the experiences of impact investing in East Africa. Second, we examine the challenges in a specific sector, ecotourism. Third, we examine the challenges of measuring the positive impacts of impact investments in a policy context.

### Impact Investing in Eastern Africa[2]

One of the most promising attributes of impact investments is their ability to address important economic, social, and environmental issues in emerging markets. As mentioned earlier, very little impact investing activity is happening in middle-income countries and even less in low-income countries. We can learn much by looking at the opportunities and challenges encountered by impact investing efforts in East Africa.

The East African Community is an intergovernmental organization that comprises six countries in the African Great Lakes region: Burundi, Kenya, Rwanda, South Sudan,

Tanzania, and Uganda. Adding Djibouti, Ethiopia, and these countries together account for the fourth-largest GDP ($326 billion) in Africa behind Nigeria, South Africa, and Egypt. And this group of East African nations has had annual GDP growth averaging almost 6%, compared with only 3% for the continent overall.

East Africa's proximity to the Middle East and Asia, along with its internal infrastructure development in terms of rail, port, and air freight, means that these largely coastal nations are poised to continue to lead Africa's economic development in the coming decades, offering an excellent market for investors.

This opportunity aligns well with impact investors' interests in emerging markets. The expansion of the East African economies presents attractive prospects for investors seeking to invest now in anticipation of future growth. Countless opportunities exist for impact investors, but the current impact investment landscape is rife with challenges that prevent the industry from fully realizing impact within its investments. In particular, institutional capacity, financing infrastructure, and deal maturity all need strengthening.

Impact investing in East Africa is more of an art than a science at this point. Among the key challenges that still prevent impact investing from fulfilling its potential, three of the most important ones are (1) access to quality deals, (2) alignment among owners, investors, businesses, and needs, and (3) investment readiness.

**Challenge 1: Access to Quality Deals.** Too many investors do not see the value of making an internal investment in staff or offices on the ground. As a result, their teams must use third parties, fly into the region as outsiders, set up meetings for short periods of time, and then fly out without ever fully understanding the culture, politics, and nuances of the investment market.

Iungo Capital's Steven Lee is one impact investor who decided to build a team on the ground. He was a part of the Bid Network model, which scheduled investment trips from the Netherlands to East Africa to connect with businesses and make seed investments. Lee decided that to really understand the market, and to find the deals that made the most sense from an impact perspective, he needed to be on site. He identified a set of deals, ranging from $50,000 to $500,000, using an unorthodox method of walking and talking to businesses and assessing what fits best from a 'gut feeling' perspective.

Although rigorous investment requirements must still be met, the approach has changed how investments affect companies that would not otherwise have access to this type of capital. In Lee's words, 'Our long-term objective is to prove to the world that one can cost-efficiently deploy smart capital with a tangible social impact into lower ticket size investments in these markets with a reasonable financial return'.

**Challenge 2: Alignment.** Three types of alignment are relevant, based on the Amani Partners investment group's experience in the East African market: (a) between owners and investors, (b) between businesses and investors, and (c) between capital structure needs and the investors' scope (transaction size, tenor, pricing, etc.). In the investment community, there are ongoing complaints that there is capital in the market but no qualified deals. Meanwhile, business owners contend that solid businesses exist but that investors are not interested in those ventures. This is the most rudimentary misalignment, and it is of a social nature. There is a clear disconnect between the expectations of the business owner and those of the investor, and too often the result is limited common ground on reasonable investment criteria.

The second alignment issue is between the business itself and the investor selection criteria. Investors have pre-established targets in terms of the industry, sector, and type of business in which they wish to invest. A vast majority of businesses in emerging markets are geared toward trade, leaving few options for investors to choose from.

The third alignment issue concerns the fact that most local firms put little effort, time, or resources into structuring the business to benefit from surrounding or external resources. When a business begins, it often has very little equity and may even be funded with debt, including shareholder debt. This works for only the first year or so, after which owners realize how much pressure interest payments place on the income statement. The pressure continues to grow. By the time the firm is looking for outside capital, its actual primary need is to restructure or completely buy out the debt. Investors interested in those scenarios are nearly nonexistent in East Africa.

To illustrate this challenge, consider a local stationery manufacturing company that started with no equity and mostly debt. Once its operations began, it opened a working capital line at the local bank and obtained a letter of credit, but it soon learned that it could not expand as fast as it wanted to based on the locally available commercial capital. The reason? Specified debt-to-equity ratios and single-borrower limits on total outstanding loans. The owners' original strategy was to list their equity as shareholder loans, due to the local tax regime, and reduce their tax burden. Clearly, a new legal structure is needed to support greater impact investment into these markets.

**Challenge 3: Investment Readiness**. The business culture in East Africa is ruled by informality. Couple this with the fact that trade is the primary business activity, and there is little incentive or desire among micro, small, and medium enterprises (MSMEs) to establish proper internal reporting systems, proper documentation, effective management controls, good governance practices, or any formalized business processes. This approach to business formation, which exists throughout the region, is not in sync with business administration norms in most Western societies. This East African business culture demonstrates why the region needs to enhance investment readiness so that investments will be placed in firms that are creating an impact but cannot provide the necessary documentation to convince investors. Specific challenges to investment readiness also include extended origination times, under-skilled labor, and limited market knowledge.

It was Amani Partners' original thesis that deals could be transacted within 12 months. However, the company soon realized that the gestation period for deals requires upwards of 36 months. This timing hinges on the owners' comfort level with advisors and investors, in addition to their degree of preparedness with regard to documentation. Weak governance is frequently reflected in the naming of children as shareholders and directors. This arrangement leads to non-responsive boards with little power or authority to oppose the decisions of the board chair or create changes in the firm's operations.

The labor pool in East Africa is also not as experienced as investors expect it to be. Because of this, firms cannot grow and scale up. Many managers have no experience managing large amounts of cash, which require stronger controls, robust systems, and arm's-length transactions. A limited knowledge of markets adds to the pressure put on smaller firms seeking to expand and understand how to work with new customers.

In summary, opportunities abound for impact investors in East Africa if adjustments could be made in protocols and investment criteria so as to accommodate local conditions, practices, and priorities. The market is maturing in terms of its institutional capacity, and its growth prospects are the best in the world, albeit with substantial risk. Examples in the digital financial services and healthcare industries demonstrate that local entrepreneurs, if supported with less restrictive capital, can build companies that deliver much-needed value, products, and services to the local market. Even with the speculative opinions issued by the large ratings agencies, investments can thrive if local advisors are present to ensure transparency and local knowledge to support investors. Investment funds would benefit from establishing local partnerships with professional advisors.

Impact investors can expand investment opportunities by creating innovative financial products that are tailored to the local market and employ innovative technologies to support distribution and outreach. However, investors themselves must move away from traditional screening guidelines and must adopt clear criteria responsive to local conditions. Opportunities for impact investment are endless for investors willing to customize their products, engagements, and investment criteria for the local market. If we can think and act differently about how we approach impact investing in the East African market, we can deliver more value, more deals and, therefore, positive effects on the communities that impact capital is intended to serve.

---

### BOX 2.1 ECOLODGES EXAMINED

Il Ngwesi II Group Ranch, Kenya
CAMPFIRE Tholotsho North, Zimbabwe
Campi ya Kanzi, Kenya
Garonga Safari, Greater Makalali Private Game Reserve, South Africa
Kuzuko Lodge, Elephant National Park, South Africa
Apoka Safari Lodge, Uganda
Campo Ma'an, National Park in Cameroon
Treetops Lodge, Aberdare National Park, Kenya
Angama Mara, Maasai Mara, Kenya
Mfuwe Lodge, Zambia
Clouds Mountain Lodge Bwindi, Uganda

---

### Impact Investing in Ecolodges

Ecolodges offer a promising target for impact investors and Africa is a popular destination for those seeking close interactions with wild animals. The development community favors them for the jobs they create and the added investments they bring to underserved communities. Environmentalists favor them for the contribution they make to reducing environmental damage and carbon emissions and increasing conservation and biodiversity. The hospitality industry favors them as potentially profitable business ventures tapping into consumer interest in 'eco-friendly' products and services. But how should ecolodges be organized and managed to ensure sustainable financial, social and environmental returns on investments?

One interesting—yet understudied—aspect of the ecolodge business model is the impact that can result from the support for NGOs and MSMEs that promote conservation (i.e., conservation enterprises). In general, conservation enterprises are associated with specific positive outcomes as described in Table 2.1.

*Table 2.1* Positive Outcomes form Ecotourism

| | |
|---|---|
| Development | jobs |
| | promotes entrepreneurship |
| | promotes entrepreneurship for women |
| | economic growth |
| Environment | flora and fauna conservation |
| | biodiversity |
| | carbon reduction and mitigation |
| Tourism | improved financial performance |
| | reduced operating risks |
| | reduced financial risks |

The promise of successful business operations for impact investors is supported by a strong understanding of how to design and operate ecolodges successfully that have been associated with generous financial returns. But despite their track record of profitability, ecolodges face numerous challenges that illustrate the challenges face by impact investments more generally.

For example, are the type of conservation enterprises which provide business value to the ecolodge the same as the ones with the greatest opportunities for scaling up their business operations? The literature discusses examples of conservation enterprises that have proved—and others that have not proved—to have positive impacts on the environment and communities. But the assessment of what constitutes success is mostly from the perspective of development, conversation, and/or sustainability. Those findings might inform the selection of which conservation enterprises to support and invest in, even if the selected firms may not have the best prospects for growth and expansion. Protecting flora and fauna, reducing and mitigating carbon emissions, providing income to needy communities, and supporting entrepreneurship can all accomplish sustainability and conservation goals and could create business value for an ecolodge. But there is no evidence that these same conservation enterprises have good prospects to grow and become an attractive investment for impact investors. Incorporating the focus on growth that investors require could results in supporting different conservation enterprises from those identified in and endorsed by the development and sustainability literatures.

Or, in a related situation, are the management teams proficient in operating conservation enterprises supported by the ecolodge also qualified to manage them as self-sustaining businesses? The literature does not address management issues related to the operation of ecolodges or partnerships with conservation enterprises. The management paradigms employed in operating non-profit organizations differ from those used in for-profit entities. There has been an effort over the last 30 years to encourage NGOs involved in development programs to operate in a more 'businesslike' fashion. But time has shown that managers working for non-profits may display management competence or excellence but may not possess the skills and experience required to operate a successful business—and that they may exhibit no interest in obtaining these skills. For this reason, the management team hired to operate conservation enterprises when they are initially funded by the ecolodge might need to be replaced at some point by a different management team better suited to operate a business. But firing people who have built up a social enterprise for the ecolodge has obvious negative implications and could undermine community support for the project.

These two examples of impact investing in specific contexts demonstrate how a potential impact investment that looks good on paper may not be a good investment and may not produce the social benefits associated with it after all. Many ecolodge customers like the idea that local entrepreneurs are supporting enterprises that make the world a better place—stimulating the local economy, supporting conservation efforts, and protecting local animals from poachers. But the costs and risks involved in financing such operations present real threats to the profitability of the entire ecolodge operation. Ecolodges provide a clear example of how impact investments that can provide impressive financial returns and substantial social and environmental impacts when considered separately can actually work against each other in practice.

A third context for understanding the challenges to impact investing is public policy. The determination of which impact investments are successful is also influenced by whether people take a market-based or policy-based perspective of impact investing. When impact investments are viewed as just another financial product offered to investors, then success is whatever the investor thinks it is. When an investment is made purely with the intention of receiving a financial return, then success means getting the greatest net return, in the shortest period of time, with the least amount of risk. But adding social impacts into the equation muddies those waters. It might seem that simply adding in the criterion of 'greatest social impact' would be sufficient. But social impacts themselves are so unique to the circumstances and the individuals affected that they are not easily compared across projects. Of course, it is possible to narrow the assessment of social impact to a simple measure, such as how many jobs are created, but that only ends up trivializing the quantification of the social benefits.

In contrast, when impact investing is viewed through a policy lens, then the success of impact investments is easier to assess against any given standards. Taking a policy perspective on impact investing places investors in the position of substituting for government policy and acts of charity. That perspective is one way to redirect impact investing and imbue it with a more precise purpose and mission. But the multitude of different and sometimes competing policy interests means that success is judged based on one's policy preferences, which are not always comparable. You cannot judge whether providing education to young girls in remote communities is better than combating climate change. In this instance, success becomes whatever the policy preferences say it is.

Impact investors can showcase many creative and thoughtful impact investments that keep fidelity with the idea of impact investing. But these are an outlier to the vast set of investments that face many difficult challenges in broadening the approach beyond a niche market. We believe these challenges can be overcome and impact investments can flourish. We have studied both the theory and the practice of impact investments and there is much to be learned from small but inspiring set of innovative impact investors blazing new trails to discover and finance projects that embody the idea of impact investing. There is also a lot to be learned by understanding the challenges that impact investments face and translating them into lessons learned so we can all avoid re-inventing the 'flat tire' when it comes to developing new approaches to impact investing.

## Notes

1 These findings draw from "Mobilizing Commercial Financing for the SDGs." *Impact Investing in Brief*. May 4, 2020. https://business.gwu.edu/sites/g/files/zaxdzs5326/files/GWSB_ICR_Impact _Investing_brief_v2.pdf
2 This section draws from the Working Paper, "Impact Investing in Eastern Africa." John Forrer and John Brittell. GW ICR (2022).

# References

Calvert Impact. (n.d.). *The Community Investment Note*. Calvert Impact. https://assets.ctfassets.net/4oaw9man1yeu/2XWqLgelMX909a0ouU2csD/fafa42652ee3a9e2617646bceef050bf/Calvert_Impact_Fact_Sheet.pdf.

Forrer, J., & Brittel, J. (2021). *A Closer Look: Impact Investing in Eastern Africa* [Unpublished Manuscript]. George Washington University.

Islam, S. M., & Rahman, A. (2023, February 5). 'Impact investment deal flow and sustainable development goals: "Mind the gap?"'. *Accounting & Finance*, acfi.13068. https://doi.org/10.1111/acfi.13068.

'On the rise: Navigating the wave of green washing and social washing'. (2023, October). *RepRisk*. https://www.reprisk.com/news-research/reports/on-the-rise-navigating-the-wave-of-greenwashing-and-social-washing?mtm_campaign=content_greenwashing_report2023.

Soil and Water Outcomes Fund. (n.d.). https://theoutcomesfund.com/.

# Chapter 3

# Lessons Learned

Examining the theory and the practice of impact investing evokes feelings of inspiration and discouragement. Impact investing has great potential to bring new money into communities that otherwise have little or no chance of attracting investment. Unfortunately, in actual practice, it has usually become more about checking boxes than functioning as an innovative force for change. On the positive side, however, countless innovations in the field are transforming the lives of people and communities.

We can learn much from past experiences to inform strategies that will move impact investing away from checking boxes and toward meaningful innovation. Examining both failures and successes for the lessons they can teach us will help us rethink and 'reboot' impact investing so that it has a better chance of realizing its ambitions.

## Impact Investing Is Not a Tweak

If the conventional approach to investing is described as an ice cream sundae, then much of impact investing as practiced today is an ice cream sundae with a cherry on top. That is one of the main reasons why impact investing has yet to launch. Representing impact investing as just a minor adjustment or 'add-on' to conventional investing is an understandable approach. Most of the parties promoting the idea would prefer not to present it as radically different from established practice. The path of least resistance to impact investing involves making it as easy as possible to adopt, regardless of whatever lofty rhetoric and ideals might accompany descriptions of what impact investing is and the changes it could bring about. For now, impacting investing has retained the processes, norms, priorities, criteria, calculations, and culture of conventional investing and simply added the task of identifying and documenting the positive social impacts that would be produced.

But if impact investing is to be something different, clearly distinguishable from other concepts—socially responsible investing, green investments, sustainable financing, ESG—that seek to add additional investment criteria to conventional investing decision-making with the aim of expanding positive outcomes, then we have to recognize it as in fact a radical departure from conventional investing practices. And this difference should be embraced if impact investing is going to fulfill the hopes pinned to it.[1]

To elevate impact investing, we have to conduct our practice very differently from the current approach. And to do it differently and get the results to which we aspire, we have to rethink how we do impact investing, including a better understanding of how to create meaningful social impacts—ones that go beyond being incidental or intentional—we would say purposeful combined with a competitive financial return. It also includes looking at

DOI: 10.4324/9781003276920-4

investment opportunities that have higher risks than conventional investments. That should not be surprising; investing in innovative ideas and untested business models will almost always be riskier. But in these instances, the investment has to be structured so that the hoped-for returns will be superior, so as to offset such risks.

If we embrace the fact that impact investing is very different from conventional investing, then we must invariably accept the corollary that fewer investors will be interested. Impact investing is not for the faint of heart, because it calls on investors to finance new and untested approaches to achieving the positive impacts we seek. But expanding the pool of mediocrity is not as beneficial as a focused set of high-performance impact investments that break new ground, provide proof-of-concept, are replicable, and serve as the vanguard for other, more risk-averse investors to follow.

## 1. Impact investors don't make more money by increasing social impacts or by increasing the assurance of social impacts

It is generally recognized in conventional investing that investment opportunities with higher risks must offer higher returns. Some investors are willing to take on the additional risk to achieve higher gains, while others want greater assurance that a return on their investment will be realized and thus eschew higher risks. But this is not the case with regard to social impacts and risks.

In current impact investing, the risks of achieving social impacts vary across the set of investment opportunities. But promising higher social impacts does not necessarily decrease the risks associated with the proposed financial returns, nor do higher social impacts translate into greater financial returns. Given these circumstances, it is not surprising that the scale and scope of social benefits offered have tended toward becoming a *de minimis* proposition.

If you cannot get greater financial returns from greater social impacts, there is limited incentive to work hard to expand the social impacts for any project or to improve the likelihood that social benefits will be achieved. Of course, some impact investors deeply value the social side of the equation, and accordingly they will favor investments that offer greater social impacts. But current practice is dominated by the 'check the social impact box' crowd. As long as one can establish some intentional social benefit—reducing carbon emissions is a popular and ubiquitous one—there is no financial reason to push the boundaries or do any more than the minimum.

## 2. Limited funding for developing innovative impact investments

One major frustration for many people seeking impact investments is they cannot secure enough funding to support the development of a full proposal that contains sufficient detail and specifications to warrant a review by impact investors. There are entities that attempt to fill that gap, for example, the Swiss Impact Lead. In their own words,

> We link capital with innovative and scaleable [sic] start-ups, which have positive social and environmental impacts. If you are a Private or Institutional Investor, or Asset Manager, seeking impact start-ups, we are happy to assist. We offer: access to best CEE impact start-ups, start-ups' impact reporting & auditing, assistance in start-ups growth, and SIL Certification™ – Impact & ESG Certified.
>
> (Swiss Impact Lead, n.d.)

But Swiss Impact Lead and others can only address a relatively trivial share of the pool of entrepreneurs seeking impact investments. Many great candidate projects, whose projected financial returns and social impacts align with the goals of impact investing, go unfunded, with the result that the targeted communities who would benefit remain in need. Obviously, finding funds to develop good ideas into a fully fleshed-out proposal is always a challenge. And there is no shortage of great ideas with innovative approaches that could qualify for impact investing but don't have the hard numbers to demonstrate their viability.

However, there are additional explanations for why this situation exists and persists. First, many of the people promoting an investment opportunity do not have a strong—or even a fleeting—understanding of finance. Often, they are practitioners with a deep understanding of the problem being addressed, the previous attempts to address the problem, and why and where those efforts fell short. Moreover, their innovative ideas are often grounded in an extensive understanding of what works and doesn't in providing services to underserved communities, and of the local context for designing service delivery. This understanding and grasp of the local circumstances is invaluable to structuring activities that have good prospects for filling a gap and accomplishing social impact goals. But these same entrepreneurs often fail to grasp what information investors—even impact investors—need to see before they can decide whether to invest.

Second, more often than not, the project and investment data that most impact investors would want is simply not available. For example: a basic discounted cash flow (DCF) model sets out what equipment and facilities would need to be purchased, the cost of their operation and maintenance, the level of production of goods or services associated with the expanded production capacity, the price at which goods and services could be sold, and the future demand for those goods and services[2]. Collecting the requisite data is one more expense in developing an investment proposal for which funds need to be found. There are plenty of people who could conduct such analyses, but typically, data collection is very expensive (sometimes prohibitively so) and, given the questions around data quality is also subject to reliability concerns.

---

### BOX 3.1  NOT ENOUGH JUICE?

For example, a project that costs $150,000 to prepare the analysis and documentation for an investment of $500,000 means the cost of preparing the investment is an additional 30% increase in project costs that needs to be paid back without any of that money being available to contribute to social or financial returns. Such project preparation costs are intolerable. One impact investor observed that when the cost of project preparation is so large compared to the total investment required, pursuing these opportunities is more like a hobby; it is an untenable method. It is no wonder that many great projects will never be funded, given the current approach to impact investing.

---

A third and largely overlooked reason is that most projects proposed for impact investing that are actually innovative and would offer real benefits to underserved communities do not have enough 'juice' in them to make the investment worthwhile. By lack of 'juice', we mean that an impact investment might bring about real and tangible benefits to a community—for example, a smart cocoa farming project in sub-Saharan Africa could reduce carbon emissions and include ecotourism lodges—thereby generating greater economic prosperity for local communities. But when you consider the hoped-for financial returns and the social impacts against the costs of preparing the investment proposal, it just doesn't generate enough value to make the effort worthwhile. And while one potential solution is to expand the size of the investment, many times the entrepreneurs who developed the idea have limited capacity to manage larger operations. The issue isn't a lack of potential community benefit, but that the cost of developing and securing finances for the project is far too great for the total social benefits being promised.

### 3.    A Paradox of Social Impact Metrics

We know that providing a convincing assessment of the prospects for achieving the social impacts sought by impact investments is a cornerstone of the entire impact investing process. One reason for the close scrutiny of potential social impacts is the presumption that achieving a positive social impact comes at the expense of financial returns. Many investors are willing to make such a sacrifice and embrace the philosophy that they can use their money and purchases to do good in the world.[3] But the sacrifice of financial gain is not made lightly.

If financial returns are to be forsaken, then the corresponding social benefits should be assured. The presumption of an unavoidable trade-off between financial returns and social impacts is one reason for such an exaggerated focus on measuring the positive impacts of impact investments. When we say 'exaggerated', we are referring to the level of precision and exactness expected in reporting social impacts. The GIIRs+ framework and methodology provides a good example. A brief description is provided in Box 3.1.

---

**BOX 3.2    IRIS+ MAKES IT EASIER FOR INVESTORS TO TRANSLATE THEIR IMPACT INTENTIONS INTO IMPACT RESULTS**

All investors and companies create positive and negative effects on society and the environment. Impact investors seek to maximize the positive and minimize the negative by using the IRIS+ system to integrate social and environmental factors into investment decisions alongside risk and return.

Credible, comparable impact data are needed to inform impact investment decisions and drive greater impact results. IRIS+ solves for this by increasing data clarity and comparability, and it provides streamlined, practical, how-to guidance that impact investors need, all in one easy-to-navigate system. It is a free, publicly available resource that is managed by the Global Impact Investing Network—the global champion of impact investing (GIIN, n.d.).

---

The IRIS+ guidelines for what social impacts could be measured associated with investment targets are sophisticated and granular. We are not criticizing GIIN's framework for measuring social impacts. Rather, we are keenly aware of the paradox that has evolved in impact investing: the greater the comprehensiveness, precision, and reliability required of the metrics of social impact, the more expensive the project development costs become, and the higher the barrier for innovative projects to attract impact investing.

Now, it could be argued that this is the proper order of things. Projects that cannot attract funding for conducting the proper analysis of their social impacts, so as to provide good assurances to impact investors, perhaps are simply not a good risk—the market is speaking.

But measuring social impacts is not such a clear picture. Even if 'best practices' are adopted to measure social impacts, troubling challenges remain. As we noted earlier, the difficulties of collecting adequate and reliable 'on the ground' data to be used to report on project impacts can be formidable. Data collection is often very expensive and unreliable.

The US State Department and the Institute for Corporate Responsibility at George Washington University cosponsored a series of roundtables to look at practical impact investment opportunities in cocoa supply chains, particularly in West African nations. Attendees represented a diverse set of actors, actively involved in promoting sustainability and cocoa supply chains, including: Grameen Foundation, Fair Trade, Green America, Farm Grow, World Cocoa Foundation, Mars, Divine Chocolate, Rainforest Alliance, and USAID among others. All the organizations were either funding or operating programs to promote sustainable cocoa supply chains. There were discussions about the best way to achieve that goal—sustainability certification, conservation, microloans to farmers, fintech solutions, smart farming. But all agreed on the difficulty and high-cost of collecting data on the results of their efforts. And even when the data were collected, reliability was often disappointingly difficult to ensure.

Another aspect of unreliable and/or unavailable data is the mismatch between what social impacts an investor may want to have reported on and what phenomena are reportable. For example, impact investors may want to know how many women and girls are beneficiaries of investments in pay-as-you-go home solar panel projects. But because many countries allow only men to sign contracts, that statistic is very difficult to provide with exactitude. Or some impact investors may want to know what ethnic groups or people of color (treated as proxies for members of marginalized communities) are beneficiaries. But often, the beneficiaries' view of their identity does not correspond with those of investors. Sometimes they balk at identifying themselves by the racial or ethnic categories presented to them, which have often been developed by Western government agencies and philanthropic organizations.

Despite all the sophisticated frameworks, standards, and techniques that are available to measure social impacts, we cannot, in fact, measure our way out of these problems. Too many unavoidable conditions inhibit our attempts to measure certain types of impacts accurately and reliably. And efforts to solve the problem by expanding the sophistication of the measurement methodologies are only 'gilding the lily'. There is no good reason why metrics used to measure the social impacts of impact investments should strive to meet the same levels of precision that conventional investing requires. Deciding to be an impact investor already signifies a willingness to back away from the approach of trying squeeze every nickel out of an investment. Impact investments are not public policy and do not need to be held accountable for the use of funds in the same way as public spending might be expected to be. The efforts to provide detailed and robust metrics on social impacts are intended to provide comfort to investors that they are getting both financial and social 'bang-for-their-buck'. But the current approach to measuring impact sets out unrealistic expectations for what could be measured and what impact investors should reasonably expect. Our current approach to measuring social impact hobbles the expansion of impact investing and offers a false sense of precision that simply cannot be achieved.

The social impact of investments will need to be measured and reported accurately and faithfully if these opportunities are going to attract impact investors. But impact investing needs its own social impact paradigm that helps to identify reasonable ways to measure the success of an impact investment and what type of information can reasonably be collected and analyzed to provide assurances that that the promised social impact has been achieved.

4.  Impact washing and impact 'fluffing'

'Greenwashing' is a common term used to criticize activities that are promoted as eco-friendly but, in reality, are not very green at all. Similar concerns are directed at impact investments, over what could be called "impact washing." Given the issues we have raised about the ambiguities over what qualifies as an impact investment and the serious challenges investors face when attempting to create positive impacts, these concerns are, are unfortunately, well-founded. Of course, some impact investments will not live up to their billing. For example, energy companies often promote their embrace of renewable energy and associated reductions in carbon emissions, while, at the same time, acquiring fossil fuel other fossil fuel-based energy companies.

---

**BOX 3.3   EXXON'S HISTORIC SHALE DEAL SIGNALS NEW WAVE OF OIL MERGERS**

Exxon Mobil Corp.'s $59.5 billion acquisition of Pioneer Natural Resources Co., the biggest US energy deal in decades, is poised to usher in a new era of industry-shifting takeovers.

The shale sector is a hotbed of consolidation talk as cash-rich oil companies compete for the best drilling portfolios in the Permian Basin, North America's biggest source of crude. Output from that region of West Texas and New Mexico has doubled in just six years to the point where it yields more oil on a daily basis than OPEC heavyweight Iraq. (Crowley et al. 2023)

---

But falling short of delivering expected social impacts does not necessarily imply malfeasance or an intentional effort to defraud investors. Not every impact investment that falls short of the projected outcomes should be branded as impact washing. Just as with projected financial returns, there is always the chance of something going wrong, and investors accept the risk of underperformance.

But we suspect that more is going on here than firms overselling the social impacts of their investments or intentionally touting misinformation to deceive investors. Just as green marketing creates a blur between authentic eco-friendly outcomes and the exaggerated and/or imprecise claims of environmental impacts, we have observed the same phenomenon with impact investing. The roots of impact washing do not have to be nefarious. Those proposing an investment opportunity that they believe has great potential will naturally want to put their best foot forward and think positively about the possibilities.

In some—perhaps many—instances, we believe both the seller of the impact investment opportunity and the buyer are fully aware that the hoped-for positive social benefits may not materialize fully and that the claims of impact may be uncertain. And yet they are both willing to participate in the transaction. We might call it "impact fluffing," because this is not the same as intentionally misleading an investor. The phenomenon of impact fluffing reveals that many impact investors may want their investment to bring about a positive social impact but also have limits on how much effort they are willing to dedicate to making sure it actually happens.

It may seem odd that investors would take such a stance, but not when impact investing—just like green investing—is becoming a marketable brand. Currently, in the global bond market, 'Green bonds' command a premium price just by being labeled as "green." When it becomes desirable for funders to classify their investment as impact investing, it is worth paying extra money, even when the impacts are uncertain. Just being seen as an impact investor may be more valuable in some cases than the actual impacts. For impact investors, it may well be that a "feel-good" premium has emerged.

For those who are strong advocates for the power of investing to bring about real, positive change in the world, this type of branding would be understandably offensive. But impact investments are made by two consenting adults (or organizations of adults). If an investor wants to purchase a financial product labeled "impact investing" and knows that the impact prospects are risky, where is the "impact washing"? There is no blame if an investor knowingly places money in an inferior investment when it comes to assured social outcomes. And the investee or investment advisor is not to blame for selling the customer what they want: an impact investment about which they can be casual about and still feel good about it.

The observable shortcomings of some impact investments' outcomes should not be written off as impact washing. In fact, such a simplistic assessment works against the prospects of mitigating true impact washing. When the presumption is that impact washing is due to primarily deceit and bad faith, then the future becomes a self-fulfilling prophecy where people will continue to make investments based on their preferences for how much they care whether the projected impacts are realized; and critics will continue to attack impact investors as bad actors with poor intentions. This vicious-cycle leads nowhere.

Beyond the relative merits of any particular investment, impact washing has implications for the entire industry. If investors do not believe in the integrity of the promised positive social impact, this undermines the reputation of a true impact investment. If investments qualify as impact investing, but don't deliver on their impact, it is more difficult to elevate them as a more desirable investment option and even harder to persuade some investors to accept some reduction of financial returns. In addition, impact washing will only drive up the cost of providing a convincing case that any given impact investment will in fact deliver the intended impacts, which in turn lowers the anticipated financial returns further and makes impact investments less attractive.

The future of impact investing must devise more transparent and practical standards about how the social impact of impact investments is assessed and reported. But impact investments as a financial product cannot survive if each impact investment transactions invents its own definition of what constitutes an impact investment. It is an unfortunate conclusion, but we have seen that impact investing is too often more about making money by selling business services that claim to measure social impact, than offering authentic investment opportunities that make money and makes the world a better place.

## Subtraction by Additionality?

A key concept in development studies is additionality, which means that the funds going toward the delivery of some good or service should be in addition to what is currently provided; or more technically accurate, in addition to what would have been provided in the future. The concern is that the parties receiving funds to provide some goods or services might use those monies to provide the specified goods or services, while then redirecting to other purposes the funds currently used to provide those same goods or services. The concept has migrated to the impact investing world, with the result that for some people, social impacts resulting from impact investing only count when they are in addition to what is currently in place.

However, additionality has many different meanings depending on the field of study or its application. In the context of impact investing, we rely on the following definition: "In order to qualify as additional, capital investments need to generate an activity (with a positive impact on climate change or other sustainable development goals, for example) that wouldn't have occurred without that capital." (Lawton 2023)

We want to confirm the benefits that impact investments can create by making a capital investment and generating additional impacts beyond what is already in place. When an impact investor is expecting additionality, the reporting should make very clear what these real additional impacts were and how the additionality was determined. And that requires some projection of what would have happened in the future with and without the effect of an impact investment (T. Rowe Price, 2023).

But the insistence that impact investments must always and only produce additionality has stymied billions of dollars of impact investment opportunities unnecessarily. We find the idea of additionality perfectly reasonable and appropriate under the right circumstances: when there is concern regarding accountability of government spending; when a corporation is providing added value to an investment through the use of its supply chains, market position, and/or customer and B2B networks; when an investee receives non-financial assistance beyond the capital investment of an angel investor such as mentorship or networking; or when one is measuring impacts of government spending to understand the extent to which projected impacts would be the result of private activity absent government involvement.

But we also think that additionality plays an oversized role in the impact investment space that should be curbed. Impact investing serves two masters: those who are focusing on the positive results that come from investing in a firm, fund, or project, and those conducting a proper accounting to determine who should receive credit for these same results. Many times, there are tax implications for an investor over whether additionality occurred.[4] Or there may be a specific goal to use impact investing to expand the level of investment in a particular country, region, or sector. You would not want to count new investments as achieving any of those goals if they were accompanied by an equivalent reduction of funding elsewhere and a corresponding lower level of performance. And if impact investments are to bring some positive impact beyond conventional investing, it would be important to ensure that any alleged impact is really attributable to the new investment.

Plus, the over-emphasis on additionality in impact investments is the result of not giving enough consideration to the perspective of the investor. If we accept the motivation of impact investors is to use their investments to create positive outcomes, then the investor would rightfully be concerned about the linkages of their own investments to their impacts. For example, if an impact investor was to purchase a solar farm and believe that their funds were linked to carbon emission reductions, they would be correct. But the results could be that whoever sold the solar farm might in the future use a fossil fuel-based energy source, and thereby simply swapping the positive outcomes of a solar farm from one source of capital to another – no additionality.

But it is hard enough to convince conventional investors to change their investment strategies to include impact investing without require them to ensure that there will always be additionality. It places a analytic burden on the development of impact investments that raises the cost of the investment and creates disincentives to becoming an impact investor. Of course, achieving additionality is the ultimate goal, but expanding the community of impact investors is a critical goal as well. And we might focus on the other party in this solar farm transaction. Why not put pressure on the solar farm seller to pledge not to take a step back from supporting carbon emissions as a part of their own 'social responsibility'?

The reliance on additionality is intended to provide a reasonable resolution of both concerns. Instead, it compels the rejection of a ready-made set of impact investment opportunities. Many projects generating significant social impacts rely on uncertain funding sources. Impact investors provide an invaluable way to support funding for programs that could be at risk of losing their existing funding.

Substituting impact investments for other sources of funding to support positive social impacts is the equivalent of, and could be treated as mimicking, refinancing for conventional investments. By eschewing the unnecessary 'additionality mandate,' not only would we expand potential high-social-impact and low-risk investment opportunities, but the funding that impact investments substituted for could be released and redirected to other activities with their own social impacts. In essence, the additionality is not absent but is shifted to other types of social impacts. Accordingly, greater attention should be devoted to how new, attractive investment opportunities for impact investors can produce a net positive result—including the redirecting of other funds—for underserved communities.

## Conclusion

We have seen firsthand the power of impact investments to produce positive change and benefit individuals and communities who otherwise would be poor prospects for conventional investments. However, our central observation about the current practice of impact investing, based on the lessons learned that we have discussed in this chapter, is that the definition of impact investing is too loose and the practice too tight. The overall results are relatively lackluster—compare to the lofty aspirations—in terms of both the level and actual impact of impact investments, good intentions notwithstanding.

Allowing impact investing to be considered applicable to such a broad range of investment opportunities undermines its attractiveness to investors. When it is so easy for investments to qualify as "impactful," this lowers the incentive to really leverage the power of investments to bring significant improvements to people's lives. Why spend the time and effort to design an impact investment that is innovative and meaningful when nearly any investment could be called impactful with little or even no additional effort?

The generous nature of the working definition of impact investments also creates a vulnerability for impact investing in the future. If the impact investing "brand" is allowed to become so diluted, it will lose its credibility as a distinctive and positive approach to investing. We see early signs that this phenomenon is already happening. Unless we can reconceptualize what distinguishes impact investing from conventional investing, embrace the challenges that impact investing presents, and use the lessons learned to develop a new approach, we fear that impact investing will slowly diminish until those who advocate for calling *all* investments impact investments will get their wish. In that case, the term won't mean that all investments have positive social impacts, but simply that all conventional investments are viewed as impactful.

For impact investing to achieve its goals, we need to forego the legacies of conventional investing and the analytical and administrative protocols that have been adopted as the best way to authenticate the actual social impacts of impact investments, because they are so costly, exacting and particular as to present a very high bar that only a limited number of projects can get over. We need to reimagine what a new impact investing paradigm could look like, what models we would use to guide the development, financing and operation of future impact investments, and clarify the tools and techniques that could be applied to achieve the vision that has inspired so many to support and embrace the idea and the practice of impact investing.

## Notes

1  A useful analogy can be found in the public governance literature with regard to public-private partnerships (PPPs) and cross-sector collaborations more generally. The popularity of PPPs and networking governance as new approaches to governance has expanded rapidly. But the adoption of these governance modalities has been undertaken in practice as if they differed little from the traditional bureaucratic models of governance that have been prevalent in US and other Western governments for over a century. PPPs and network governance are radically different approaches to governance, requiring very different methods of leadership, forms of accountability, resource allocation, and organizational capacities (Forrer, Key and Boyer 2014). The failure to recognize the radical differences between governing in a bureaucratic structure informed by 'hierarchy' (Weberian bureaucracy) and 'heterarchy' (collaborative governance) helps to explain the sorry gap between the promise of collaborative governance found in scholarship and the failures that litter this field in practice.

2  This type of financial analysis is associated with the pre-feasibility stage of investing. It is meant to be a 'quick-and-dirty' assessment of the potential profitability and IRR (internal rate of return) investor might expect. We discuss this and other related topics in detail in Chapter 8.

3  We recognize that the idea of an inherent trade-off between financial returns and social impacts has been rejected by many as not necessarily an inherent attribute of impact investing. This is a key assumption of what we will propose as a different way to think about and organize impact investing. But unfortunately, too many of the funds and financial advisors who argue that investors do not have to sacrifice financial returns to make impact investments do so at the expense of the actual social impacts.

4  As nearly 70% of impact investments are made in the renewable energy sector, it is easy to see how additionality has become a fixture. The accurate measurement of carbon reductions caused by investments in renewable energy is of paramount importance. 'Solar renewable energy certificates (**SRECs**) are a performance-based incentive that allow you to earn additional income from solar electricity generation'. Accurate calculations are specifically tied to the size of the financial credit, and the emissions reductions need to be actual, but just a shifting assigned SRECs from one entity to another.

## References

Crowley, K., Wethe, D., & Ferman, M. (2023, October 11). 'Exxon's pioneer deal ushers in new era of oil mergers'. *Bloomberg.com*. https://www.bloomberg.com/news/articles/2023-10-11/exxon-s -historic-shale-deal-signals-new-wave-of-oil-mergers#xj4y7vzkg.

Forrer, J., Kee, J.J., & Boyer, E. (2014). 'Governing cross-sector collaboration'. John Wiley & Sons.

GIIN. (n.d.). 'IRIS+. IRIS The GIIN'. https://iris.thegiin.org.

Swiss Impact Lead: Home. (n.d.). 'Swiss impact lead'. https://swissimpactlead.com/.

'The importance of additionality in impact investing | T. Rowe Price'. Accessed 14 November 2023. https://www.troweprice.com/financial-intermediary/uk/en/thinking/articles/2023/q1/the-importance -of-additionality-in-impact-investing.html.

# Chapter 4

# Reimagining Impact Investing

To avoid the pitfalls of a weak conception of impact investing (Chapter 1), overcome the barriers identified (Chapter 2), and benefit from the lessons learned from prior experiences (Chapter 3), we propose a rethink of the whole idea of impact investing. We have seen that the idea of impact investing, as it is currently practiced, has limited potential to bring about the revolutionary change in investing that many foresaw for it. Socially responsible investing, green investing, sustainable investing, and even ESG all advocate for considering the impact investments will have on social and environmental issues. We believe that impact investing can be reimagined to make possible a fresh start as a new paradigm for investing.

In this chapter, we present our reconceptualization of impact investing and what it could be. This is not a modest task, but it is not drawn from our imaginations either. Many impact investors have been developing better ways to achieve the desired goals, or they have wanted to adopt new practices but found out the hard way that few investors have been receptive to their ideas. These entrepreneurs and innovative thinkers have inspired us to reconsider what impact investing could really be.

## Refocus

Impact investing as currently practiced will continue to find projects for investors and will make claims about the positive social impacts: the low-hanging fruit. But if impact investing really wants to distinguish itself from other approaches to investing, it should focus on a specific method that is aligned with its vision. We propose that future impact investing should target investments in communities where finding solutions for local problems is not so obvious: the 'high-hanging fruit'.

This term refers to the communities, and their problems, that the current approach to impact investing can never reach: the risks are perceived to be too high, the revenues too small, and the business climate too unfavorable. But it is precisely because of these challenges that impact investing should dedicate itself to finding innovative solutions for such communities. We need investments that will realign value chains so that farmers and their families can enjoy greater prosperity, reduce carbon emissions, make communities more climate-resilient, expand microfinancing opportunities and financial services to the unbanked, improve access to healthcare services, expand affordable housing, improve food security—the list is endless.

Such investment opportunities exist in middle- and low-income countries—in struggling urban and rural communities in high-income countries as well—and they offer reasonable investment returns, but they are often not embraced by investors because the information

DOI: 10.4324/9781003276920-5

needed to assess their risks and return prospects is not easily available, and devising solutions that fit local communities' preferences and priorities takes time and money—sometimes a lot of it. High-hanging fruit investments are not necessarily bad investments, they are simply less favorable compared to other investment opportunities. Impact investing should focus intentionally on those types of investment opportunities that are overlooked by conventional investors.

Many times, these communities are marginalized politically and have little sway with government leaders. Their prospects for substantial government grants and investments being made in their communities are poor. Or they are perceived as being very risky when examined through the lens of an investor—conventional or impact. Those communities have no political power to wield and no market power to leverage. This is where the need for impact investments is greatest.

When impact investors focus on the low-hanging fruit because it is more profitable, they overlook underserved communities where the greatest need for investment is located. Such 'investment deserts' have limited prospects for receiving the assistance they need, based on the generally established practices of conventional and impact investing. We understand why the difficult investments are looked over in favor of the more profitable and less risky investments—but that is why a refocus on what impact investing is all about is necessary.

Refocusing impact investing would galvanize efforts to finance start-ups and innovative projects that provide sorely needed benefits and give impact investors a real purpose for making their investments. It would make impact investing singular among all the other investment strategies we have discussed. Focusing on the high-hanging fruit would present substantial challenges of course, but that should be a badge of honor for impact investors, not a source of discouragement.

## Rebrand

The best way to promote and communicate this new focus is to rebrand impact investing as a specific approach to investing. We propose 'Investing in Innovation for Impact'. Adding innovation to the brand sends a clear signal that impact investments are different from conventional investments in terms of what they invest in. We will use the shorthand term 'I3' for this rebranding, making it easily distinguishable from the current approach to impact investing (which we will call I2). We will use these acronyms from here on as we discuss how to implement the I3 approach in contrast to how I2 is being implemented now.

The I3 brand is associated with projects that offer greater social impact and greater financial returns at lower risks than other types of impact investments. But for that very same reason, I3 investment opportunities are not for the average investor. Today, impact investments (I2s) are marketed as one among many financial products. Of course, their marketers want to sell to the greatest number of investors possible. But I3s have greater uncertainty about them as they are innovative, doing something different, and often located in communities where risks have been perceived to be high already. Typical investors are conservative, and even among those who are enthusiastic about making investments that create positive social impacts, their tolerance for investing in whole new approaches will be understandably limited.

So in contrast to I2s trying to expand and attract the most investors possible, I3s should target investors who can *see around corners* (we will call them SAC investors)—people who can see the benefit of the innovative approaches before any discounted cash flows are completed; who trust their gut and their instincts on when there is a promising innovation to invest in that others have passed over. There are a small number of SAC investors who relish the idea of investing in something that will be both different and profitable and will make the world a better place. So I3s need to market themselves to this smaller set of potential investors and partners. For I3s, more isn't better—better is more.

SAC investors are willing to accept the relatively higher uncertainty about success (although not necessarily in their own minds—they may believe the investment is actually a lower risk than others who don't see what they see) in exchange for the higher financial returns and higher social impacts. Once the project has been successful and replicated in other locations, then the perceived risks of investing in such projects will be lower, attracting more traditional I2 investors. And once that change in perceptions occurs, I3s will look less risky and will be more attractive to conventional impact investors.

SAC investors are the avant-garde who share a vision with the project originators and partners on what is possible, even when others are skeptical. Their pioneering investments can open up future I3 investment opportunities to conventional I2 investors. It is commonly stated in the field of impact investing that eventually all investments should be impact investments. I3 projects—financed by SAC investors—are one way in which that ideal can become reality.


## Redefine

Given the substantial changes we are proposing on how impact investing should be thought about and conducted, and how harsh we have been regarding GIIN's definition of impact investing, it would follow that we would offer a new and improved definition for I3—but we do not; or at least not a traditional definition. In fact, we believe that pre-determining what qualifies as an I3 investment presents unnecessary limitations on apply innovations in different and creative ways that are responsive to communities' preferences and priorities.

No matter how thoughtful a set of standards are designed to reflect the benefits associated with impact investing, as soon as such standards are codified, many investors will see those standards as a 'ceiling'. And that means crafting their investments to assure they can advertise them as meeting the new I3 requirements but without embracing the I3 approach—which is the whole goal: using a different approach to impact investing.

Rather than establishing a pre-determined set of criteria that define I3 and then arguing about whether any given investment does or doesn't qualify, our vision for expanding the role investments can play in making the world a better place focuses on the I3 investment process. For us, I3 investments are not about 'checking boxes', but discovery.

Because I3s start with a focus on developing solutions to problems faced by communities, the proposed outcomes and the theory of change that describes how these outcomes will be achieved become paramount at the very beginning of the investment process. And they are accompanied by probing questions such as: what specific activities require investments?, how large an investment?, how are those investments structured?, how can the social benefits be expanded?, what additional revenues could be generated?, what other funds are available to contribute to these efforts?, what additional investments could be made that would de-risk the original investment?, etc.; the answers to these questions evolve over time as the I3 investment process proceeds. It is a matter of continual improvement in the design, financing, and operation of the project.

The simple answer to the question of 'what is an I3 investment?' is that it is one that was made using the I3 approach to guide the investment process. The more reliant the investment process is on the I3 approach, the more the investment will look like an I3 investment. We understand that our use of the I3 approach to identify I3s—as opposed to a predetermined set of conditions and/or results—still leaves some wiggle room for stating unequivocally whether an investment qualifies as an I3 investment. But concepts like green investing, socially responsible investing, sustainable investing, and ESG all have a level of ambiguity. What is the actual value to an investor of using definitions to classify different types of investments except to establish their expectations for the impact of their investment? We have already noted that the whole point of defining what counts as impact investments is to distinguish them from 'other' investments. But even with a more concise and rigorous definition of impact investing, what is the value of pre-determining certain types of investments? And in futures chapters, we spend extensive time describing what investors can expect from I3 investments.

Our concern is with promoting the understanding and the use of the I3 approach. Plus, we do not have to rely on this method for identifying I3s for long. As I3 investments are made in the future and there is an inventory of established investments, it should be possible to use that data to discern patterns and trends in I3 investments and that information and experience could support a more specific definition of I3 in the future.

## Reposition

I3s are designed to attract investment for projects. We have no objections to the investments that are currently made, or the celebration of positive impacts when they are produced. But for I3s to achieve their Holy Grail goal, we have argued, there must be an innovative approach to solving problems in communities that would not otherwise be considered a good investment. Moreover, the I3 approach aims to solve problems that are the priority and preference of the local community. It is something completely different from just investing in a firm that makes solar panels.

---

### BOX 4.1   COCOA, CARBON, AND COMMUNITY (C3) PROJECT

*Background:*

Just over a century ago, Trinidad and Tobago was globally renowned for its ability to produce large quantities of fine-quality cocoa. At the turn of the twentieth century, some estimates placed the country third in the world for the quantity of cocoa produced and exported, with 30,000 tons of beans produced annually on 90,000 ha of land. However, due to a series of issues—financial difficulties during the Great Depression, the outbreak of deadly crop diseases, and the discovery of oil and gas deposits—Trinidad and Tobago's hundreds-year-old history of cocoa production began to sharply decline in the latter half of the twentieth century. Today, only several hundred tons are produced annually.

*Opportunities:*

Trinidad and Tobago's location, business-friendly climate, natural resources, and supply of skilled cocoa farmers present enormous opportunities and 'fertile ground' for growth. With the right business model, collaboration, and investments, a revival of Trinidad and Tobago's cocoa industry could propel the country's economy forward and position it as a major player in one of the world's most traded commodities.

**Mission:**

The Cocoa, Carbon, and Community (C3) project, a 3-year, USD 450,000 project funded by the Inter-American Development Bank plans to create a sustainable business model for impact investments in the Trinidad and Tobago cocoa sector while improving farm management, diversifying crop production, and modernizing farming practices to be more sustainable. Also, we are identifying strategies and additional investment opportunities to decarbonize the cocoa sector and work with local partners to develop and finance projects and activities to 'build cocoa community resilience'.

**Vision:**

Targeting external and local impact investors, the C3 project will identify profitable investment opportunities in cocoa farms that also improve greater energy efficiency, lower carbon emissions, and help build cocoa community reliance. We are working on creating an investable pipeline for projects and properties across the entire value chain and expanding exports of fine-quality beans and chocolate.

**The Way Forward:**

We aim to achieve this by:

1. Engaging cocoa farmers in Trinidad and Tobago and assessing their impact investment opportunities
2. Meeting with potential impact investors and identifying investment opportunities in the cocoa sector
3. Working on investment opportunities for decarbonizing cocoa farms and their supply chains
4. Studying how to 'de-risk investments' in support of investments in cocoa farms including biochar, flowers, agroforestry, and plant material, among others
5. Washington D.C. region as a test market for exporting Good Will Chocolate. Conducting market analysis and engagement for exporting chocolate products to the

Positioning I3s to be an attractive investment does not exclude businesses from participating in I3 projects. In fact, commercial enterprises are expected to be key partners in I3s. Businesses and start-ups can play a critical role in the overall set of activities funded by I3s.

For example, in the C3 project, the prospects for creating a market for biochar was explored. One proposal was to support the establishment of small enterprises that would collect the biomass material that would become the feedstock for the biochar process. It is a way to bring development to the cocoa communities where the investments in the farms were being planned. But this business opportunity for local entrepreneurs would not have been possible without an effort by project partners to link the business model of the biochar investment to local start-ups. And the biochar project is linked to reducing carbon emissions and selling the associated carbon credits as another revenue stream. The impact investment also supported new, small businesses, and integrated business activities into the project in order to achieve the overall investment goals.

## Reaffirm

We have argued that one weak spot of the current approach to impact investing is the difficulty of distinguishing its approach from conventional investments. One way in which I3 makes the distinction clearer is its emphasis on the use of innovations to target and solve local problems. Impact investments should be made in new, bold, innovative ways. I3s would not invest in projects that conventional investors also invest in. Innovations are needed if the existing barriers and disincentives to investing in the low-hanging fruit communities are to be overcome.

One reason why so many global communities are investment deserts is that it has been determined that the potential returns and risks associated with an equity investment made there are not sufficiently appealing when compared to other alternatives. Or the actions taken to mitigate the perceived risks can raise interest rates so high they cannot be borne by the investees. If an impact investment only makes a better effort to identify positive social impacts but still structures the investment in conventional ways, this won't be enough to overcome the existing barriers to investments that underserved communities face. If investments in the high-hanging fruit are ever to look appealing, they need to promise significant advantages over how they are now perceived by investors. This is where innovations are the essential change agent. Innovations are at the core of I3 because they are the source of the value creation required to improve financial returns and social impacts.

Of course, we appreciate the challenges involved in developing just such innovations. Investors are always sourcing and screening potential deals. Competition is fierce to discover possible investment opportunities. Some investors will jump on a plane at a moment's notice to personally vet a possible investment in a far-off location. In such a marketplace, one might assume that if there existed any credible innovative approaches to making investments applicable to communities in investment deserts, they would have been found already. But it is not the case, and we recognize that such innovations do not grow on trees.

The innovations that drive the value creation in I3s are not simply found; they are *discovered* as new approaches and new opportunities that come about through collaborating with partners and stakeholders who share the same interests and values associated with a potential investment. And they catch the attention of SAC investors. The value creation is born out of an understanding of local conditions, markets, norms, and preferences. And this understanding comes from the information and ideas that are shared among trusted partners. The I3 approach anticipates the nurturing of relationships and the mulling over of possible new ideas: it is an iterative process.

As we have mentioned already, it takes patience and resources to develop an I3, and that is not the *modus operandi* of many investors. I3s look for wholly different ways to structure investments to make them better and more attractive, but most investors would rather invest in projects that are tried and true. I3s look for SAC investors who are willing to explore investment opportunities based only on the 'big idea' and their own intuition about future success, whereas most investors seek concrete proof of an investment's prospects before they will give it any serious consideration. Investors may be willing to chase new investment ideas with the goal of beating their competitors to the punch, but they also have a narrow view of how they want deals to be structured—not inventing new structures—and they need to make snap decisions about whether to spend more time investigating an investment opportunity or moving on to other prospects.

For I3s to distinguish themselves from conventional impact investing, innovations are showcased to investors as the reason why financial returns can be higher, the social impacts greater, and the risks lower than with alternative investment opportunities. These innovations are then nurtured through a bottom-up process of engagement where the knowledge, insight, and understanding about how to do things better, smarter, and cheaper resides.

## Redirect

It is typical for impact investments to start by establishing a favorable prospect of financial returns. With that condition established, it is then time to look at what positive social impacts could be documented and reported. This procedure may seem logical; after all, there is no sense in spending much time elaborating on the possible positive social impacts of an investment if the prospects for a reasonable financial return are poor. But I3s take the opposite approach. They identify the reasonably expected positive outcomes that investing in a project could produce first, and then they follow up on that highlighted feature by demonstrating ways to generate revenues that are used to pay back I3 investors.

Employing the 'social first' approach provides the best chance of developing projects that achieve the Holy Grail. The success of the I3 approach depends on garnering information from local partners and stakeholders. And the best way to establish a healthy and productive exchange of information and constructive engagement is to demonstrate that the first priority of the I3 investment is to generate goods and services that solve community problems in accordance with community preferences and priorities.

We discussed earlier how a distinction has been made between impact-first and investor-first types of impact investors; but social-first is different. The idea around impact-first investors is that they are willing to take lower financial return—or assume greater risks around those returns—to better assure that the positive social impacts are achieved. But adopting a social-first approach in no way assumes that financial returns will need to be compromised. On the contrary, a social-first approach is adopted explicitly to improve the chances of generating higher financial returns than conventional investing. A social-first approach believes there are powerful synergies that can be conducted between the activities that deliver positive social impacts and those that generate revenue.

People understand that an investor—even an impact investor—wants to make money. The main concern in target communities regarding impact investments is that the financial returns are a far higher priority than the promised social impacts. In some instances, local communities see projects labeled as 'impact investments' are all about the marketing and lobbying for a conventional investment—the claimed social impacts are only window-dressing. Another suspicion is if troubles with the investment arise, the investors will take steps to protect their financial interests and that the social impacts will take a back seat. In such situations, one can hardly expect the local stakeholders to be very forthcoming with their ideas and innovative thoughts when they do not believe in the authenticity of many proposed impact investments. Rather, they are likely to be somewhat stand-offish and adopt a wait-and-see attitude.

The potential lack of trust—or perhaps cynicism—held by many stakeholders when dealing with proposed investments is the very reason why I3s make a point of engaging stakeholders and learning about the local problems and challenges, gauging local priorities and preferences, establishing and documenting the anticipated social impacts first, and then looking for ways to generate revenue. Of course, in practice, the development of an I3 opportunity does not have to be so rigid. And it is often the case with I3s that the potential profitability has been scoped already. The key point is that an I3 project must not wait to discuss or look for positive social impacts until after the financial analysis is completed. The social impacts must be integrated into the design of the I3 investment opportunity. And the prospective investors must signal that they will make the I3 investment only if there are reasonably expected outcomes that reflect local community preferences and priorities. I3s take the approach that the reason for the impact investment is to bring about positive social impacts; once the ways to secure the social impacts have been established, then attention is turned to how much money could be made.

## Replicate

In the beginning it takes a lot of blood, sweat, and tears to develop an I3 project. The resources required for a first-time investment will almost certainly be higher than for conventional impact investments. The efforts to learn about local community preferences and priorities take more time than assuming what types of social services communities might need and the most effective responses to those needs. Engaging stakeholders, learning about their interests, addressing their concerns about the project, identifying ways for them to participate, and working with them to develop complementary projects that could attract additional impact investment—all this takes a lot more work than convening some perfunctory meetings or having no serious engagement with stakeholders at all. Searching for the Holy Grail of impact investing requires a lot more energy and resources than settling for financial returns and positive social impacts that reflect past experiences. Looking for impact investment opportunities in communities that are most desperate to receive it but also pose the biggest challenges is a lot more difficult than focusing on the low-hanging fruit, where there is more experience and information to inform the prospects of success.

All these challenges can be expected, but they do not eliminate the hope that the additional resources required to develop an I3 project will provide higher financial returns and greater social impacts, all with lower project risk. The extra effort to understand local conditions, prices, markets, politics, norms, and penchants translates into better I3 project design, financing arrangements, and operations. But even though the higher level of effort required by I3s leads to better prospects for investors, those higher costs can be a deterrent to investing in I3s compared to other investment opportunities.

With this reality in mind, I3s specifically develop business models that undergird the investment opportunity so that it can eventually be applied and replicated elsewhere. A preliminary business model is developed during the pre-feasibility stage of project development and is used to explore where similar conditions exist elsewhere that might enable the impact investment to be repeated elsewhere. Of course, we know that local conditions can have a powerful influence on the attractiveness of an investment. We do not claim that an I3 project that succeeds in one community can simply be parachuted into another community, country, or hemisphere. But the I3 business model developed for one project will reveal other opportunities for the theory of change applied in that project, and it provides a starting point for exploring whether it could then be adapted and applied to other situations.

When potential investors in an I3 project know that the project developers are not limiting themselves to securing investments in one project, but that they have ambitions to use the initial project development work to secure I3 funding for multiple projects, this type of scaling makes the additional costs of the first investment much easier to accept and absorb. Since each future replication of the I3 project will be cheaper than the first iteration, based on the learnings from the original project, investors can see future cost and risk offsets to their original investments. One approach in this regard is to focus on replicating projects by creating an investment pipeline. As the project business model is being developed, there are likely to be multiple investment opportunities in one community. Under conventional approaches, the investors would seek and pursue the best of those opportunities. For I3s, the business model can be used to assess the relative attractiveness of the different investment opportunities and rank them in terms of their readiness, thereby creating a pipeline of projects.

We believe that our suggestions offer a promising pathway to rescue impact investing from slowly dwindling into a mostly hollow brand name. As noted, it has been suggested that in a better world, every investment would be an impact investment—that is, all investments would consider their potential to provide positive social outcomes. But unfortunately, the trend we have observed is that more and more investments that are not particularly impactful are nevertheless being branded as impact investments. If the promises and hopes associated with the inspiring idea of impact investing are to be realized, we believe the I3 approach is the best way to get there.

# Chapter 5

# I3 Approach Model and Framework

One of the main shortcomings of the current approach to impact investing that we have highlighted in previous chapters is that the idea, and the associated investment products, can mean so many different things to investors and financial advisors. Ambiguity over what should be considered an impact investment has allowed the term to become so ubiquitous that it is often hard to distinguish from conventional investing—except, of course, for the marketing used to sell 'impact investment' products. One of the sources of this problem is the absence of a rigorous model that describes how investments could be organized to generate both financial returns and social impacts.

Our proposal that people should adopt the I3 approach to achieve greater success with impact investing must, if it is to avoid the shortfalls demonstrated by the I2 approach, be supported by a general I3 model. In the case of the I3 approach, the shared interests are the Holy Grail—investments that provide higher financial returns and greater positive social benefits with lower risk. A proper model should describe the actions taken by different participants, the goals associated with those actions, the inter-relationship of those actions, their effects on the decisions and actions of participants and stakeholders, how those actions and relationships create incentives that align the interests of the participants, stakeholders, and beneficiaries, and what outcomes we should expect.

Our I3 model is in fact a theory of change—or what we prefer to call a change model—for impact investing.

Given the frustrations associated with the inadequacy of the current I2 practices to achieve the goals and ambitions associated with it, we have developed our own change model that describes what actions should be done differently and how those changes will produce different outcomes.[1]

Several challenges are involved in constructing a model on how to design, finance, and operate projects so as to accomplish the I3 goals. First, you have to identify the level of incentives required to induce participants to adopt specific practices. For example, in private financing of public infrastructure,[2] the P3 model calls for financing to be fully private. The idea is that such a feature gives investors strong motivation to ensure that the project is designed properly, with high assurance that the project's Key Performance Indicators (KPIs) will be achieved.[3] But what are the consequences of including 5% government co-funding? Or 10%? The exact level of private financing of a project needed to establish the necessary incentives will vary from project to project, but the P3 model includes the feature of full private financing to ensure that the private-sector investors' success is tied to the success of the project. Our I3 approach is designed to create the necessary incentives—adapted to the local circumstances—to achieve success.

DOI: 10.4324/9781003276920-6

---

**BOX 5.1   SOCIAL IMPACT BONDS**

Social Impact Bonds are unique public-private partnerships that fund effective social services through performance-based contracts. Impact investors provide the capital to scale the work of high-quality service providers. Governments repays those investors if and when the project achieves outcomes that generate public value.

Whether they are focused on helping mothers experiencing poverty achieve healthy births, supporting immigrants and refugees through job training, or retrofitting homes, Social Impact Bonds transfer risk from the public to the private sector and align project partners on the achievement of meaningful impact (Social Finance 2023).

---

Second, as with any collaborative project, performance and financial risks are incurred by the different participants. One constant concern under such circumstances is that participants will attempt to push risks onto other partners, if possible. Taking Social Impact Bonds as an example, in the selection of the performance standards that must be achieved to trigger payments to the service provider, some parties might push for lower standards to reduce the risks and improve their likelihood of being paid, even at the expense of providing a lower level of social benefits. Our I3 approach is designed to frustrate efforts to shift risks onto participants and to allocate risks to the partners who are in the best position to manage those risks. In this way, partner success is dependent on the success of the project and vice versa.

Third, understanding the preferences and priorities of stakeholders is essential. Generally, people making conventional impact investments are aware of the roles of stakeholders as they relate to the investment. But in our experience, the common motivation to consider stakeholders is one of risk assessment—that is, understanding how governments, advocates, or others might support or oppose the proposed investment and thereby potentially lower or raise project costs or delay its execution. In these circumstances, stakeholder engagement is perceived as a 'cost of doing business'. Drawing again on our experiences, we want stakeholders to be sought out as potential partners and their interests and priorities to be included as part of a value-for-money calculation. Our I3 approach identifies stakeholders' interests in the investment as a strategy for increasing financial returns, expanding the positive social impacts, and lowering the risks—the three 'Holy Grail' goals.

## The I3 Model

Our I3 model seeks to describe the elements of an investment strategy that could be used to accomplish our three Holy Grail goals simultaneously. It sets out the features of an investment such that investor success is grounded in project success. The I3 model draws on research insights and on our personal experiences in developing and financing impact investments. We have also been inspired by pioneers who have adopted some of the I3 model's features—even if they were not aware of it at the time.[4]

We present a detailed description of the I3 model in this chapter, many of the elements being an operationalization of the concepts we discussed in Chapter 4. And then in Chapter 6, we offer more detailed descriptions of the tools and techniques, accompanied by specific examples that should be useful in the adoption of the I3 model. We have identified five key elements of the I3 model:

1. Positive-sum strategy
2. Integrated and iterative
3. Impact Investing Solutions
4. Assurable outcomes
5. Innovation and Investment Platform

The five features should be thought of as a package. Each one of the elements makes its own contribution toward achieving the Holy Grail; yet, for the model to be fully effective, all five would be adopted. They are interdependent and the success of one feature relies on the presence of the others.

## Positive-Sum Strategy

The first feature of the I3 model draws its name and inspiration from *The Positive-Sum Strategy: Harnessing Technology for Economic Growth* (1986), edited by Ralph Landau and Nathan Rosenberg. The book is a collection of papers that focus on the 'relationship between technology and economic growth'. It is a rebuttal to an earlier popular book by Lester Thurow, *The Zero-Sum Society: Distribution and the Possibilities for Change* (1980). Following two recessions and amidst a period of 'stagflation' during the late 1970s, Thurow argued that the macroeconomic reforms necessary to put the US economy on a low-inflation and steady, long-term growth path would require a major shift in the current state of politics so as to break the existing 'zero-sum' stalemate. He contended that certain segments of society would have to absorb an inordinate share of economic sacrifice (e.g., through taxation) even though they held sufficient political influence to block such actions.

In contrast, adopting a positive-sum strategy in I3 projects means that they will embody two critical characteristics. The first is an emphasis on using innovative technologies and techniques to increase financial returns and expand and improve social impacts. I3 investments support a calculated strategy that adopts innovations[5] as a means of improving the status quo. These innovative solutions will create additional value that can be captured—in part or in full—by project participants and even by stakeholders and in turn monetized.

Second, I3 projects can be initiated and participants engaged with the knowledge that the future does not involve a win-lose situation. Rather than a Thurow-ian worldview that anticipates that someone's gains will have to be offset by someone else's losses, a positive sum strategy rejects the premise that impact investing entails lower financial returns as a 'necessary evil' to produce positive impacts. Projects can be credibly advertised that the goal is to make all participants better off than they were before, embracing the endless possibilities of developing I3 projects that achieve the Holy Grail.

Employing the positive sum strategy is an attractive approach for investors because the focus on generating more value means the ceilings on financial returns could be raised any time during project development, and even afterwards. It also allows for considering including investments in activities that might have greater risk but could be made acceptable if corresponding financial returns can be raised based on the adoption of new innovations.

## Integrated and Iterative

The investment process is traditionally conceptualized as a sequence of events, starting with sourcing potential investments and ending with managing and monitoring the investment after it has been made. This is considered the most efficient way to winnow down investment opportunities as quickly as possible. Investors know they have to spend money to learn about the specifics of any given investment opportunity, but they want to spend only enough money to learn whether it is worthwhile to move to the next steps in the process. Taking a potential investment through all the stages of the investment process only to reject it in the end is—in retrospect—an unnecessary waste of the money spent.[6]

But I3 investments are not developed simply in sequenced stages. Rather, they progress in an integrated and iterative way along the journey of bringing an idea to market and making it investment-ready. I3 investments are created and discovered, not just run through a standard operational template. We take our inspiration again from the P3 approach. Typical public contracting for public infrastructure divides the tasks contracted out to vendors into three phases: a design contract for an architectural firm, a construction contract for a construction firm, and operations and maintenance by a facilities firm. But a P3 puts all those tasks together into one contract and asks the bidders to bring together a team with all these competencies and make one bid. The advantage is that it allows firms to explore and propose ways in which they can lower project costs and risks and improve service delivery by taking an integrated view and discovering efficiencies and advantages by considering how all three aspects of a project—design, financing, and operations – can be leveraged and complementary.

For example, when a design firm is creating blueprints for a new facility, it has no incentive to think about the costs associated with changing the filters for HVAC systems based on where they are located. But if the same firm had to bear the operations and maintenance costs related to the facility's HVAC systems, they would have a strong motivation to design easy access to the filters. The same idea is applied to I3s. We explore the project design, financing, and operations together, bringing together experts and possible partners for the project from the beginning. Building the right team and coalition is discussed in more detail in Chapter 6. For now, our main point is that the I3 approach considers all three facets of a project simultaneously and ensures that all aspects are integrated to the ultimate advantage of the beneficiaries: the investors, stakeholders, and partners.

As a result, the project must be developed iteratively. Ongoing assessments are made of the possibilities for increasing financial returns, expanding social impacts, and lowering risks. One implication of this iterative method is that all participants need to be flexible and adaptive. Different combinations of activities funded by impact investors will need different business models and will have to accommodate different forms of blended financing. And the financing to be structured to accommodate the project design—not the other way around. For some, the potential for continually changing the activities to be funded, the outcomes measured, the business model employed, and the blended financing arrangements, might seem quixotic—all these efforts cost money and time. This is true, but the trade-off is the development of investable projects with higher financial returns, expanded social impacts, and lower risks.

## Impact Investing Solutions

The title given to this third component signifies that developing an I3 starts from an understanding of a problem or need, and a plausible idea on how to bring about the desired changes. Undoubtedly, most impact investors would say that they do this already, as this concern seems central to what conventional impact investing is all about. But Impact Investing Solutions is different.

Our I3 approach is grounded in solving a pressing problem and understanding what set of actions will produce the desired outcomes that are preferred by, and a high priority for, the local community. We develop those solutions by working closely with stakeholders and local experts to identify the current barriers to solving problems and what innovations could be adopted to overcome those barriers.

In our experience, identifying solutions to local problems is not, in fact, the most difficult step. People working in business, government, NGOs, or applied research academies usually have a good sense of the nature of problems, why they exist, barriers to solving them, and potential solutions. The challenging part is to develop the design, financing, and operating plans attractive enough for someone to pay for it. Government agencies have their established policies and everyday politics and rarely have the flexibility to change their approaches in dramatic or innovative ways. NGOs have donors with their own program priorities, and constant concerns about raising enough funds to operate, so they may not be so open to changing business-as-usual as one might think. And businesses have their own markets and strategic goals to deal with and can't easily veer off into other pursuits without a strong business case. Yes, of course there are foundations and family firms offering funds for new ideas and new approaches, but these are not easy for most people to acquire and often are only for short-term durations.

These are the reasons why I3s rely on a value creation and capture approach and embrace the Holy Grail as the best way to develop I3 projects that can attract impact investors. Once the possible I3 solutions are clarified and stakeholders have expressed support for the project, then it is time to figure out how to make money doing it. Of course, in developing an Impact Investing Solution, we are always mindful that in the end we have to fund it. Impact Investment Solutions cannot be fanciful, pie-in-the-sky dreams. They need to demonstrate the likelihood of success first to the stakeholders, and then to impact investors. Impact investment Solutions are practical and doable, but also imaginative and innovative.

We came up with the Impact Investing Solution idea for very practical, not idealistic reasons. When you are working to help solve and finance local problems, strong partnerships are an invaluable source of information, insights, and innovative approaches. Collecting information about possible solutions to local problems, market conditions, local politics, stakeholder roles and efforts, and past practices is difficult and expensive under the best of circumstances, and despite best efforts, it can yield incomplete and unreliable information that is difficult to validate. Partners who believe that an Impact Investing Solution could actually work and be beneficial to them and/or their organization or community are motivated to share their best information that contributes to designing the project. Alternatively, if a potential impact investment is viewed as 'window dressing' for what is actually a conventional investment where the investors make all the money and the impacts are limited and/or intangible, there is limited incentive for stakeholders to help in developing such projects.

As a result, the Impact Investing Solution method improves problem solving, but it is also a knowledge creation device that is more reliable and many times cheaper than conventional approaches to sourcing and screening potential investment opportunities. And the results of the methodology can then be adapted to other communities with similar problems. Any given Impact Investing Solution can be adapted and fit to the circumstances just as any business model has to be modified to the specific circumstances and situations of other markets.

## Assurable Outcomes

One of the greatest challenges to impact investing is measuring its impacts. One main source of this challenge, among the many we have already discussed, is the uncertainty around what can actually be accomplished with a high-level of confidence and those accomplishments translate into desired outcomes. The typical response to that uncertainty is to increase efforts to attempt to produce better metrics on the social impacts generated by the investment. Notice that we say 'attempt' as there are serious limitations on the degrees of accuracy and the level of precision that can be achieved under the best of circumstances when measuring and quantifying positive impacts of impact investments. With apologies to the English language, we invented the term 'assurable' because we know that positive social impacts can never be absolutely assured or guaranteed. But we can give impact investors the confidence they need to believe in their investment and its results were as they anticipated.

As discussed earlier, we cannot measure our way out of overcoming the challenges of documenting social impacts. We need other tactics. First, I3s rely on strong theories of change to give impact investors the confidence they rightfully seek that their investments will provide positive social outcomes. I3s are better able to construct rigorous theories of change because they work closely with stakeholders to ensure that local circumstances are understood and incorporated into the project design. These efforts take more time and cost more money, but the reduction in the uncertainties of what is reasonable to try to accomplish and what is outside the realm of reasonable expectations. If a projected outcome of an impact investment was uncertain from the very beginning, it is no surprise that quantifying those impacts with precision will be very difficult.

But we see no meaningful added value in collecting information on the precise number of beneficiaries or the exact services received. The positive social impacts of a well-designed I3 project will happen whether we measure them or not. The use of resources in the project design phase to construct a strong theory of change is a much better use of resources than chasing after an elusive precision on social impacts.

Second, I3 projects work with high-quality partners who have experience and deep knowledge of the issues being addressed by the investment. Having strong relationships with local partners who share the interests and the values embedded in the project and its outcomes is critical. As is understanding the reputation of potential partners. There is always a history that serves as the context for how any impact investment is perceived. Some partners may have an interest in participating in an I3 project and they may have the proper technical skills to contribute, but how are they viewed by potential stakeholders and others in the community. Our point isn't that I3 partners must have spotless reputations, but other partners and stakeholders need to feel good about collaborating with a team if they are to fully contribute to determining which assurable outcomes should be promised.

Because conventional impact investing is transactional, it is understandable that precise, accurate, and comprehensive reporting on the social impacts achieved would be the expected standard. But the I3 approach, because of its engagement with partners and stakeholders, is more collaborative than transactional. For this reason, there is more awareness and buy-in about the approach to achieving social impacts, and more trust in the intentions and commitment to success in the project. We call this concept 'Trusted Partners' and discuss it further in Chapter 6.

Third, it's important to remember that impact investing in general and I3s specifically are not a substitute for achieving public-policy goals. I3 investments are framed around accomplishing specific outcomes that have been vetted and endorsed by project partners, stakeholders, and beneficiaries. The aim of the I3 approach is to accomplish the type of benefits that investors believe are achievable and align with the preferences and priorities of the local communities. The fact that I3 projects accomplish outcomes that mirror many public policies does not mean that they should be viewed through the same lens. They focus on achieving outcomes that they know can be achieved.

We are not arguing the I3s will not be an essential method for attracting investments that will help achieve the SDGs or be responsive to local community development needs. But we are arguing that in order for I3s to provide assurable outcomes, they need to be guided by what the project can deliver with confidence at that point in time and under the existing circumstances, and what is outside the scope or expertise of the project to accomplish. One implication of advantage that adopting the 'assurable outcomes' approach is that it may narrow the range of claims made regarding the positive impacts, but it also will go a long way in eliminating the concerns over 'impact wash'.

We have argued that the high cost of conducting experiments and assessments to demonstrate the prospects of creating the desired social impacts adds a substantial burden for project developers. We have also mentioned how expensive data collection can be and how, despite participants' best efforts, the data may nevertheless be unreliable. Maybe at some future point, blockchains will be as common as electronic spreadsheets are today, and these issues will become moot. But for now, it is reasonable to ask: what is the point of being so comprehensive and precise in measuring social impacts?

It has been our experience that impact investors might seek more precise social metrics when determining their level of confidence in the project, but once they have that confidence, ranges and approximations should serve the reporting requirements. We must be realistic about our actual ability to make precise measurements, no matter how much people may want us to do so. We believe, based on our experience, that settling for 'assurable' outcomes will remove the biggest barrier to the growth of impact investing.

## Innovation and Investment Platform

A signature feature of the I3 approach is its capacity to provide larger financial returns and greater social impacts, all with lower risk for the investor. This feature results from a purposeful effort to invest in multiple activities that will produce multiple outcomes benefiting both public and private participants. Furthermore, engaging in multiple activities creates multiple revenue streams. Another consequence of this approach is that the number of stakeholders also grows and expands, and this may call for more work to consider these stakeholders' interests and incorporate them into the project's activities and outcomes.

A useful way to conceptualize the 'multiples' strategy is to think of each I3 project as an Innovation and Investment Platform. When an I3 project is being developed, the search is always on for identifying additional investment opportunities, that, in turn will create their own investment returns and their own positive outcomes. We have used this tactic for our Cocoa, Carbon, and Community project in Trinidad and Tobago. We have established the impact investment opportunities in cocoa farms, described how those same investments could reduce carbon emissions, and identified activities that would provide positive social outcomes for the local communities.

With that investment opportunity in place, we began to explore additional opportunities for impact investors, using our original I3 project as the platform for building greater impacts and more investments. We show the number of additional impact investments we discovered (so far) in Figure 5.1.

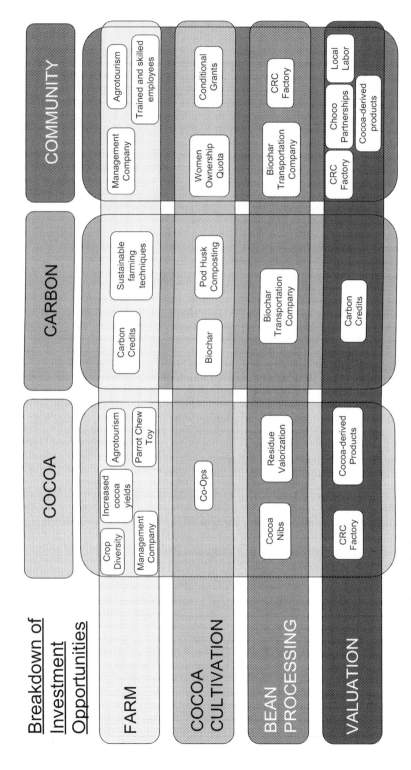

*Figure 5.1* C3 Innovation and Impact Platform.

The original impact investment lent itself to spinning off and informing over a dozen other investment opportunities. Some are directly related to reducing the risks around the original project, such as investing in growing cacao plantings in response to the expanded cultivation on cocoa farms. And others were identified based on discussions around efforts to produce 'net-zero carbon chocolate', such as investing in biochar production. But they all are born of the Innovation and Investment platform. These additional investment opportunities—and their corresponding impacts—in the case of the C3 project provide multiples revenue streams, multiples avenues for carbon reduction, and multiple social impacts.

The idea of multiple social impacts is not a new concept. For example, in projects seeking to accomplish the SDGs, the interconnectivity of health, water, and poverty is well-recognized.

---

**BOX 5.2   IFPRI BLOG: ISSUE POST**

**The SDGs on Zero Hunger and Clean Water and Sanitation can't be achieved without each other, so where do we start?** (Choufani and Ringler 2018)

In reality, water and nutrition are closely interlinked, and achieving SDG targets for water could well constrain efforts to reach SDG targets on nutrition—and vice versa. In fact, it has become increasingly clear that progress toward those two SDGs can only be achieved if efforts to meet one support—and do not undermine—efforts to reach the other.

Water and nutrition are linked in multiple ways, but few of these interlinkages are well understood. An evidence base is developing for several key water-nutrition linkages, such as those between water, sanitation, hygiene, and nutrition; and one is starting to emerge for irrigation and nutrition. But little is known about several others, including the associations between water pollution and health, and between water resource management and nutrition. Even less is known about the interactions across these various linkages

The big challenge is how to meet both water security and food and nutrition security goals, while also protecting and improving water-based ecosystems.

November 16, 2018, by Jowel Choufani and Claudia Ringler

---

Despite these advantages creating linkages between outcomes, in our experience, such integrated approaches are the exception rather than the rule. One reason is that many NGOs specialize in one area of expertise and would not have the capacity to develop projects addressing other topics. NGOs conducting programs with positive social benefits that would make them a good target for I3 projects do not have the resident expertise in other types of activities. Of course, the large international development and humanitarian organizations (IDAHOs) and large consulting have expertise and experience across a wide range of development issues, but funding for development projects are often as silo and addressing only one issue in isolation of others.

A second reason is that often the funding received from governments, international programs, or foundations is focused on addressing one issue. When NGOs receive funding of this sort, they have to follow the mandate and goals of the funding source. Governments are renowned for operating in silos, with the result that funding awarded to improve water security cannot be applied to nutrition issues. Moreover, because of these programmatic silos, attempts to interlink program goals require working across a series of bureaucratic agencies and their respective stakeholders, who do not typically collaborate with each other.

Third, we have noticed that many IDAHOs are risk-averse. Presumably, this tendency reflects the funding ecosystem within which they operate. Government agencies and private foundations all want to report the success of their projects as an important factor in justifying their own funding decisions. And the successes of NGO activities are easier to communicate convincingly if they are framed in familiar, tried-and-true narratives and metrics. Although public foundations may have more leeway to be creative, they also have internal reviews of how effective their funding decisions have been. And striving for multiple social impacts makes everything more difficult to measure; the more complex the theory of change, the more variables and the more risks that have to be anticipated and managed. It should not be so surprising the IDAHOs opt to select the straightest line between two points.

But when impact investors are assessing an I3 project, more social benefits mean a more significant contribution to the local community for any level of investment. And because I3s are not implementing public policy—although the outcomes typically align with public policy goals—the problems related to bureaucratic silos are usually not as much an issue. The I3 approach embraces the complexities of delivering multiple social benefits and sees in these complexities opportunities for synergies and leveraging to create more than one social benefit. In Chapter 6, we will discuss numerous tools and techniques to help us overcome the barriers described above.

When it comes to multiple revenue streams, we have noticed that most discussions of conventional impact investing are not enthusiastic about generating multiple revenue streams.[7] We surmise that this attitude is grounded in the ethos of venture capital investing in start-ups and in the field of entrepreneurship itself. According to this view, start-up firms, and even small firms looking to raise capital to expand, face intense competition in the market. This competitive pressure leads to an imperative to be single-mindedly focused on building a business product or service that is better and more profitable than what the competition offers. Given this perspective, multiple revenues streams appear as distractions. The established wisdom is to be hyper-focused on your business and squeeze out as much revenue as you can; do one thing and do it better than anybody else.

But for I3 projects, we see the benefits of leveraging investments in facilities, products, and services that can create additional revenue streams. Just like individual products that offer multiple social benefits, looking for multiple revenue streams can identify synergies and leveraging opportunities in project development. We learned this lesson from the X-Car project with Ford Motor Company. A vehicle could charge money for delivering packages to remote communities while also bringing a community nurse to provide healthcare services. Or, once the car was in the community, it could use its batteries to charge cellphones or collect data on the diets of residents for a fee for nutrition companies. Once you start looking for additional revenue streams, the possibilities are endless.

There are also ways in which the provision of social benefits and the creation of revenue streams can be synergistic. We call this Reciprocal Value.[8] When one is designing an impact investment solution for an I3 project, investments would pay for a combination of facilities and/or equipment that are used to provide the social benefits. With those resources anticipated to be in place, the next question is how to use those same resources to leverage private value. For example, if a facility is built to house job skill training activities, the same facility—with some expansion and additional upgrades—might be rented out for commercial activities. And if those enhancements are undertaken, that provides additional resources that could be used to provide further social benefits, such as counseling and/or health services.

Conventional impact investing has not only perceived social benefits and financial returns as an unavoidable trade-off, but has viewed the activities that create social benefits and those that generate profits as separate and stand-alone. Reciprocal Value looks for synergies and new opportunities to create public and private value through leveraging the resources used for an I3 project. This is one of the ways in which multiples are created by the I3 approach.

The five elements we have described above comprise our I3 model. It is by adopting these components of the I3 approach that the goal of achieving the Holy Grail becomes possible. But following the I3 approach and organizing impact investments in that fashion may not be intuitive for many potential impact investors. For example, we understand that promoting multiple revenue streams form an I3 project may make sense, but just how you do that may be less clear. Chapter 6 provides descriptions of a number of tools and techniques that can be used to accomplish the different elements of the I3 model.

## Notes

1 The distinction between a 'theory of change' and a 'change model' is subtle, but we feel that theory of change suggests an uncertainty about ultimate success, whereas we are confident based on experience that the I3 approach works.
2 In the US, Canada, and Australia, these projects are called P3s (a variation on public-private partnerships); the rest of the world refers to them as PPPs.
3 The P3 model also contains payments to the private-sector partner linked to achievement of the KPIs.
4 In particular we want to acknowledge the innovative work on impact investing of Quantified Ventures, Grameen Foundation, and Calvert Impact
5 As conceptualized by the study of information diffusion, technology is understood as 'the application of scientific knowledge to the practical aims of human life or, as it is sometimes phrased, to the change and manipulation of the human environment.' (https://www.britannica.com/technology/technology) The importance of this distinction is that innovative technologies encompass techniques—including management techniques—in addition to hardware and/or software.
6 A more nuanced observation is that business value can be created by reviewing a potential investment—even if it is rejected—through the knowledge gained that can be applied to the review of future investment opportunities. Nevertheless, normally investors want to find out as quickly and inexpensively as possible whether an investment is a good fit for them.
7 Some businesses thrive on producing multiple products from the same conversion processes, such as refining petroleum. But these multiple revenue streams are typically derived from products that have an established demand.
8 We intentionally choose this term in the spirit of Porter and Kramer's (2010) 'shared value.' Their proposition was that businesses could create social benefits while they were conducting their business, in ways that improved the firm's competitiveness.

## References

Choufani, J., & Ringler, C. (2018, November 16). 'The SDGs on zero hunger and clean water and sanitation can't be achieved without each other, so where do we start?' *Ifpri.org*. https://www.ifpri.org/blog/sdgs-zero-hunger-and-clean-water-and-sanitation-cant-be-achieved-without-each-other-so-where-do.

Porter, M. E., & Kramer, M.R. (2011). 'Creating shared value: Harvard business review'. From the Magazine (January–February 2011).

Social Impact Bonds. Social Finance. (2023, February 10). https://socialfinance.org/social-impact-bonds/.

# Chapter 6

# I3 Tools and Techniques

The I3 approach model that we described in Chapter 5 has five key features that support the achievement of the Holy Grail of investing: larger financial returns, greater social impacts, and lower risks. The five model components describe the attributes I3 projects should have:

1.  Positive-sum strategy
2.  Integrated and iterative
3.  Impact Investing Solutions
4.  Assurable outcomes
5.  Innovation and Investment Platform

Now that we have articulated the main features of the I3 approach, we next describe the tools and techniques used to activate those features. A dozen such tools and techniques are described in this chapter. Some of them are fairly technical in nature and it takes some time to explain them, and others are likely to be more intuitive and can be summarized in short order. They are by no means exclusive to I3. In fact, many of them have been used in other contexts. Nor are they the only tools and techniques that facilitate I3 projects. Undoubtedly, countless others could be applicable to I3 of which we are unaware or that have not yet been invented.

In listing these tools and techniques, we address the common frustration that arises when someone proposes a specific approach without indicating what methods can be used to carry it out. In one way or another, each of the tools and techniques addresses issues associated with the design, financing, or operation of I3s such that they align with the I3 Approach model—in some instances they are applicable to two and sometimes all three facets.

## Value Creation and Capture

The I3 approach is all about creating and capturing more value—both private and public value. Learning the techniques for creating and capturing value is essential given the I3 approach of developing solutions to problems first and then devising ways to generate sufficient revenue to satisfy investors. Many ideas and tools can be used to discover where additional value could be created or how to monetize it.[1] But it is also valuable to recognize that businesses can internalize value and take it to their bottom line without monetizing it: reducing political risk, enhancing reputations, generating market information, etc. Some specific ways to create and capture both public and private value that could be applied to I3 projects include:

DOI: 10.4324/9781003276920-7

1. *Monetize an externality.* One person's waste is another person's valued feedstock. Technological innovations and/or local market conditions can help in transforming goods with limited market value into valued products. Human and animal waste can be converted into methane gas and become a source of energy; old clothing can be down-, re-, and up-cycled into new products; sewage can be converted into drinking water—and other valuable materials—through an Omni processor; food and material can be converted into high-quality fertilizer; agricultural by-products, such as straw, rice, husks, or sugar, can be converted into high-value materials for building or other industrial uses; plastic water bottles are recycled as materials in automobiles or clothing; and biomass can be converted into biochar. The possibilities are—literally—endless. Of course, the economics of applying any one of these and other conversion technologies depends on the specific locale and local and global markets at any given time.

2. *Create or expand markets.* Current markets for goods and services can be expanded or new markets created when an entrepreneur is willing to take on greater risk or believes that existing risk assessments are off target. Micro-finance, micro-insurance, and micro-banking are all examples of new businesses born out of seeing opportunities to create new, profit-making products and services that others could not discern. Establishing a farm management services company can help regularize labor shortages and enhance yields on farms. Capturing methane from manure pits and using it as energy is a proven method, but in some communities, the demand for gas is too small to make such operations profitable. But partnering with existing mobility networks and establishing distribution networks that expand the markets for gas purchases at low-marginal costs can create the market for a profitable operation.

3. *Reduce operating costs.* IDAHOs and other organizations providing humanitarian relief and managing development programs often focus on one or a few services that they provide or support. For this reason, multiple organizations, each with their own programs and overhead costs, may be providing services to one community. Collaboration between multiple organizations on service delivery efforts can reduce operating costs significantly. Vehicles used to drive to communities may be used only a few days a week, and sometimes never on the weekend. Outsourcing transportation services can offer significant cost reductions. Reducing operating costs and increasing the effectiveness of service delivery improve both financial returns—since lower costs mean higher profits—and improved social impacts.

4. *Higher utilization of capital.* Government or philanthropic funding for projects may be used to purchase equipment in support of program operations, such as refrigerators, vehicles, or computers. But rarely are these assets fully utilized. Refrigerators may not be fully stocked; automobiles cars may carry only one or two passengers, or may be driven only a couple of days per week; computers have excess storage or computational capacities; or facilities are left unused for hours every day. Most such assets are left unused during nonworking hours, like vehicles sitting in a garage all night. If private-sector partners were found that could utilize this excess capacity, a reasonable user fee could be charged, reflecting their market value. Carrying products to destinations in vehicles with less than full payloads is another example: the marginal costs of transporting additional products in the vehicle is nearly zero. Greater utilization means opportunities to charge fees for services provided at nearly no additional cost to the provider.

5. *Avoiding future costs with better results.* Finding more cost-effective ways to deliver services that create value for the targeted community reduces operation costs and increases positive social impacts. A classic example is the cost of recidivism to taxpayers. Every year, some people sentenced to prison are repeat offenders. Since it is expensive to provide prison services, the lower the recidivism rate, the lower government expenditures will be. However, many governments do not have the funds (or the political will) available to institute robust recidivism reduction programs. This is where the 'avoided cost' technique comes into play. There are companies that specialize in providing rehabilitation services to prisoners with the aim of reducing recidivism. One value creation and capture technique would have the government sign an agreement with a firm to reduce recidivism by a specified amount.[2] If the contractor achieves its target, it is paid a specified fee for services; if it fails, then it does not receive a fee (targets and fees can be tiered as well). In this way, the contractor takes on the performance risk. Due to the lower recidivism rates achieved by the contractor, government expenditures for operating prisons are reduced, and some of the savings can be redirected to pay the service fees of the contractor.

These are only a few examples of how impact investments can be made with a focus on accomplishing positive social impacts while still generating sufficient revenues to provide reasonable financial returns.

## Trusted Partners

This term might sound platitudinal—of course, everyone wants to work with partners they can trust. But we use this term to describe establishing a specific relationship between partners and the project so as to build trust. It is important to remember that I3 investments are voluntary and that any partners participating in the project could leave at any time for another partnership to join that provides greater value.

Establishing a 'trusted partners' relationship in an I3 project means that all the partners work collaboratively to achieve shared outcomes, but also that they collaborate to achieve the goals of individual partners. The identification of the project outcomes is a group process that evolves over time. The outcomes represent what the partners believe they can achieve through their collaboration.

One important factor influencing the determination of I3 outcomes is the reputational risks of the partners. If an impact investor makes an investment in a project that does not produce the projected social impacts, it is no bad reflection on them. But partners in I3 projects have their own organizational reputations, and a failed I3 project could reflect poorly on the partners themselves.

Regarding the actual terms of such collaboration, they are often just common sense. Sometimes they are as simple as scheduling events to accommodate a partner's travel schedule or giving visibility to one or more of the partners in a media event or release. Or they may involve incorporating the provision of social benefits aligned with the mission of an NGO partner, or with the CSR program of a local business.

The goal is to form closer bonds among partners by helping all partners achieve their various goals through the relationship. By linking the success of the I3 project with the success of all partners, a natural incentive is created for partners to make a strong commitment to the immediate success of the project and to explore additional I3 opportunities.

## Stakeholder Involvement

Considering which stakeholders could influence the profitability of an investment or impose substantial risks on project operations is a standard due diligence activity. Even when we are looking at just one type of risk—political risk—there are many factors to consider. For example, local interest groups may object to the investment and provoke local government officials to become involved. Such activities slow down the investment timetable and add to project costs. Or local government officials may attempt to negotiate funding from investors for local projects—or even straight-up bribes. Or protesters and demonstrations could disrupt operations or supply chains.

The typical approach to addressing these risks is stakeholder management. This means trying to address the concerns and assuage opposition among those stakeholders who have sufficient power, urgency and legitimacy to delay and disrupt the completion of the investment. I3s embrace stakeholder engagement and actively reach out to stakeholders, engaging them as partners where possible. One reason for this greater openness in I3 investments is the redirecting of priorities entailed in impact investing. Rather than starting with a potentially profitable investment and then adding positive social impacts to it, I3s start with providing positive social benefits that are the priority and preference of local communities, and *then* they look for ways to provide a reasonable return to investors.

When an I3 partnership engages stakeholders from the very beginning of the project as partners, when it is clear that the positive social impacts are the focus of the project, and when stakeholders are listened to and their interests are considered, there is almost always greater receptivity. If those stakeholders include governments and well-regarded local institutions, businesses and NGOs, and local investors, there is a much greater chance of success. Of course, not all stakeholders can be effectively engaged, and some stakeholders will not want to engage. But designing I3 projects that create meaningful social benefits and investments in local communities that reflect stakeholders' priorities is a recipe for success.

## iBlend

iBlend is different from, although not totally unrelated to, 'blended financing'. Blended financing is used to describe two different structures regarding a financial investment. First, it can refer to the combination of both debt and equity. The types of investments can come from one investor or can combine the investments from two different investors. Not all investors have the authority to make both types of investments. The second structure involves a combination of non-concessionary (market-rate) and non-concessionary (below market-rate) investments. The idea is to reduce the financial risk for impact investment opportunities by reducing the cost of capital for the project and/or shifting some of the risk to the concessionary lender. These are good ideas too, but we have something else in mind.

A limitation we discovered in our practical work was that the common financial instruments available for making an impact investment (e.g., investment funds and debt instruments) were designed for only a few of the sources of capital that could support an impact investment. If we wanted to expand the participation of funding sources in support of impact investments—for example, bringing in money from government grants, foundation gifts, or crowdsourcing—we needed a flexible financial structure that could receive a wide range of funds in a wide range of forms from a diverse set of funders. That is what we refer to as iBlend.

An iBlend arrangement could receive funds from multiple sources, allocate the proceeds to various entries, and manage the use of those proceeds. The advantage is that all the activities in an I3 project do not need to be funded from just one source, with its own expectations and preferences as to how a project's financing is structured. An I3 project involves a range of activities, not all of which can easily be funded through conventional investing financial structures. The iBlend aligns funding with different elements of an I3 project, mixing and matching the various sources' funding expectations, mandates, and requirements.

We acknowledge that having multiple funding sources for a project increases the complexities of administration. It can also make assessing project risks more challenging, as the funding sources support different but interdependent activities. The trade-off for the greater complexity is, of course, gaining access to additional funding for project activities from entities who have a mission to accomplish a specific outcome, but who may not have any specific interest in the broader investment itself.

## Wraparound Projects

Public-private partnerships have been used for nearly three decades as an innovative financing method to mobilize commercial financing for investments in public infrastructure projects.[3] Variations on this procurement model have become standard practice for financing infrastructure in most places around the world. The overwhelming demand for public infrastructure projects in emerging economies in support of SDGs such as clean water, power, transportation, water treatment, and internet networks could benefit greatly from an innovative financing method like P3, but infrastructure projects are expensive and often raise concerns from local communities regarding negative effects on the environment and communities. Those protests can delay projects and/or raise their costs and thereby dissuade institutional investors from investing in a project.

We argue that combining P3s and impact investments—what we call wraparound P3s—into one investment will be more attractive to all parties—P3 financiers, impact investors, developers, owners, service providers, governments, and local communities. Wraparound P3s will also open up new opportunities to combine private, public and/or philanthropic funding for projects. Wraparound P3s lower the overall cost of capital, operations, and project risk while increasing positive social impact. Uniting P3s with impact investments in a single project creates new opportunities to deliver greater infrastructure services and social impacts than if they were financed separately, as they are now.

Wraparound P3s can unlock private investment for public infrastructure projects in communities that desperately need expanded infrastructure facilities and repairs to existing facilities. Wraparound P3s are beneficial to both types of investors—institutional and impact—beyond the benefits offered by traditional investment opportunities. For P3 investors, they produce social benefits tailored to be responsive to specific local community concerns, and they are sustainably financed for long-term impact. For impact investors, they offer high-quality investment opportunities that are well designed, managed, and operated, at a lower cost and lower risk than conventional standalone projects.

The advantages offered by wraparound P3s can attract both private and public support because they result in services (e.g., infrastructure and social services) with superior design, financing, and operations. The results include not only the mobilization of commercial capital for infrastructure projects, but also higher performance from both private- and public-sector perspectives. Research on Wraparound projects that show promise include:

affordable housing, urban university campus revitalization, smart cities, sustainable mobility networks, and energy equity and storage. But bringing together impact investors and institutional investors to co-invest in projects that provide basic public services also has a demonstrable positive impact on the local communities is a promising approach that has many different applications.

## De-risking Investments

I3 projects face risks like any other investment, and I3s look to mitigate those risks like any other investment. But the I3 approach is constantly looking to de-risk projects by investing in additional activities. For example, agroforestry can play an important role in de-risking investments in agriculture. Agroforestry is the practice of intentionally integrating plants and trees into crop and animal farming systems. It provides opportunities for farms to diversify their production systems so as to mitigate risk—when executed properly—and improve the local environment.

For example, climate change is threatening coffee production around the world. Arabica coffee can only tolerate mean annual temperatures of up to 75°F; hotter than that and the beans ripen too fast and the trees are damaged. Recent analysis by the Stockholm Environment Institute (SEI) claims global Arabica coffee production climate change could be reduced by 50% and global Robusta bean production reduced by almost 25%. Higher ambient temperatures and more extreme droughts and rainfall are the reasons why. Farms located in the 'coffee belt' that grow and harvest coffee may not have suitable conditions to continue as early as 2050. Agroforestry is one approach to mitigating the risks faced by coffee farms by making them more resilient by providing enhanced food security, additional income opportunities, the provisioning of ecosystem services, and biodiversity conservation. (Idle 2023)

De-risking investments can also be applied to specific risks in a supply chain associated with an investment opportunity. For example, using the I3 approach, the C3 project has identified several de-risking investment opportunities applied to making investments in cocoa farms in Trinidad and Tobago. One concern raised regarding cocoa farms in Trinidad and Tobago is the shortage of cacao planting material that would be required for expanded cultivation. The potential shortage poses significant risks to the profitability of cocoa farming, but it also suggests a de-risking investment opportunity.

Currently, the Ministry of Agriculture, Land and Fisheries of Trinidad and Tobago grows cacao plant material and sells it to local farmers at highly discounted prices. Although the below-market prices for planting material lowers investment costs for expanding production or replacing old trees, there is a perpetual shortage of plant material. We are exploring options for investing in a private cacao plant material nursery that could produce the material at one-third of current costs and enough to meet current and future demand. The market price for the plant material would be more expensive, and our pre-feasibility calculations show such a cost increase would decrease investor returns. However, given the already large subsidy the government is providing cocoa farmers currently, it could retain that policy to provide a subsidy to keep the cost of planting material low and, under the circumstances, still lower government expenditures; the investors in the nursery make a nice financial return; and the investment in cocoa farms is de-risked.

We are not claiming that every risk associated with impact investing can be mitigated with additional investments. But taking the time to learn about local preferences and priorities and engaging stakeholders to learn about their concerns and interests can reveal new investment opportunities that can strengthen supply chains that are beneficial to the community and to the original I3 investment.

## Impact Investment Solutions Fund

We have discussed our concept of Impact Investing Solutions. The idea is to develop innovative solutions to problems that align with local preferences and priorities and then, once established with stakeholder, secure revenue flows that provide a financial return to investors. We are proposing that this approach be extended to and inform the way impact investments in I3s are structured.

The creation of investment funds with a mandate to invest in I3s projects could be expected. But we recognize that the perceived risk of I3s and their innovativeness will make many investors wary. Other funds that are looking for investments that could have significant social impacts have looked to address this issue by attracting 'catalytic capital' as a way to buy down the risks of projects[4]. But the success of I3s is grounded in working with quality partners, successful stakeholder engagement, and the support of local communities due to the significance and relevance of the social benefits they generate. Relying on conventional investment funds that place a top priority on the financial returns of their investors and the profits to their managers could prompt doubts about the commitment of I3s to delivering on the promises of social impacts.

Our suggestion for employing an Impact Investment Solutions Fund is grounded in lessening the profitability of the fund itself. We do not want investors in I3s to take lower profits in exchange for creating positive social outcomes—we want the fund and its partners to take lower profits. Of course, we recognize that a Social Impact Solutions Fund needs to have highly skilled analysts and managers, so we are not suggesting it to be a 'budget' investment fund. But consistent with the I3 approach, including thinking of investment opportunities as Innovation and Investment Platforms and looking for Positive Sum Strategies, an Impact Investment Solutions Fund could be structured as a not-for-profit entity.

Limiting the profitability for fund partners could allow for investments to be made in 'investment desert' communities with high social impact but lower returns. Running the Impact Investment Solutions Fund has other benefits as well. It would present a more attractive option for local investors who would be aligned with an investment fund that puts community first. In addition, it would set aside funds to be used by NGOs and universities to nurture new investment opportunities and provide guidance on how to accelerate investment opportunities through an investable pipeline. That funding support would go beyond what might be typically expected to be expended by conventional investment funds in technical assistance.

## ESG Impact Reporting

Any investment in an I3 project or an Impact Investing Solutions Fund should anticipate requests from investors for documentation on the I3s projected ESG performance and policies. Unfortunately, the ESG reporting space is fraught with confusion and ambiguity. This is not because there are not enough acceptable ESG Guidelines and Frameworks—but because there are too many to choose from. (Zero Circle 2023) There are so many options without any clear or obvious advantages associated with one or the other. Or more precisely, whatever advantages might convey using one ESG standard over another are case-specific and difficult to determine in advance. A second reason is that most ESG frameworks are directed toward assessing investments in firms. And while some of the specific ESG criteria can be adapted to project activities, there isn't always a comfortable fit.

Our advice is for I3 projects to develop their own indicators of ESG practices. We call this inside-out ESG reporting rather than outside-in. Relying on indicators of ESG performance that are taken from existing standards means deferring to broad global considerations at the expense of local preferences and priorities. Attempting to achieve the standards listed in existing ESG standards can be challenging in emerging markets. Existing ESG standards tend to be focused on large corporations and assume certain organizational capabilities. GRI is a very popular ESG framework, and in its own words, 'The aim was to create the first accountability mechanism to ensure companies adhere to responsible environmental conduct principles, which was then broadened to include social, economic and governance issues'. (GRI, n.d.) But many firms and NGOs do not have the capability or the funds to adopt ESG practices at the levels proposed by GRI. That is what we mean when we say doing ESG reporting outside-in.

Rather, we suggest I3 projects identify the impacts that matter most to their partners and stakeholders. These impacts may take account of local histories and norms that are outside the consideration of typical ESG standards. Once these metrics have been identified, they can be reframed using the existing criteria from ESG Frameworks that are more familiar to the investment community. We would anticipate that impact metrics developed with an inside-out approach will have overlaps with other familiar ESG standards such as carbon emissions, good corporate governance, and fair and non-discriminatory Human Resources policies. Developing the real performance indicators that speak to the values and interests of I3 partners and stakeholders in specific terms and metrics that resonate locally is critical to I3 success. Restating these same impacts in the language of existing ESG frameworks that are familiar to investors is simply a matter of good communication. We believe most investors in I3s would prefer that their performance is aligned with the expectations of partners and stakeholders as it offers confidence in the investment's ultimate success, but these same investors might need these metrics translated into ESG-speak as a requirement of their own organizations.

Finally, we strongly suggest that any ESG performance reporting system use blockchain technology for collecting and verifying the accuracy of data measuring impacts. I3s rely so heavily on trust with partners and stakeholders, that blockchains add a level of reliability and transparency that is consistent with the I3 approach.

## Aligning Supply Chains

Our suggestion to work on unifying supply chains is applicable to I3s that address social issues involved in business activities that are part of a larger supply chain—the farming of commodities is just such a case. For many farms that are the starting point of a supply chain along which a commodity is exported, processed, packaged, shipped, and sold, there are considerable concerns about their sustainability. Labor conditions can be unhealthy, wages low, environmental damage considerable, carbon footprint large, and community development weak.

Such a condition would be an obvious target of I3s to identify and adopt innovative solutions to these problems and attract impact investments. But making a strong case for the financial returns can be difficult given the typical volatility of global commodity prices and the expanding risks faced by global supply chains due to extreme weather conditions. Taking steps to unify the supply chain can reduce some of those risks and provide greater confidence impact investors. For example, in the C3 project, the expanded cultivation of cocoa farms will mean a greater yield of cocoa beans. We have been working with local chocolate manufacturers to secure an agreement that they will purchase the additional beans provided they follow the sustainability protocols specified in the impact investment.

The expanded cocoa production will also provide new opportunities for chocolate products to be exported—along with the beans—to Caribbean and Latin American countries, the US, EU, and other global markets. To that end, we have organized webinars targeting tree-to-bar and bean-to-bar chocolatiers in Trinidad and Tobago on different practices regarding sustainable packaging options and practices in the US and EU. And we are fostering B2B discussions between chocolate vendors in the Washington, DC region with the goal of establishing partnerships focused on featuring Trinidad and Tobago (e.g. 'Chocolate island') chocolate.

These and other efforts are just a few examples of how unifying supply chains can help increase confidence that impact investments made in I3 projects will have robust financial returns despite the clear risks associated with investing in global commodities.

## Value for Money

The term value for money is used casually to express the basic idea of getting a good deal. But we are suggesting its use as a specific project assessment technique in developing I3 projects. Value for money (VFM), as with many concepts is defined in various ways. We prefer the definition and explanation of the National Auditing Office (NAO) in the United Kingdom because of its laser focus on outcomes and its commitment to quantifying those outcomes:

> The National Audit Office (NAO) uses three criteria to assess the value for money of government spending i.e. the optimal use of resources to achieve the intended outcomes: Economy: minimizing the cost of resources used or required (inputs)—spending less; Efficiency: the relationship between the output from goods or services and the resources to produce them—spending well; and, Effectiveness: the relationship between the intended and actual results of public spending (outcomes)—spending wisely.
>
> (NAO, n.d.)

Combining all three considerations when assessing the value of an impact investment adds depth and sophistication you cannot achieve with only a cost-benefit analysis or by only measuring changes in efficiency.

In addition, NAO's view of VFM includes, where applicable one more 'E'—'Equity: the extent to which services are available to and reach all people that they are intended to—spending fairly. Some people may receive differing levels of service for reasons other than differences in their levels of need' (NAO, n.d.). The additional consideration of equity acknowledges that one-size may not fit everyone: some people might need assistance in order to use the service provided; some people might need descriptions of the services provided and how to access them in a different language or using different terms; or, the level of service provided to one group or community may differ from that of another group or community despite having similar needs.

Because I3s emphasize innovative approaches to solving problems, the VFM technique is a natural fit. VFM calculations are always pushing questions about the project and its impact: is there a cheaper way to do it? Are we really providing what people need? Are different people with different needs getting the appropriate service? Is there a way to expand the number of impacts without spending more money? Are people eligible to receive services being treated fairly? VFM calculations are always seeking a better set of outcomes with a lower cost—exactly the same two issues of prime interest to impact investors.

In our experience, employing a VFM calculation is particularly useful when comparing past practices in delivering services with a new I3 approach. In both public and private sector organizations, going with what has worked in the past is a common norm. And suggestions of adopting an innovation approach can meet with resistance from those who are used to and like the tried-and-true. But VFM can reveal where an alternative approach can improve outcomes without necessarily raising the cost of services delivered—sometimes it can be done cheaper—and quantify those impacts so they are tangible benefits. Even if a formal and full VFM calculation is not undertaken, taking a VFM mindset and asking lots of questions about whether there is a better way to solve problems is useful.

## Cross-sector Collaboration

I3s are project-based investments, and they are built around collaborations with partners and strong engagements with stakeholders. Cross-sector collaborations have grown in popularity as an alternative to the direct provision of services by governments, but understanding the different forms of cross-sector collaborations and the implications for how organizations can work together. We suggest that I3 organizers consider this issue from two perspectives: first, what form of collaboration is to be expected with the government, and second, what form of collaboration is to be expected with other project partners?

Impact investments may mean that the private sector is financing a major share of the project, but it does not mean that government agencies and public officials will be interested in—and potentially assert themselves into—how the project is designed, financed, and operated.

We suggest that proponents of I3s anticipate a possible role for the government and, at the earliest stages of project development, engage relevant government officials. The spark for creating an I3 may be borne out of a frustration of under-performing government programs and policies, or the dedication of insufficient funding to addressing a problem, but government agencies can make important contributions to an I3. For example, for the C3 project, many cocoa farms do not have adequate connections between their property and public roads. If cocoa farms are to expand their production, some of the investment will be needed to build roads on private lands, but government agencies could be engaged as partners and approve building or improving the same roads but on public lands. For these types of arrangements, we recommend public-private partnerships as the preferred form of cross-sector collaboration.

Collaborating successfully with partners on an I3 project is not guaranteed. People who work for not-for-profits, businesses, entrepreneurs, philanthropies, and social enterprises have different norms and expectations of success, and sometimes conceive the motivations of other organizations in stereotypic ways. While collaborative partnerships might share the same interests and values, working together can pose challenges. We typically recommend that network governance is the most appropriate form of cross-sector collaboration for I3 partnerships.

Network governance is a collaborative arrangement that involves non-governmental actors working interdependently to achieve outcomes that are perceived to be superior to what any individual organization can accomplish on its own. Networks typically organize themselves in three different ways: 'self-governed', where network members are collectively involved in their own governance and are cooperating in solving a problem; 'lead organization', where one entity coordinates the rest of the network's operations; and 'network administrative organization', where a designated entity (with designated staff and responsibilities) supports and governs the network's activities. The best way to organize any given governance network depends on the set of activities undertaken, the complexity involved in producing the outcomes, the resources available to support the governance network operations, and the flexibility organizations have in selecting what types of actions they may undertake. And the local conditions and circumstances—including the history of past problem-solving actions—inform the best form of network governance to adopt. (Forrer et al. 2014)[5]

## Project Branding

Creating a brand for the initiative you are looking to finance as an impact investment can be a major asset. A compelling brand can facilitate stakeholder engagement and inspire impact investors. And a clever and evocative brand can make messaging much easier. Of course, a clever brand has no effect on the fundamentals of the project, and some might completely dismiss as a gimmick the suggestion that branding is important. But the experiences of impact investing tell a different story.

Investors in Green Bonds pay a premium of three to five basis points based on recent research, even though the use of the proceeds has no discernable additional value than that with other investment instruments. Why? Branding. A growing number of investors want to place their money in funds or projects that are associated with more sustainable business practices and outcomes. And when the opportunity arises, they are willing to pay a little bit more for the opportunity to secure such green investments. Of course, as with any branding, if it is done disingenuously or dishonestly and amounts only to 'greenwashing', there is no benefit. Our suggestion for brand impact investments is simply taking the lesson of Green Bonds and applying it to the I3 Approach.

Using branding for the C3 project has been very helpful in communicating to people what our goals were and how we were different from others who had considered investing in Trinidad and Tobago cocoa farms. Many impact investments in agriculture explore what opportunities may exist to create carbon credits and sell them. But by incorporating this interest into the name of the project, we showed concern not only for expanding production on cocoa farms, but also for the environment. We built on that interest by promoting our goal of producing 'Net-Zero Carbon Chocolate'. This was an aspirational goal, and we recognized that the actual determination would be highly dependent on how we designed the analysis. We had to develop the methods ourselves to do the calculation, but our branding signaled our strong interest in linking our impact investment with addressing climate change.

Eventually, we settled on 'Chocolate Island' as the meta-branding we used to refer to our broader vision for the Trinidad and Tobago cocoa sector. There was plenty of justification. The islands are home to what many consider the premium cacao species, Trinitario. Chocolate made from the pods of these cacao trees has been treasured for centuries. When you think of Brazil, you think coffee; when you think of Scotland, you think of Scotch whiskey. Now, when you think of Trinidad and Tobago, you will think … Chocolate Island! The branding also expressed that the range of business opportunities and potential investments extended well beyond the cocoa farms themselves. 'Choco-tourism' sites and events could be expanded. New foods and beverages could be crafted out of cocoa or out of the cacao pod. Existing cocoa-based products could be more widely marketed.

The branding brought a sense of excitement and possibilities to the impact investment opportunity. It helped people see that our effort cared about more than money, and that the environmental and social elements of the impact investment were not a sidebar. 'Cocoa, Carbon and Community', 'Net-Zero Carbon Chocolate', and 'Chocolate Island' helped to engage stakeholders and give them a sense that the project was about new possibilities and discoveries. It embodied our seriousness about partnering with other businesses, government agencies, entrepreneurs, and farmers to promote and advance their goals as a vehicle for making impact investments in Trinidad and Tobago even more attractive.

## Notes

1  An extensive discussion on value creation and capture is available in *Global Governance Enterprises* (2016) Routledge. This section draws on discussions in that publication.
2  Agreements structured in this way are often referred to as Social Impact Bonds
3  Private finance initiatives (PFIs) were first launched in the UK in the early 1990s. This infrastructure financing model is referred to today as P3s in countries such as the U.S., Canada, and Australia. For other countries, the more common designation is PPP.
4  "Catalytic capital is defined as debt, equity, guarantees, and other investments that accept disproportionate risk and/or concessionary returns relative to a conventional investment in order to generate positive impact and/or enable third-party investment that otherwise would not be possible." https://www.macfound.org › programs › catalytic-capital...
5  *Managing Cross Sector Collaboration*

## References

Circle, Z. (2023, July 12). '5 best ESG reporting frameworks explained with examples – 2023'. *LinkedIn*. https://www.linkedin.com/pulse/5-best-esg-reporting-frameworks-explained-examples -2023.

Forrer, John, James Jed Kee, and Eric Boyer. (2014). *Governing cross-sector collaboration*. John Wiley & Sons.

'GRI - Mission & history'. Accessed 14 November 2023. https://www.globalreporting.org/about-gri /mission-history/.

Idle, T. (2023, August 25). 'Future-proofing coffee through agroforestry and innovative finance'. *Innovation*. https://www.innovationforum.co.uk/articles/future-proofing-coffee-through -agroforestry-and-innovative-finance.

National Audit Office (NAO). 'Successful commissioning toolkit assessing value for money'. Accessed 14 November 2023. https://www.nao.org.uk/successful-commissioning/general-principles/value -for-money/assessing-value-for-money/.

# Chapter 7

# Ideation Phase

## Ideation—The Initial Phase of Appraising a Project or Social Enterprise

The ideation phase is the initial appraisal phase for a project or enterprise. There will be subsequent phases, such as the feasibility phase, when increased rigor and different criteria are used to test whether a project or enterprise should be approved to move to the next phase and eventually to being implemented. Although the rigor increases with each phase, the tendency is that at later phases, projects are not rejected outright as much as they are required to reconsider the makeup of one or more project components. As such, the ideation phase is most often where enterprises and projects get rejected. In this chapter we outline the important features of the ideation phase, so that good ideas will have an opportunity to move to the feasibility phase.

As the name suggests, the feasibility study phase provides the entrepreneur with a good understanding as to whether the social enterprise or project will achieve its two main objectives—i) to intentionally achieve a positive social or environmental outcome that is measurable; and ii) to achieve financial sustainability so that principal repayment can be made to investors, along with a return, on the loan capital. Although it is not uncommon to have financial, economic, and distributional appraisals done separately, this book uses an integrated approach that views all three as part of the same evaluation.

At the end of each phase there should be a formal go/no-go decision-making process, each with its own indicators. The process uses the information collected along with the analytical results to decide whether to continue to the next phase. A no-go decision does not necessarily mean dropping the project as it does a recheck or reverification. These decision points are often called phase gates when a go/no-go decision needs to be made. It is important to note that a phase gate is about validation and verification that then leads to a 'yes' or 'no' decision to the project. For instance, if the causal logic is verified to not be strong this will likely lead to a no-go phase gate decision and either the project will be stopped or the causal logic improved.

The feasibility phase is broken out into two sections—1) pre-feasibility study, and 2) detailed feasibility study. Although part of the same phase, there will be a go/no-go decision-making process after the completion of the pre-feasibility study. Others have broken the two out into separate phases which is also acceptable. The important issue is that the investment appraisal team fully understand the objectives of the two phases.

The pre-feasibility study is meant to obtain an inexpensive overall potential of the net social benefits of the business or project. It should provide the project team with sufficient information to decide as to whether to proceed with the much more costly feasibility study. The pre-feasibility study will primarily use desktop research to obtain biased estimates that

DOI: 10.4324/9781003276920-8

reflect the higher-end amounts of all of the key and secondary variables, and especially for those variables with significant uncertainty.

The pre-feasibility study specifically biases the data used in the modeling so that it does not accept projects based on outlier or overly optimistic estimates of benefits and costs. It uses a downwards bias for benefits and an upwards bias for costs.

The pre-feasibility study uses desktop research to obtain data that reflects the probable magnitude of the identified key variables. It will also provide a good measure of whether the project will meet its objectives and will justify the investment in collecting additional secondary data, as well as primary data. The feasibility study is all about improving the accuracy and understanding of the key variables.

The project or social enterprise is assessed on its merit of achieving expected financial, economic, and social benchmarks. Financial tools, such as sensitivity analysis, are used to identify and understand how key variables will affect the intended outcome results.

It is at the end of the feasibility phase that a decision is made, based on financial and net social benefit criteria, on whether to approve the project and begin detailed design and structuring of the project investment instrument for the project or social enterprise.

## Ideation Phase

The ideation phase is about how the project or social enterprise will solve a difficult social issue. There are two main attributes that need to be evident. These are the effectiveness of the idea and its efficiency. The interventions need to be effective so that above-average results are achieved. Secondly, they need to be efficient in that the cost of achieving social benefits is less than other current options.

In order to understand proposed interventions, a document is prepared that describes how the desired results will be achieved. This is often called the Theory of Change (TOC) and it describes the causal logic of how and why these interventions will achieve improved outcome level results.

This chapter provides an overview of the TOC and the theoretical models that help explain it. Although we list the theoretical models, the results chain model is used in the examples provided. After the overview of the TOC and supporting results chain, there will be an overview of the practical steps in developing a TOC. Box 7.1 provides the basic elements of a TOC.

Every project has activities that lead to achieving an output, and when these outputs are combined, along with a behavioral change of key stakeholders, there is an outcome that is achieved. The TOC provides the detail on how this will happen and begins with the end in mind. It identifies the desired long-term impact and works backwards to figure out what outcomes must be achieved along with the cause-and-effect logic between outcomes and outputs. In addition to being put into a narrative, these can be modeled in various ways, for instance, using theoretical models—logic model, logical framework, outcome models and frameworks, and a results chain.

---

### BOX 7.1   BASIC ELEMENTS OF A THEORY OF CHANGE

A theory of change can be modeled in various ways, but all of them maintain the basic elements which are i) causal logic; ii) assumptions; and iii) contextual influences and conditions.

These theoretical models provide a framework for identifying the activities or interventions that will lead to outputs and outcomes and contribute towards achieving long-term goals. This approach provides for improved planning as the cause-and-effect allows the planning team to go through and ask 'if' we do this, 'then' this will be the result. It can also help in evaluation as progress can be measured towards the longer-term goals.

In Figure 7.1 there is a simple results chain where financial, human, and other resources are mobilized as part of the project inputs that will support the activities. Work is undertaken in the form of activities that will convert the inputs into planned outputs. As an example, consider the activities required in developing a new math curriculum. The inputs would include an approved budget, a multi-organizational team, and the facilities for the team to work. The activities might include curriculum development, training of teachers, and the printing of the new textbooks. These inputs and activities would lead to outputs that are measured by the number of teachers trained, and the number of textbooks delivered to the schools.

The outputs, as seen from the example, are the product of converting inputs and activities into a measurable and tangible result. The intermediate outcomes are achieved by the logical sequencing of the outputs by a specific stakeholder group. To continue with our example, the outcomes might include i) teachers using the textbooks and curriculum in the classroom; ii) students understanding the curriculum; and iii) improved student performance on mathematics tests. It is important to note that these outcomes are not fully under the control of the service provider. There is a need for behavioral change to occur in order to achieve the intended outcome. In other words, the implementation of the project consists of the inputs, activities, and outputs; whereas, the development outcomes also require behavioral change

# RESULTS CHAIN

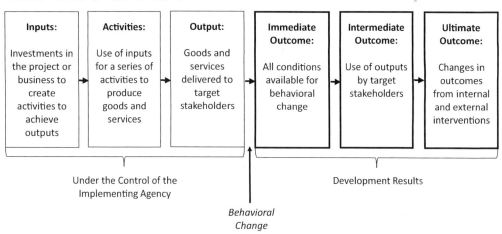

*Figure 7.1* The theory of change can be modeled using various theoretical models. The use of a logical framework is often used but in all instances the model will demonstrate the causal logic, those interventions the project has control over, and any key assumptions.

*Source:* Authors, drawing from multiple sources.

of key project stakeholders. This interaction between the project implementation and the successful behavioral change will determine the results and the project impact.

Too many service providers talk about the impact of their projects based on what they were able to accomplish—the number of teachers trained and books distributed—rather than on the behavioral change and the impacts that result—improved math test scores and teachers' continued use of the new curriculum. Implementing service organizations that use implementation results as impact may or may not have achieved genuine developmental results, and will certainly not be able to make changes to continually improve project outcomes.

The use of a results chain or other theoretical model can be useful in the process used for developing a TOC. A TOC will begin by identifying the expected project intermediate outcomes and then working backwards. Figure 7.2 shows the steps that are taken in developing a TOC.

The importance of the TOC is that it clearly defines all the necessary and sufficient conditions required to achieve the intermediate outcomes. The TOC depicts a sequence of activities and events that lead to outcomes. This 'backwards mapping' requires the design team to take the project from its desired intermediate outcome objective through the steps shown in Figure 7.2.

The team makes explicit the causal logic behind the project and maps the project interventions along a logical pathway of change. Experienced practitioners will make every effort to fully involve stakeholders when putting together the TOC as doing so will further refine the project design and provide improved insights into changing behaviors. When these consultations are done well, they will provide the design team with insights into the best interventions and outputs. While developing this pathway of change, the participating stakeholders will include their assumptions which will be examined and refined and the remaining assumptions then classified and tested.

## Developing a Theory of Change

- Identify the expected project outcomes – ultimate/intermediate/immediate
- Backwards mapping/preconditions for success – outcome/output/activities

- With stakeholders identify the basic assumptions
- Classify assumptions – i) outcome connectors; ii) precondition validation; iii) activity links

- Develop a logical causal pathway involving stakeholders for behavior insights
- Further refine assumptions to recognize the hypothesis being made for the project

- Indicators to monitor the project and to evaluate results
- Inclusion of stakeholders in the selection of the indicators

- Narrative that explains the logic of the project
- Citing of learning from other projects that verify assumptions behind causal pathway

*Figure 7.2* The theory of change is meant to be participatory in that all key stakeholders bring their unique perspective to its development. Each of the steps brings a further refinement and clarity to how the interventions are to deliver the desired results.

*Source*: Authors, drawing from multiple sources.

In addition, the assumptions will include any evidence from literature reviews of similar projects, as well as risks that might affect achieving intended results, and will be classified as being i) outcome connectors—improving the movement from immediate outcomes to intermediate and then ultimate outcome; ii) precondition validation—the necessary evidence that preconditions for success have been met; and iii) activity linkages—project activities have evidence-base for supporting outputs and outcomes. In many projects, the implementing team knows the sector's best practices and will consider the use of proven activities for achieving industry-standard outputs as being a well-designed project. Often, very little consideration is given to outcome connectors or precondition validation.

The logical causal pathway will become evident as project design team members work with stakeholders in an iterative manner. The TOC approach to planning is meant to provide incentives for further defining and providing clarity to outcomes throughout the process. Every population has its own specific data and a uniqueness that must be unpacked and investigated. Naturally, the time frame for achieving success needs to be taken into consideration when developing the TOC. This attention to detail is important in the financial and risk analysis. Experienced investors will always be interested in knowing the length of time for achieving intermediate outcome goals.

The use of a theoretical model, such as a results chain, is helpful in selecting the indicators that will be measured along the chain. A results chain sets out the sequence of inputs, activities, and outputs that are expected to improve outcome level results. Indicators are used to i) monitor program implementation, ii) manage performance, and iii) evaluate results. It is important to identify indicators all along the results chain. The project design team needs to keep in mind the objective of the indicators being selected. The monitoring of project implementation will be focused on inputs, activities, and outputs. In most cases, this information will be used for reporting to investors and others. For performance management, the scope is squarely on improving results and the purpose is to learn so that results can be continuously improved. The impact evaluation indicators are for assessing the impact and the purpose in most cases is for transparency and accountability. Much more will be discussed in Chapter 12.

A well-articulated TOC will be of great assistance to the implementing and managing team. It provides everyone with a common vision for the project, its objectives, and the path to achieving intended outcomes. The TOC informs the design team whether the project might not be able to achieve one or more intended outcomes as the causal logic could not be substantiated and clearly shown in the TOC. The inadequacy of the project will become evident and as difficult as it might be, the project should be rejected if appropriate changes cannot be made to the design. Although a project might make it through this initial stage, the feasibility study would further identify its weaknesses and substantiate the recommendation for project rejection as a 'no go' at the feasibility stage gate.

Once the TOC has been drafted, it is helpful to get feedback from all major stakeholders. A helpful exercise includes holding interviews with the stakeholders affected by, or in some manner benefit from, the project. In some instances, there will be stakeholders negatively affected and these people should also be interviewed. The interview may include staff, donors, clients, government ministries, and key partners. Usually 10–15 interviews bring sufficient breadth for key themes to emerge. The purpose of the interviews is to gain a 360-degree perspective of the organization's work and impact to date as well as to gather other landscape factors that may inform the assumptions under which the project interventions take place.

Once the interviews have taken place, any gaps within the TOC can be filled by having an organizational team come together for a 'sensemaking session'. A series of three 2-hour sensemaking sessions with staff will consolidate the TOC. The focus of these meetings is three-fold:

1.  Taking stock—to reflect on key themes emerging from the interviews and explore link-ages between the themes. The focus should be on linking the interventions to areas of impact as well as surfacing assumptions
2.  Getting clear—to present options or iterations of the TOC and to reflect on areas of resonance and surface any ongoing dissonance or areas for further discussion
3.  Moving forward—to validate the final TOC narratives (if possible, accompany it with a diagram—see example below) and identify indicators for measuring impact

## Performance Indicators

The results chain identifies the expected impacts resulting from behavior change and the project or business outputs and activities. It will be important to measure these expected impacts, but before being able to do so, a decision needs to be made on the purpose of the measurement and how the impact data will be used. In some cases, it is because a donor is requesting that the project measure certain impacts. For others, it might be to learn and improve impacts. Both are legitimate and once the purpose has been determined the appropriate indicators can be selected.

Indicators are too often thought of for monitoring program implementation and to make sure the project is 'going to plan'. For monitoring, the focus is on inputs, activities, and outputs and the project management team can know whether they are implementing the project according to plan. Monitoring is most useful for reporting purposes.

The use of a performance management system puts the emphasis on development results and instead of a focus on implementing to plan, it is asking the question of whether the project is on track to achieve its intended outcomes. Performance management is all about learning and finding new ways of improving the project results, especially at the outcome level.

Regardless of the system being used, there is a need to select indicators along the entire results chain. It is important to be able to understand the causal logic of how outcomes are achieved. When outcome indicators are measured along with implementation indicators, the project manager gains insights on how to improve the results of the project. In developing indicators, engaging project stakeholders is important as they will have unique and helpful experiences. Key stakeholders will make sure that the indicators are good measures of performance.

A widely used method of developing good indicators is to make sure they are SMART. SMART KPI is an acronym for specific, measurable, attainable, relevant, and time-bound (SMART) key performance indicators (KPI).

An indicator needs to be 'specific' as the information should be operational and narrow in focus so that it clearly indicates the *who* and *what* of the intervention. The *how, where,* and *who* should also be part of the indicator as these will provide for the action of the intervention.

A measurable indicator is more than being aligned with a ranked value that can show change over time. The design of a measurable indicator must also take into account whether the project time frame will allow for these results to be achieved. It also must consider whether the indicators are realistically achievable.

The 'A' in SMART is sometimes referred to as 'achievable' although it also needs to include 'attributable'. There is a strong relationship between these two concepts. There are times when a project will overestimate its impact because of other activities taking place in the same area. These inflated outcomes cannot be attributed to the project. Many impact investors are wary of claims of unrealistic achievements. This is the reason for many investors wanting to use an experimental approach to evaluating the project. Such approaches, if designed properly, can ensure that the results attributed to the project are strongly linked to the project's efforts.

To be 'relevant', an indicator should link back to the theory of change and the outcomes of the project. To be a valid measure of different levels of results it needs to tie into those used in the theory of change. This will often include making sure the data can be obtained in a timely fashion, with reasonable frequency, and at a reasonable cost.

The concept of being 'time bound' is important for several reasons, including that—i) the data must be collected at regular time intervals so that it can be used for decision-making; ii) there might be a predetermined timing of the collection for certain data; and iii) there can be a time lag between outputs being delivered and the intended outcome being achieved. As such, indicators must be selected that will reflect these dynamics that are at play.

As mentioned, it is important to select indicators all along the results chain. Without indicators being in place throughout the results chain, an impact evaluation will only be able to determine whether the predicted results happened and not be able to explain the logical sequencing that took place.

# Chapter 8

# Scoping Phase

After a decision has been made to investigate the use of impact investment financing for a proposed project, the next step is to do a landscape or scoping analysis. A scoping exercise can provide added confidence by ascertaining those other actors, whose involvement is critical, are interested and available to become involved in the work being proposed.

Since no two entrepreneurs or initiatives are the same, the number of actors needed to support a business or project will vary, depending on the proposed work and how it will be financed and structured. For instance, one social enterprise entrepreneur might not require the participation of any other actors, whereas another might need assistance from a business accelerator. In the latter case, the entrepreneur would need to confirm that these services are available and that the social enterprise is eligible to participate. Thus, the scoping exercise can save time and resources.

When the term social entrepreneur is used, most people immediately assume that the reference is to a business or a social enterprise owner. However, the term can also be used for people designing new social programs to be implemented as impact investments. The Center for the Advancement of Social Entrepreneurship, housed within the Fuqua School of Business at Duke University, defines social entrepreneurship as

> the process of recognizing and resourcefully pursuing opportunities to create social value. Social entrepreneurs are innovative, resourceful, and results-oriented. They draw upon the best thinking in both the business and nonprofit worlds to develop strategies that maximize their social impact. These entrepreneurial leaders operate in all kinds of organizations: large and small; new and old; religious and secular; nonprofit, for-profit, and hybrid. These organizations comprise the 'social sector'.

In Box 8.1 David Borstein explains the role of the social entrepreneur. As discussed earlier, the social entrepreneur must determine whether the proposed undertaking is an impact investment. To apply an impact investing model, a project or business must have two primary objectives:

1.  To pursue a positive, measurable social or environmental outcome
2.  To achieve financial sustainability so that investors can receive repayment of their loan capital along with a financial return

The structure of an impact investment will be determined by the instrument that is used. There are instances when an impact investment can have several participating actors that can range from one to six and in some cases more. In a relatively simple case, an entrepreneur might have everything needed to start a social enterprise except investment capital. In

DOI: 10.4324/9781003276920-9

a more complex design, an entrepreneur might be seeking to use an impact bond, which is part of the family of results-based financing (RBF) or payment-by-results (PBR)[1] and will require several supporting actors. Later in this chapter we will talk specifically about impact bonds and those actors that are involved in making it a success. For now, it is important to know that using an impact bond will require an outcome payer—this might be a government ministry, government donor, or other institution that agrees to pay for predefined results usually at the outcome level—investors, a service provider, an independent evaluator; and a community to be served by the project. In many instances, an intermediary is also needed to coordinate the many aspects of the SIB or PbR.

---

**BOX 8.1   ROLE OF THE SOCIAL ENTREPRENEUR IN DRIVING SOCIAL CHANGE**

What business entrepreneurs are to the economy; social entrepreneurs are to social change. They are driven, creative individuals who question the status quo, exploit new opportunities, refuse to give them up, and remake the world for the better.

David Borstein, Author, *How to Change the World: Social Entrepreneurs and the Power of New Ideas*

---

In this chapter, we will define each of the types of possible actors and will discuss what entrepreneurs may want to look for as part of an impact investing partnership engagement. Since building successful partnerships is so crucial, we will give attention to this topic in the latter part of the chapter. Understanding the different means of engaging in impact investing is important to the scoping phase, as entrepreneurs will want to select the best approach to sustaining social outcomes. At the end of the chapter, we provide a brief discussion of impact measurement as it pertains to this early scoping phase. Impact measurement will be discussed in greater detail in Chapter 12.

Since impact investing is growing and, for the most part, receiving positive feedback from professional institutions and the media it is not surprising that many organizations are claiming to be a social enterprise or an impact investing project. Although some business entrepreneurs might refer to themselves as social entrepreneurs because their product or service is socially or environmentally friendly, this in itself would not be a sufficient condition to qualify as an impact investment. In impact investing, the social entrepreneur's *intentionality* is the most overlooked aspect. Social impact doesn't just happen; it must be carefully planned. In many instances, businesses might be providing positive economic and social benefits, but these elements are not intentional in the design and implementation plan. Instead, these entrepreneurs identified an opportunity for making money and there are economic and social benefits, as would be expected. The key question in determining whether a business is a social enterprise is its intentionality to maximize net social benefits. This is consistent with the criteria mentioned on the previous page.

A social entrepreneur must consider whether the products or services they are selling actually support social needs. Here are some good questions to ask:

- Do the business and products have a defined social purpose?
- Are profits largely reinvested in furthering the social cause?
- Does the financial investment arrangement intentionally include plans to achieve a positive social or environmental impact?

As we saw in the previous chapter, a theory of change and logic model are key parts of the process of mapping out intentionality.

Social entrepreneurs recognize the need for innovation and novel applications to solve social challenges within a community. Like other entrepreneurs, they must be willing to take on risk, especially in the early stages of implementation, when their initiatives are often educating target audiences as to the needs and there might not yet be full acceptance. For instance, social entrepreneurs that work in vulnerable communities to reduce the onset of Type II diabetes will need to begin by educating people about the dangers of diabetes and then introduce lifestyle changes that will significantly reduce the likelihood of being diagnosed with this chronic disease. In this example, the entrepreneur recognizes the importance of prevention and will collect data on key performance indicators. Once the social entrepreneur has verifiable evidence of their success the project might further refine their approach through the use of impact investing and the use of a results-based financing instrument.

There can be several reasons for social entrepreneurs to want to use an impact investing financing instrument. Many social entrepreneurs have had disappointing experiences with the traditional process of seeking a grant to implement a project. Too many institutional donors approve or decline the proposal based largely on how well the proposal was written. This has incentivized many organizations to hire consultants to write the proposal. Another downside to traditional grants is that what is written in the proposal becomes part of a contractual agreement and changes to the project activities and outputs can only be made with a written request justifying the changes. After this justification is written it will then be reviewed by the donor, and if approved, a letter of concurrence is sent to the service provider. Donors do not take into consideration that every project experiences a new reality once they begin the implementation phase, but the traditional grant provides little flexibility on how the implementation will take place. Ironically, the focus is not on the project outcomes which is the most important objective of the project. Once a contract has been signed, the service delivery organization is held accountable for implementing the steps (or outputs) agreed to in the proposal. Making any changes requires detailed explanations and contract amendments that will often take weeks for approval. The donor will be convinced they are doing the best for the project community by holding the service delivery organization accountable for the activities that were described in the proposal. The monitoring system being used has the service provider reporting on the implementation of activities and outputs against the proposal plan.

In contrast, social entrepreneurs are focused on serving communities and working with them to find innovative means to improve outcome-level results. The focus is on achieving results, not on *how* the results are achieved. This is not to suggest that implementation is not important, but when the evidence shows there is a better means of implementing then there is a freedom to do so. The social entrepreneur will monitor and document their processes carefully, but experimenting, learning, and making changes at the output level are at the discretion of the project manager and team. There is no need to request donor concurrence before adjusting the project plans. The social entrepreneur has the freedom to respond to the social, political, and cultural context and to use performance data to make changes to the theory of change and to reallocate the budget so that improved outcomes can be achieved. In other words, the social entrepreneur is determined to find the right combination of outputs and associated costs that will maximize effectiveness and the net social benefits, and to distribute them so that the poor and marginalized are the primary recipients.

Effectiveness and efficiency are important to all entrepreneurs, but not for the same reason. For the business entrepreneur, very often the objective is to maximize profits. For the social entrepreneur the primary objective is to *maximize net social benefits*. Figure 8.1

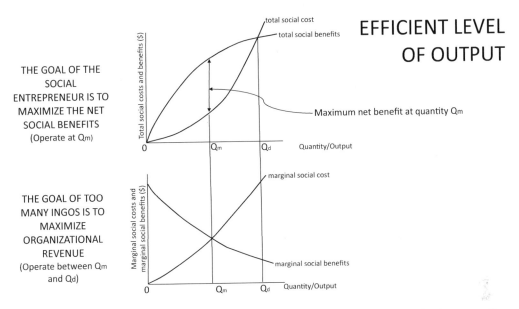

Figure 8.1 Adequate funding is needed to respond to humanitarian emergencies and development efforts, but how assistance is delivered will demonstrate whether a project is designed to make a maximum impact. Too many organizations presume that more funding equates to more impact, and although that might be true, the impact might be deployed inefficiently. Development practitioners need to change their thinking from how to secure the most funding to how to make the greatest impact.

Source: Authors, drawing from multiple sources.

shows that net social benefits are maximized when marginal social costs are equal to marginal social benefits, or where there is the largest positive gap between total social benefits and total social costs.

The social entrepreneur is different not only from the business entrepreneur, but also from many INGOs in how they are motivated. When a social entrepreneur is calculating a project budget there is a strong motivation to get the most out of every dollar. This motivation comes from incentives that impact investing inherently has as part of its makeup, but also those that the design team have included in the project. Too many NGOs write proposals with the intent on getting as much funding as possible. At times, even donors will encourage NGOs to increase the budget. This will often happen at year-end. These organizations do not recognize that increased revenue does not necessarily translate into increased impact. The social entrepreneur does understand this concept very well.

## The Actors

During the scoping stage, the social entrepreneur will meet with other impact investing actors, especially those that may play a critical role in their initiative's success and whose partnerships are thus essential.

By definition, impact investing requires investors. In this section we will identify the different investors and the role they play in impact investing. After that, we discuss service providers and the criteria used in making this selection. In many cases, it is the service provider that initiates an exploration into impact investing. As we will see, some service providers have a firm foundation and are ready to begin the process of becoming investment-ready; whereas, others will have some prerequisite work to complete before they can begin the process. Very often, this work involves collecting verifiable data of their project's impact.

The use of an impact bond will require several different actors and the role of each will be discussed along with the critique of how expensive it is to design and implement. There have been some excellent reviews of impact bonds and whether they are a useful development financing instrument. Well recognized institutions, such as the Brookings Foundation, have done some excellent work on evaluating the use of impact bonds.

Although it is not too surprising that social entrepreneurs and investors are at the core of impact investing there also must be someone who is willing to pay for outcomes using an impact investment. Increasingly, local governments are looking for a means of improving development outcomes, especially in those areas for which they are responsible. Therefore, we include a discussion of local government authorities' interest in innovative financing tools. Some of the most exciting projects currently taking place include local government and are using an innovative twist on the familiar public private partnership (P3). One of these instruments, impact bonds, have proven to be a very valuable tool for work in low- and middle-income locations, as well as in Western countries including the UK and the US.

The last actor we examine is the intermediary. An intermediary is often the impact investing partner that understands the big picture—that is, it has the experience and expertise to work with other actors in building their own capacity while also coordinating with all the actors to achieve the intended development outcomes.

### Investors

Experienced social entrepreneurs may have their own network of potential investors, but they may also rely on established networks, such as the Global Impact Investing Network (GIIN). Personal networks provide entrepreneurs with established relationships, which are often crucial in initiating an investment opportunity. To broaden one's personal network, institutional networks are a good starting point.

Various online tools can assist in the search for prospective investors. For example, Crunchbase and AngelList enable an investor search that automatically populates as filters are selected.

Many start-ups look for initial capital from family and friends. For most entrepreneurs, the focus is on getting the enterprise or project off the ground. Crowdfunding can be another source of capital.

## Angel Investors and Venture Capitalists

Angel investors are individuals who invest in start-ups. Some angel investors work with social entrepreneurs. In most cases, those who participate in impact investing will prefer to get involved at an early stage. Angel investors often fill the gap between the initial help from family and friends that gets the enterprise or project off the ground and the point when one is ready to approach venture capitalists.

Angel investors may provide Series A financing, or the first significant round of capital financing, intended to make the enterprise operational or get the product developed. Series B financing then takes the enterprise or product to the next level. Series B is often triggered by strong achievements that take place after the Series A round. Finally, Series C financing further develops new products, expands into new markets, and pursues interest from venture capitalists; it will often require the assistance of an investment appraisal expert.

Venture capitalists (VCs), when considering an investment, focus on getting to know the management team and assessing its ability to execute the business plan. A VC might commit to an enterprise for ten years. Most often, a VC is a private equity investor that provides capital to impact investments, with high growth potential, in exchange for an equity stake. Typically, the VC will actively invest for three to four years but will be involved in the business, such as on the board, for about ten years. After this time, the VC liquidates its assets and maximizes its ROI.

## Family Offices

There is an investment trend amongst the wealthiest people that has them eliminating the middlemen, those who have managed their wealth, by creating their own 'family offices', or what is described as a personal investment firm. With such intimacy between the family offices and the individuals whose wealth they manage, there is a closely aligned set of motivations when the family office searches the world for investment opportunities. It's estimated that family offices have over $4 trillion in assets of which a very small, but growing amount is being targeted for impact investments. Some of these offices have a handful of staff; whereas, others have hundreds of people in their employ. It is estimated there are upwards of 10,000 family offices in North America, Europe, and Asian hubs such as Singapore and Hong Kong. Not too surprisingly, given the world's wealth distribution and investment experience, most family offices are located in North America.

The family office is set up to handle investment and wealth management for a family with usually over $100 million in investable assets. In most cases, this privately held company has as a key objective succession planning and the growth and transfer of wealth to the next generation of family members.

The family is always at the heart of family wealth management. Increasingly, the younger generation is looking at different models and means of investing that would be aligned with the family image. Impact investing has provided families with a principled approach of socially responsible investing that goes beyond simply not investing in tobacco, alcohol, gambling, or military products. Although family offices are private wealth management advisory firms, they also have an important distinction and that is the pulse of what is important to the family.

Family offices have a history of investing directly in start-ups, as well as in venture funds. These investments are often very strategic in that the family office is adding value based on their networks and other businesses.

## Fund Managers

As impact investing continues to grow in popularity, it has begun to attract interest from investment fund managers. For example, Vital Capital is a leading private equity fund focused on sub-Saharan Africa. In 2020, the fund celebrated its tenth anniversary of involvement in impact investing. Other notable impact investing firms include Triodos Investment Management, The Reinvestment Fund, BlueOrchard Finance S.A., and Community Reinvestment Fund, USA.

## Foundations

One can hardly talk about impact investing without mentioning the Rockefeller Foundation, which hosted the retreat in northern Italy where the term was coined. The Rockefeller Foundation and others have been promoting impact investing as an industry for the past 25 years, hoping to help this idea grow in a similar manner to how foundations helped grow the microfinance movement.

Many entrepreneurs, investors, and others hoped that foundations would play a prominent role in helping to get good projects financed and making sure that bad projects didn't get financed. However, project and enterprise investment appraisals have not been of consistent interest to foundations or government and other institutions that have shown an interest in furthering the development of impact investing.

## Pension Funds

In recent years, pension funds have shown increasing interest in impact investing, partly because pension holders began to demand a more diversified portfolio including impact investments. In addition, pension funds realize that the long-term nature of the investment is in alignment with their fund goals.

---

**BOX 8.2  PRESS RELEASE FROM RESPONSABILITY INVESTMENTS**

Zurich, 14 June 2021 – Convinced that targeted private investments can contribute substantially to the development goals of the UN Agenda 2030, Swiss impact asset manager responsAbility Investments, the Swedish International Development Agency SIDA and Danske Bank have joined forces to launch a novel social bond. Through the social bond, USD $177.5 million will flow to capital-constrained companies in developing countries. The selected companies' business models are characterized by their products and services achieving a measurable positive social impact. The launch builds on the recent popularity of social bonds in the capital markets and responsAbility's expertise in structuring impact investment solutions at scale, in lending to companies in developing countries and in managing credit risks.

---

A 2021 announcement by the Swedish pension funds Alecta and Afa Försakring demonstrated a paradigm shift in how pension funds view impact investments. Julian Jonsson, the portfolio manager at Alecta, made an interesting comment in a 2021 press release:

Alecta's, and other large investors', investments in social bonds have increased during the last couple of years. As long as we find good structures with credible partners such as responsAbility, we will continue to invest in products that give a stable return and enable solutions to pressing societal challenges. The problem, from our point of view, is that there is a lack of suitable products to invest in, not a lack in capital or will.

In other words, the big issue for large investors is gaining confidence that the deals presented to them have been properly appraised and structured. Box 8.2 provides the press release from responsAbility Investments

Pension funds have a fiduciary responsibility to protect their members' retirement resources. Unlike family offices and foundations, they do not offer subsidies to attract other investors. However, many pension fund managers view the fundamentals of impact investing as closely aligned with their fiduciary duty, mainly because of the long-term perspective associated with these investments. Pension fund members who are early in their careers will not begin collecting their pension for 40 years. The long-term nature of these investments allows pension funds to take on significant social issues, such as climate change, that require decades of focused attention. This long-term commitment combined with financial opportunity creates the opportunity to participate in solving big challenges. Pension funds are acutely aware that this can also mean big returns. When we add in concerns for strategic diversification and risk mitigation, impact investments could have considerable appeal to pension funds.

## Development Finance Institutions

In 2009, at the meeting of the Clinton Global Initiative in New York, the Global Impact Investing Network (GIIN) was announced along with a new asset class that would be known as impact investments. At the time, the network's 20 or so members included big banks, philanthropic institutions, and non-profit impact investment funds that were focused on investing in social enterprises that serve low-income individuals. The goal of GIIN is to share information on what works and what does not, along with creating a common language, and to find a means of impact measurement. In more recent years, the GIIN Annual Impact Investor Survey routinely reports that pension funds or insurance companies and development finance institutions (DFIs) manage the largest amount of impact investing assets.

DFIs play an important role in the international impact investment ecosystem, promoting economic development in underserved regions globally. They provide catalytic capital in markets where private sector investment is weak, drawing on comprehensive institutional knowledge and strong relationships in traditionally underserved markets. They adopt environmental and social standards for their investments to varying degrees, and they play a crucial role in leveraging partnerships between public- and private-sector stakeholders for larger-scale investments.

## Service Providers

Although service providers can be either for-profit, non-profit, or public-sector, most are non-governmental organizations (NGOs) or international non-governmental organizations (INGOs). Since NGOs and INGOs often do similar work, we will use the term 'NGOs' for both unless specifically referring to one or the other. NGOs have played a critical role in development, especially in rural areas of low- and middle-income countries. During the past decade, impact investing has begun to disrupt traditional grant funding mechanisms. This has impacted almost all NGOs, since they rely on grant income for programs. This new funding opportunity has led many NGOs to begin to explore opportunities for impact investing. Although NGOs have often made good partners for development projects, the introduction of impact investing has caused many of them to hesitate to become involved. The reasons are not always clear other than some have the sense that current private donors will not give philanthropically if they become investors. We have not been able to find any evidence of this happening. The reason why this is an unfounded concern is simply because investors separate their philanthropic giving from their investments. For those NGOs that are concerned that impact investing will cannibalize philanthropic giving, there appears to be a misinformed understanding of the objectives of impact investing. Primarily that the financing is from money allocated for investments and not philanthropy.

During the scoping stage, it is most useful to look for NGOs that have substantial experience in the development sector and whose commitment to impact can be clearly articulated and easily demonstrated for all their projects. The best way to identify these NGOs is to look for an evidence-based monitoring and evaluation system and to understand how data is used to make decisions towards achieving outcome-level results.

## Actors Required for an Impact Bond

We have mentioned that a common criticism of impact bonds is the costs of structuring and appraising the investment. Included in these costs is the time spent in pulling together the various actors. In this section, we highlight the six main actors that are involved in developing an impact bond. There can be others, such as a law firm who might provide a legal opinion on the financial or governance structuring.

During the scoping stage, it is important to identify the outcome payer. An outcome payer is an entity that will ultimately pay back the investors with a return on their investment. In a traditional grant scenario, the service provider would be looking to submit a proposal to a government donor or foundation, in the hope of receiving a grant. If the proposal is successful, the donor provides the financing to the service provider organization.

In contrast, when one is using a results-based financing tool, the service delivery organization approaches a potential outcome payer with a different proposition. Instead of approving a grant based on a well-written proposal, the outcome payer promises payments that are conditional on achieving predetermined results. Unlike with traditional grants, the outcome payer is only making a payment once a third-party has verified the results. In other words, the outcome payer is not paying for good intentions—which can lead to considerable cost savings. The outcome payer provides a conditional payment contract. Basically, if certain results are achieved then the predetermined amount of financing would be released. Without an outcome payer, a results-based project, such as an impact bond, cannot move forward. This is the reason why identifying an outcome payer is one of the initial steps during the scoping phase.

Social Impact Bonds and Development Impact Bonds (SIBs and DIBs) are two tools used to connect the allocation of money to an expectation of effective results. For a DIB, the outcome payer might be a government donor outside the country where the project will take place, a foundation, or even the private sector. An outcome payer agrees to purchase predetermined impact results. Since the payment is made only when the results have been validated, the service provider receives up-front working capital for the project from investors, based on their anticipation of a financial and social return. Box 8.3 provides evidence of traditional donors recognizing the improved efficiency and effectiveness of impact investments.

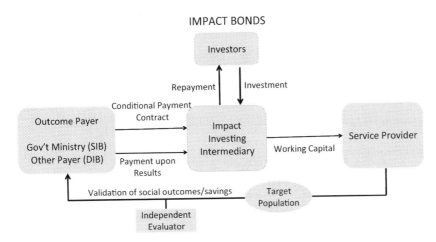

*Figure 8.2* Impact bonds are a form of outcomes-based contracts. Other names include pay-for-success financing and performance-based financing. In each instance, there are several players involved. During the early stages of the Scoping Phase, it will be important to identify a potential outcome payer and service provider.

*Source*: Authors, drawing from multiple sources.

---

**BOX 8.3    PRIVATE DONORS TRANSITIONING TO INVESTOR MINDSET**

Many private donors are starting to think more like investors, seeking better value for money and returns on investment in terms of social outcomes, and expecting NGOs to be more accountable and transparent than ever.

Patricia Tweedley, Senior Director, KPMG Development and Exempt Organizations, US

---

The difference between an SIB and a DIB involves who ultimately pays for the outcomes. In an SIB, the outcome payer is the government of the country where the work is undertaken. Box 8.4 provides an indicative list of questions that a government should answer when considering the use of a social impact bond. A DIB can be structured the same as a SIB, but the outcome payer will be an entity other than the government ministry. It might include a foreign government aid agency, a foundation, or a corporation.

Figure 8.2 provides an overview of how an impact bond works. There are six main agents, including the outcome payer that has been discussed.

---

**BOX 8.4    WHEN A SOCIAL IMPACT BOND SHOULD BE CONSIDERED BY GOVERNMENT**

*A social impact bond can be attractive to government ministries, but there are some key questions that should be considered. These include the following:*

Are there programs where there is underinvestment in prevention?

Are there promising programs that are currently underfunded or ready for scaling up?

Are there programs that get substantial funding but where there are serious concerns about performance?

Are there proven programs with a long waiting list?

Are there promising programs in other jurisdictions that should be taken into consideration?

Other actors involved in an impact bond include:

1. *Investors.* During the early days of impact bonds, the investors included were trusts and foundations. In the case of the first DIB arranged in a lower- or middle-income country, for a project to educate girls in Rajasthan, India, UBS Optimus Foundation was the investor. Since then, the investors have expanded to other categories as discussed above.
2. *The service provider*, who is usually selected based on prior evidence of achieving above-average outcome level results.
3. *The independent evaluator.* This is the validating agency that verifies the results reported.
4. *The target population* are the primary people or community benefiting from the project services.
5. The intermediary takes on an important role because of the unique nature of a development impact bond and more specifically the need to make the project into an investment. An intermediary can be a for-profit or a not-for-profit entity. Most importantly, an intermediary understands the process and can work effectively with all actors. The intermediary's primary function is to determine a project's feasibility as a high-quality investment. An intermediary works with the service provider to define outcome metrics, identify the most appropriate interventions, and to the interact with the outcome payer.

In consultation with the outcome payer, investor, and service provider, the intermediary develops the operating model, completes the financial modeling, calculates the outcome pricing, and ultimately produces a business plan and term sheets that will be used in an outcome contract and investor proposition. The intermediary also provides leadership in the legal structuring, which includes the design procurement process for outcome-based contracts and the contracting structure(s) between the payer, investor, and service provider.

Impact bonds can be an effective tool for achieving intended outcomes for these reasons:

1. Impact bonds make money more effective by tying funding to measurable results and reducing the risk of funding projects that do not work.
2. The methodology gives service providers the freedom to innovate by determining how best to implement the project. An impact bond focuses on outcomes and allows flexibility as to how to achieve those outcomes.
3. The design of an impact bond gives each of the players strong and appropriate incentives to maximize the development impact of the project.

Impact bonds can be especially effective in catalyzing a promising, innovative intervention.

As noted above, with an SIB, the host government takes on the role of the outcome payer. Having the government play this role is still relatively new in middle-income countries, although in the US and UK this approach has been growing in popularity over the past decade. The Government Performance Lab at the Harvard Kennedy School has been working with state and local governments on ways to finance difficult social programs, as well as conducting research on how government can improve results. Similarly, the Government Outcomes Lab at the University of Oxford Blavatnik School of Government is researching how governments partner with the private and social sectors to improve social outcomes.

A SIB can be a very effective and powerful tool for government ministries to improve performance in addressing social problems. A government ministry could use a SIB for those social problems where there is realistic potential for significant impact.

A SIB will succeed only if government leaders are willing to dedicate time and energy to make it work. An SIB with a government ministry as outcome payer should not be considered if the government has not demonstrated enthusiasm and commitment to achieving the intended outcomes. A lead government ministry should be involved, and other key ministries, including the Treasury Department, also need to be completely committed.

A SIB might be set up for a particular district or local geographic area, but the intent should always be to scale up to other areas. The SIB will need to apply to a service area that provides statistical precision to judge whether the intervention is successful. It should create a highly incentivized environment by tying all program funding to results and should also give full flexibility to develop and revise the design and delivery practices. The SIB is a social incubator that stretches an organization's impact, with the intent that once the necessary learning iterations have occurred, the program can be scaled up at a lower cost. Chapter 12 provides details on how SIB service providers are incentivized to innovate and perform at their highest level.

## Impact Bonds and Decentralization

Impact measurement is a core principle of impact investing and is inherent in Results-Based Financing (RBF) and Payment by Results (PBR). As discussed above, payment is conditional on achieving a certain level of performance as defined by the payment metric. In all cases, there must be a commitment to measure outcome and/or output level results. In Chapter 12, we will discuss measurement in detail and introduce a performance management system that yields near real-time insights so that program managers can make timely adjustments to improve outcomes.

Some RBF models can be used very effectively in middle-income countries that have sufficient resources for government to play the role of outcome payer. In the UK, US, and other high-income countries, these same models are being used to address difficult societal issues. Before delving into the details of RBF, let us look at how decentralization has helped to make these new tools potentially strong forces for achieving poverty alleviation.

Over the past 30 years, decentralization has become an international phenomenon with the goals of improving people's well-being and the distribution of benefits to communities. There are three major reasons for reform through decentralization:

1.  *Improve efficiency.* It allows people to participate in the process of service delivery and creates a demand for those services that are most important. Understanding this demand is important for long-term sustainability.

2.  *Improve political and financial accountability*. When government is closer to the people, there is increased accountability, which allows for a decrease in elite capture, where public resources tend to benefit those of a higher or elite social status, and other forms of corruption that divert public resources for the benefit of privileged individuals.
3.  *Improve effectiveness*. Through increased local participation, innovation, and ownership, local citizens have a stronger voice and can make their ideas known or demand services or changes to existing services.

These reform objectives create an ideal environment for impact investing and the use of impact investing instruments. Unfortunately, INGOs have largely not responded to this opportunity. For those services that have been decentralized, there is a real development opportunity.

The debate over what expenditures should be decentralized to local government has been going on for decades. During the past 30 years, initiatives in many low- and middle-income countries have sought to strengthen local governments' ability to implement and manage community services. Unfortunately, too few INGOs have shown much interest in specializing in those important components of local government. These would include: planning, budget formulation, budget execution, and budget monitoring. Citizen participatory planning and citizen monitoring are other areas of specialization that few INGOs have expertise. Instead, many of them set up parallel structures to local government and implemented their own programs, involving local authorities in a somewhat paternalistic manner to the extent that INGO deemed appropriate. In most instances, when an INGO completed a project, it would turn it over to the local authorities with the expectation that local government would be able to fund and manage operations—even though they know that most local governments in developing nations lack capacity and adequate budgets. Fiscal decentralization may have taken place, but the flow of funding has been minimal. Therefore, institutional capacity building is essential, and it could be genuinely sustainable when local public-private partnership (LP3) principles are applied along with appropriate impact investing instruments, such as a slightly modified impact bond.

One of the most significant challenges local governments have faced has been central government restrictions on borrowing. Although these restrictions are not surprising given the lack of capacity there are impact investing models that can mitigate much of this risk.

LP3 uses the traditional P3 for infrastructure such as water systems and combines it with the financial structure (also aligned with the traditional P3) of the SIB. The use of such a model requires that the decentralization components are operational, although the LP3 should include a grant component for institutional capacity building.

Partnering with advocacy and community-based NGOs can be useful in planning citizen participation as well as in citizen monitoring of local services and local budget. For communities to effectively participate in the budgeting process, there must be a robust civil society whose members are familiar with and able to contribute to policy debates.

Many local governments in low- and middle-income countries do not have authority to borrow in capital markets. The rise of impact investing has not lessened these controls, rather it has opened new avenues of dialogue with the Ministry of Finance, which controls all borrowing and would be responsible for overseeing a RBF project.

These types of innovative financing approaches are already being used in the US and other countries. The Government Performance Lab (GPL) at the Harvard Kennedy School has examined how state and local government service agencies can reform social projects and improve outcomes even with their limited budgets. Their strategy includes having GPL trained experts work with state and local government agencies for a period of up to three years.

Through this hands-on involvement with state and local government, a systematic approach to evaluation can be used to identify areas of mismanagement and provide improved insights on challenges and barriers to change. The partner governments should implement appropriate data-driven performance management tools to improve outcomes.

In the UK, there is a formal partnership between the UK Government and the Blavatnik School of Government at Oxford University, where the Government Outcomes Lab is housed. The International Network for Data on Impact and Government Outcomes (INDIGO) is a one-stop shop for data on impact bonds. Information comes from a community of peers who are working in different countries, sectors, and policy domains but have a strong desire to collaborate through sharing evidence-based results.

## Impact Investing Intermediaries

Among the many intermediaries active in project financing, some specialize in the work of social enterprises, while others focus more on innovative financing methods for social programs. All intermediaries should have expertise in investment appraisal and helping small or medium-size businesses and projects become investment-ready.

The one goal shared by all intermediaries working in this field is to determine how to produce high-quality impact investments and thereby contribute to the growth of impact investing. Creating a high-quality financial investment product requires training, institutional capacity building, and a commitment to continual improvement in those areas that will contribute toward sustainable growth. A robust investment appraisal system is needed to evaluate the quality of investments. An investment appraisal is intended to prevent bad investments from moving forward and good opportunities from being rejected unjustifiably.

In today's market, there is a shortage of high-quality investment opportunities. The 2020 GIIN report mentions that the two major areas that saw the least progress during the past decade and that remain a challenge to the industry are (1) data on investment products and opportunities, and (2) high-quality investment opportunities with a track record. Intermediaries have made positive contributions in both areas during the past decade. Meanwhile, however, we have also seen mainstream lenders and foundations enter the market without a clear understanding of these issues or of segmentation of impact investing, another challenge identified by GIIN and is increasing risk to clients.

Impact investing is part of a broader market solution and requires thinking differently from the norm. Therefore, intermediaries must be adaptive in how they relate to clients and in how they provide services. Providing clients with loan capital is not sufficient. There is also a need to understand the operating environment and to know how to respond to the challenges that will invariably arise. This often requires partnering and management skills to make sure the right people are involved in the planning and decision-making processes.

Intermediaries operate in the space between key actors, especially between service providers and investors. When a service provider is able to achieve continuous improvement in project results the intermediary should be able to further unlock their potential by introducing investors that have the capability to take the project to scale. At the same time, intermediaries can work with service providers on project design to ensure that important development themes are properly integrated to maximize the net social benefits. Also, promoting innovative collaboration is a strength of most intermediaries, as they are continually experimenting to find ways to improve and sustain development results.

## Partnering

It should be clear by now that impact investing requires strong partnerships. A one-organization approach to achieving sustainable results will be at best very inefficient. The UN 2030 Agenda for the Sustainable Development Goals recognized the need for partnership in that Goal 17 focuses explicitly on partnerships for development through multistakeholder collaboration.

The 2030 Agenda highlights the need for a new collaborative way of working among a host of actors: civil society, the private and public sectors, NGOs, academia, donors, and others. Achieving sustainable outcomes will require focusing on systemic causes and involving partners with relevant expertise.

Given the limited development resources available, project plans must be carefully examined and appraised to ensure that every dollar invested makes the highest level of impact. Therefore, partner selection must be rigorous. Moreover, each partnership must be equipped to engage with other teams of partners. The UN Sustainable Development Goals are interconnected and partnerships must be suitably broad. A team might be working on a water and sanitation project, which will require interaction with those working on health, nutrition, and agricultural projects.

Local government will always be an important partner, especially on services that have been decentralized to the local level. Basic service delivery can be complicated and difficult but is absolutely necessary in achieving sustainable results. The nature of the problem can often be affected by demand and supply constraints and other sector-specific issues. Many INGOs have chosen not to work with local governments and have instead set up their own project offices. All INGOs state that they work collaboratively with local government, but in actual practice that turns out to be no more than sharing plans and from occasionally granting local authorities the honor of cutting a ribbon. Seldom should NGO district-level offices be delivering services that are the responsibility of local government. Rather, the NGOs should be working to build local administrative and technical capacity.

## Impact Measurement

The topic of impact measurement is discussed in detail in Chapter 12. For projects that have payments tied to results, such as an impact bond, there will need to be a third-party that validates the results. Impact investing, by definition, takes results measurement seriously and in many cases involves the use of a counterfactual that allows for the results to be attributed to the project. The use of a counterfactual is discussed in Chapter 12. For now, it is important to recognize the rigor that is required for some impact investments. Because of the importance of impact measurement, it is equally important that the methodology used to measure impact is well documented and understood by the independent evaluator whose results will trigger payment, in the case of an impact bond. The reality is that different measurement methodologies can provide slightly different results that can make a significant difference in the amount that an outcome payer, for instance, will provide based on the conditional contract. In our experience, even the calculations, when using the same impact measurement methodology, have caused problems in having the payment released. The conditional contract will often include a section for disputes and an experienced intermediary will make sure that measurement disputes are specifically addressed

During the scoping phase, actors are on a quest to find likeminded partners. This like-mindedness begins with the type of business or project and the theory of change, and it extends to the impact measurement and management system being used. Impact measurement can be a contentious issue when different actors have different understandings of measurement. Many investment funds are emphasizing the need for verifiable impact. Box 8.5 expresses the concern raised by The Rise Fund about impact measurement. In Chapter 12, we provide a detailed discussion of measurement. In this phase, the emphasis should be on finding actors that recognize the importance and rationale for impact measurement and management.

---

### BOX 8.5  IMPACT FUNDS AND IMPACT MEASUREMENT

You shouldn't be able to call yourself an impact fund without getting rigorous about the impact side of your work – Maya Chorengel, Co-Managing Partner, The Rise Fund

---

The impact measurement and management process will be somewhat different for each organization, but certain fundamentals should be in place and implementation roles should be clearly identified.

## Note

1 Payment by Results (PbR) and Results-based Financing are public policy tools in which payments are based on a conditional contract and contingent on the independent verification of results. The term was made popular by its use by UKAid and the Department for International Development (between 1997 and 2020) when it was merged with the Foreign, Commonwealth and Development Office to create FCDO.

# Chapter 9

# Feasibility Stage

## Introduction

The feasibility study determines whether the proposed project should be approved for further work and whether it is ready for potential investors to be invited to review the project model.[1]

In this chapter, the focus is on the five feasibility study core modules: demand forecasting, technical, financial budget, human resources, and project stakeholders (see Figure 9.1). The upper part of Figure 9.2 shows the different stages of the investment appraisal process, which include what we call a pre-feasibility study as well as the full feasibility study.

As we cover the considerable details involved in the feasibility stage, keep in mind that we encourage an integrated investment appraisal approach, which includes financial, economic, and stakeholder analysis as depicted in Figure 9.1. In more traditional approaches to investment appraisal, the financial and economic analyses are done separately. The integrated investment appraisal, in contrast, measures benefits and costs for both the financial and the economic appraisal in an integrated manner.

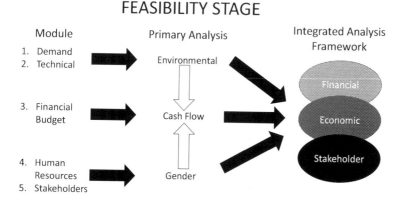

FEASIBILITY STAGE

*Figure 9.1* During the feasibility stage, the analyst works to improve the accuracy of the key variables. Unlike the pre-feasibility stage, primary data will need to be gathered, such as assessing the willingness-to-pay in an attempt to determine the demand for a product or service. Because of their importance, environmental and gender assessments are undertaken for all projects or business ventures.

DOI: 10.4324/9781003276920-10

PROJECT INVESTMENT APPRAISAL PROCESS FOR IMPACT INVESTING

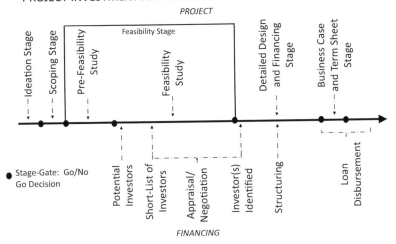

*Figure 9.2* A student of impact investing needs to understand the many factors at play during the investment appraisal process. Activities at the project level and at the financing level coincide. During the feasibility stage, potential investors are identified. As they engage in the feasibility study process, a core investor group will emerge with whom the project team will begin to structure the financing and complete the detailed design work.

*Sources*: Authors, drawing from multiple sources.

## Pre-feasibility Study

---

### BOX 9.1   EARLY QUESTIONS TO BE CONSIDERED DURING THE PRE-FEASIBILITY STUDY

1. Is the project financially sustainable?
2. Does the project contribute to local economic growth?
3. Is a positive economic NPV expected?
4. Who are the beneficiaries? Do all actors agree?
5. Who or what could negatively distort project performance?
6. What are the risks to the just distribution of benefits?
7. What are the key variables?
8. What are the sources of risk?
9. What SDG poverty alleviation goals are being addressed?
10. Is there a strong demand for the project?

---

The pre-feasibility study is the initial step prior to conducting a full feasibility study. The study framework is the same for both studies, as they cover the same subject areas and both are concerned with examining the project's overall potential. The key difference between them involves cost. The rationale for the pre-feasibility study is simple: it is a low-cost way to conduct an initial evaluation of the potential feasibility of the project or enterprise. If the pre-feasibility study justifies further investigation, then the full feasibility study can be built on the pre-feasibility study's foundation. Box 9.1 provides questions that the analyst should be considering during the pre-feasibility study.

The pre-feasibility study is an early-stage analysis that obtains estimates, often based on secondary sources, but in the right order of magnitude. It enables team members to decide whether the project is of sufficient interest to proceed to more detailed work. An attractive pre-feasibility study will be less definitive because it is based on a less exhaustive review of the potentially available information. It is only after the collection of primary data that accuracy can be improved in both the analysis and decision-making.

The pre-feasibility study may also recommend adjustments to the project's Theory of Change (TOC), along with any business operation details such as cost estimates, project risks, and key project variables. Analysts will calculate estimates using a conservative bias, so that they provide even more confidence than mean estimates of variables would do. This is especially the case for variables known to have significant uncertainty. Analysts will purposefully use a downward bias for benefits and an upward bias for cost estimates.

The pre-feasibility study will also be an initial exercise in understanding the motivations of different project actors. It's not unusual for people with vested interests in the project to want to have their ideas included in the design. This would be the case for investors, but it might also include secondary actors. The use of an evidence-based approach can help to overcome many of the pressures on project design decisions. By taking a solidly evidence-based approach, the pre-feasibility study saves time and resources and prevents special interest groups from promoting a more speculative and unverifiable approach to decision-making.

The pre-feasibility study will test the TOC causal logic and will determine whether the project components are sufficient and consistent. A proper analysis will cause the project design team to reconsider any components of the initiative that don't have a strong cause-and-effect linkage, so as to ensure that the project does not fail. Frequently, the TOC development process overlooks or inadequately considers how project risks could affect the achievement of the desired results. Although a risk mitigation strategy should have already been included, the pre-feasibility study tests whether the strategy is realistic and whether the sharing of risk is negotiated with stakeholders so as to be handled in the most efficient manner.

## Feasibility Study

A feasibility study for an integrated investment appraisal involves a detailed analysis of all the project's relevant factors, including financial, economic, and risk criteria to determine, based on evidence, whether the project is attractive to all interested parties and should be approved.

---

### BOX 9.2  IMPACT FIRST AND REVENUE FIRST ORGANIZATIONS

An impact-first organization is outcome focused and use an evidence-based approach for decision-making and determining impact achieved.

A revenue-first organization is output focused and primary strategies are for increasing revenue with the belief more activities will result in more impact.

---

The financial analysis is often considered the most important part of the feasibility study and is generally the most scrutinized component, especially for larger capital investment projects. Many organizations that want to turn projects into social impact investments or are seeking financing for a social enterprise underestimate the need for good and verifiable data on past performance. Since organizations often lack such data, development and implementation of a performance management system (discussed in Chapter 12) and other similar systems may be recommended to collect the right data. Those organizations that focus on impact will recognize the need for such systems and robust data resources to inform good decision making. Unfortunately, revenue-first organizations often exhibit a mixed reaction on this point. Some agree to invest in improved systems, but others will rely on their marketing, often to the general public, of anecdotal impact results achieved. Box 9.2 differentiates between impact first and revenue first service provider organizations.

Although outcome and performance data are important to give investors confidence that the service delivery organization has the experience to implement, the project will also need data that will allow the analyst to project the volume of outputs, inputs, and associated costs so as to understand the key anticipated cash flows of the project. Financial cash flow will, to a large extent, determine the project's viability.

Until the feasibility study, the financial analysis is based on deterministic values[2] of project variables. A proper consideration must be given to uncertainty and risk resulting in a move from deterministic rationale to a dynamic and probabilistic rationale. This is an important part of the feasibility study and more specifically the integrated appraisal. Key project variables such as the rate of inflation, market exchange rates, and budget line items for prices and quantities of inputs and outputs will change over the project's lifetime. A specific risk analysis will be applied to key risk variables.

The economic analysis focuses on assessing the project's effect on the community, district, and (in some cases) even the entire country. The economic appraisal determines whether the project will have a significant impact as measured by the increase in total net economic benefits.

The stakeholder analysis may be less precise than the financial and economic analyses, but the analyst will still make an attempt at quantifying the impacts of the project on the stakeholders. The identification of stakeholders may be quite broad, including vulnerable members of society. It's important to assess the well-being of the various stakeholders, because very few projects will benefit everyone proportionally. The analyst will be interested in knowing how the project benefits are distributed among stakeholders and whether the targeted marginalized groups received the intended benefits.

## The Core Project Modules

As shown in Figure 9.1, the five feasibility stage modules include: demand, technical, human resources, budget, and stakeholders. All five are important, but gaining a complete understanding of demand is arguably the most important step within the feasibility study. The success of a social enterprise or social program will be depended on whether people use or 'demand' the products and services provided. As such, much of this section is intentionally focused on the demand module.

## The Demand Module

Here, we will explain how the demand for goods and services is calculated. An understanding of price and quantity is highlighted throughout the discussion.

Determinants of Demand

---

**BOX 9.3   THE CONCEPT OF THE INVISIBLE HAND IN ECONOMICS**

There are market forces at work in the supply of goods, as well as in the demand, which will vary depending on price and available quantity. Efficiency is achieved when there are neither shortages nor oversupply. The presence of unobservable market forces that tend to lead toward this equilibrium state resulted in the idea of an 'invisible hand' guiding the economy, as described by 18th-century economist Adam Smith in his famous book *The Wealth of Nations*.

---

Introductory economics tells us that the amount of a product or service available within the economy is determined by the demand of consumers and the supply provided by producers. The law of demand states that at a higher price, consumers will demand a lower quantity of the good. Box 9.3 provides an overview of the concept of 'the invisible hand' that guides the economy.

If the price is high, sellers will want to provide more services and products, but the consumers may not be willing to purchase at such a high price. If the price is low, consumers may be willing to purchase more, but the producers may be unwilling to sell the quantity demanded at that price. In both of these cases, the 'invisible hand' of the market will usually adjust[3] the price and quantity to a level of equilibrium where consumers are willing to purchase a certain quantity at a certain price and producers are willing to provide the services or products at that quantity and price. This point of equilibrium will remain until it is disrupted by some outside influence.

There are many determinants of demand. Typically, the ones we think of first are the price of a good or service and the income of prospective purchasers. But there are other important determinants: population growth, access to and cost of alternative solutions, quality, and availability, to name just a few. Figure 9.3 provides a list of demand determinants used in a water supply project.

## Demand Forecasting

Demand analysis is a foundational block in the feasibility study and a central topic weaved throughout the project investment appraisal and beginning in the ideation phase. The importance of demand forecasting is obvious. Without a demand for a service or product, there is no sustainable business or social program. An analyst will want to better understand all the sources of demand, the overall nature of the market, and prices and quantities.

In all the cases discussed in this book, the demand analysis is done domestically and does not include internationally traded goods and services. For the latter, the price is largely determined by world markets and secondary data can be used effectively. For the domestic market, primary research becomes much more important. In most domestic projects, the investment appraisal team will use early community consultations during the ideation phase to get a sense of the users' preferences with regard to design, process, technology, scale and location. This information can help to provide direction for analysts, including how to prepare for later consultation meetings.

Throughout this chapter, we provide various examples to illustrate the building blocks and modules of the feasibility stage. We draw many of these examples from the water and sanitation sector, because most development practitioners have had experience in this

**DETERMINANTS OF DEMAND**

In addition to price and income, there are many other determinants of demand. The following are a few of the considerations for determining the demand for a water supply project. Each project will have a unique set of determinants.

**Factors Affecting Local Demand**

- Population and density of project area
- Number of households
- Quality of current water
- Access to and cost of alternative sources of water
- Family income
- Degree of gender equality – which family members collect water, control of family income, etc (a gender assessment will be used to identify specific issues to be included – see Ch 10)
- Cost and amount (litres) of water presently used
- Role of local authorities within a decentralized water system – eg. environmental impact assessment
- Legal issues and community responsibilities

**Factors Affecting Business Demand**

- Cost and volume of water currently used
- Type of business and whether it is water dependent
- Machinery and processes requiring water usage
- How used water is disposed, and the cost of any treatment required

**Factors Affecting Agricultural Demand**

- Type of agricultural needs (crops or animals) – area and quantity
- Irrigation systems including energy source
- Price for agricultural commodities
- Supply, cost, quality and reliability of alternative water systems
- Business legal issues

**Factors Affecting Public Service Demand**

- Number of schools, clinics, hospitals, and government offices
- Revenue collected by local authorities
- Subsidies provided by local and national authorities
- Current quantity of water being used and quantity required by institution

------------------------------------------------------

This list of demand determinants was compiled from various sources and is not meant to be exhaustive. It's intent is to provide the reader with a sense of the complexity involved in determining the most significant factors affecting demand and using this data to make key decisions. Remember, genuine community participation is critical to the success of any project.

*Figure 9.3* The determinants of demand are an intrinsic part of the theory of change. Having a complete understanding of what determines demand will influence the activities, outputs, and the behavioral change required to achieve intended outcomes.

*Source*: Authors, drawing from multiple sources.

sector. Also, the water sector provides good examples of how to do a project investment appraisal. Furthermore, water and sanitation responsibilities are usually decentralized to local government control, and innovative financing tools give local authorities in lower- and middle-income countries unprecedented opportunities to explore new means of financing projects. However, plenty of challenges remain, as we will see.

Of the many determinants of demand, the most obvious one is price, or what potential consumers say they are willing to pay for a product or service. The relationship between the quantity consumed and the price is calculated through a willingness-to-pay survey that is often administered at the household level. Figure 9.3 presents some of the determinants of demand for a water supply project.

The following are some key characteristics that will be important in understanding demand forecasting for water supply, and often for other sectors.

## Market Inefficiencies

Let's consider first why international development actors—donors, multilaterals, development financing institutions, INGOs, and others—become involved in basic water supply or other services, such as nutrition, education, or healthcare. The immediate response might be that these services are all fundamental to public health, human growth, and sustainable development to occur. This is true, but the underlying reason for these foreign entities' intervention is that the markets on their own have failed to provide a critical service to communities.

The invisible hand, as explained by Adam Smith, works best when people pursue their own self-interests. But the invisible hand's effectiveness can be limited when individuals or businesses, create external costs, such as through overproduction. In the water sector, the local government might fail to repair a leaking tap or pipe. This leads to costs that are not accounted for in the tariff price[4] of the water. As a result of these inefficiencies, along with the need for institutional capacity building, there have been very few sustainable water projects. This is even more so for sanitation.

Many NGOs have focused their attention on the humanitarian need for clean and dependable water. This has resulted in thousands of boreholes and other water systems being built every year, but with very limited attention given to the market failures and addressing institutional capacity of local authorities who are often responsible for water supply. Too often the result of such a situation is that the water systems have a dramatically reduced lifespan and need to be replaced after a short period of time.

Typically, INGOs are anxious to have a ribbon-cutting ceremony where they can take credit for bringing water to the community. INGO marketing departments can do wonders in securing donations for a much-needed water supply project. At any given time, thousands of INGOs are promoting such projects. A few responsible INGOs regularly do project investment appraisals, knowing that such a project should not be undertaken unless there is a viable solution to ongoing operational and maintenance needs. Many INGOs will not consider appraising their projects because they know the projects are not sustainable. After they have completed the water supply project, if the system is not operated properly, they will unashamedly use the excuse that operations and maintenance are the responsibility of the government and that the INGO did excellent work on the construction end. Box 9.4 highlights three categories that need to be assessed when determining demand for a project.

---

**BOX 9.4   ASSESSING PROJECT DEMAND**

In determining the demand for project services or products, three major categories of outputs need to be assessed:

1. Detailed forecast of quantities and real prices for the project life
2. Taxes, tariffs, subsidies, public regulations, technological trends
3. Environmental impacts—both positive and negative

---

In water supply projects, the demand depends on the price charged, which is a function of the cost of water supply. At the same time, the water supply is dependent on the demand for water. In other words, the demand curve for water is not linear. This interdependence should be a strong rationale for providing a thorough and careful analysis of water supply projects. There is a general consensus that clean and safe water should be provided (1) at an affordable cost, (2) using appropriate and demand-driven technology, and (3) in a manner that fits into the parameters of the willingness-to-pay (WTP).

## Use of Surveys for Data Collection

The demand module entails examining the sources of demand, the nature of the market, prices, and quantities. In the pre-feasibility study, the sole objective is to determine the projects' overall potential as inexpensively as possible. Hence, secondary data are often used. At all times, data collection should be cost-effective, but especially at the pre-feasibility stage when available funds are limited.

In the feasibility phase, additional data will be used to improve the accuracy of project analysis. It is always important to consider what data are required and the best means of obtaining them. We still want to be cost-effective, but we are more willing to spend on collecting primary data because of our initial confidence that the project or business will be financially sustainable and will provide the expected benefits to society.

The secondary data used in the pre-feasibility study can now be replaced by data obtained from a reconnaissance survey that includes on-site visits and observations. Household and business surveys are often conducted to collect data on family size, income, and needs (e.g., anticipated water use). In the case of water use surveys, information from the agricultural sector, which relies heavily on water, will be especially important.

Although initial survey work was undertaken during the ideation and scoping stages, the design team will now need to become better acquainted with the proposed project area. Further detailed survey work will significantly improve the project design. An initial survey is often referred to as the reconnaissance survey and is used to collect basic information on the area and to gain an understanding of the community on the design of a project. For a clean energy project, the choice might be between a mini-grid utility, solar panels on households, and other clean energy technology. For a water project, the design team will work with the community to determine whether the appropriate technology will be standpipes within the community or household connections. Other questions might include whether a borehole needs to be drilled, or will water be piped from a source at a higher elevation or a water tower.

The socio-economic survey will often begin during the ideation or scoping phase, but it often overlaps with the feasibility stage. It provides the design team with detailed information such as household size, quantity and quality of water used daily, expenditure on water, or waterborne disease statistics. In some cases, a specialized survey on water loss might be required. Technology allows water specialists to use acoustic loggers, a leak detection technology, to pick up vibrations that come from a leak in an attached pipe.

The socio-economic survey is the most important of the early surveys. Analysis of the information gathered in this survey sometimes causes a team not to proceed further with the feasibility study. The most common reasons for not continuing relate to the information provided on operation and maintenance costs along with administrative capacity for user fee collection. Experienced project design teams will be able to estimate whether project services are likely to fully recover these costs or if a subsidy will be needed. Although subsidies may be a viable option, the size of the needed subsidy often determines whether the project will move forward as planned or if some fundamental changes, particularly in technology, will need to be considered.

---

### BOX 9.5  EFFECTIVE DEMAND AND ACTUAL CONSUMPTION

Water consumption is the actual quantity of water consumed; whereas effective demand relates quantity of use to the price of water.

During the dry season, if the water from the facility has a bitter taste, community members may seek an alternative source of potable water, thus reducing demand.

---

The contingent valuation methodology (CVM) survey provides important data on the effective demand for a water or clean-energy facility. The CVM survey include a list of questions to better understand households' and businesses' willingness to pay (WTP) for services at different quantities. The data gathered from this survey can help the design team construct an approximate demand curve for water.

The effective demand is based on the economic cost of providing good quality water that ensures the optimal use of the water facility. There should be neither over-consumption, which leads to operational deficits, nor under-consumption, which is equivalent to a loss of welfare or social benefits in the community. The goal is to maximize the net social benefits, and this will happen when marginal costs are equal to marginal benefits. Box 9.5 describes the difference between effective demand and actual consumption.

CVM does have some drawbacks. The full economic benefits might not be completely captured in the household surveys. For instance, households might not be fully aware of health improvements that would accompany an improved water system and would thus biased answers regarding their WTP.

Identifying the effective demand requires a thorough analysis but will provide the design team with critical information including (1) the service level(s) to be provided, (2) the size and timing of investments, (3) an estimate of the project's financial and economic benefits, and (4) an understanding of users' ability and WTP. It is important to achieve the optimum use of scarce resources, such as water or electricity, by avoiding inefficiencies and waste, especially those that are in existing systems. We will return to this topic later.

### Willingness to Pay – Constructing the Demand Curve

When constructing a demand curve, an economist will use a contingent valuation survey to identify the major determinants of demand for a certain location. The determinants of demand will differ depending on the location, so the analyst will need to take this variation into consideration when constructing an estimate of a demand curve. The difference between WTP and actual demand data concerns the sources used for data collection. An actual demand curve is based on actual market conditions and observations, whereas WTP is based on data collection from surveys and other sources, such as recent research articles that have been peer-reviewed.

Collecting data can be very expensive. During the pre-feasibility study, the objective is to know whether the project will be of interest to investors. During this phase, the most cost-effective manner of making such a decision is to use secondary data, often based on desktop research. Most data, especially during the pre-feasibility study, will come from secondary sources (i.e., government, research, industry, etc.), various types of surveys (household, area, or reconnaissance surveys), and, in some cases, the collection of primary data through field observations. Primary data gathering is deferred until a firm decision has been made to begin work on the detailed design. This happens once there is investor commitment to the project. There will always be a need for accurate primary data collected directly from the community, but collecting primary data can be much more costly than other forms of data collection.

Figure 9.4 shows how the WTP survey is used as part of the investment appraisal. The amount that a consumer is willing to pay minus the amount actually paid results in the consumer surplus, which we will talk about next.

The WTP also provides planners with an understanding of what is important to the community. The planners can assess the right technology when they know the particular WTP, coupled with data that help to explain these choices.

### MEASURING PROJECT BENEFITS AND IMPACT ON POVERTY

#### CONSUMER SURPLUS OF A WATER PROJECT

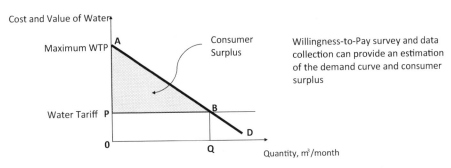

*Figure 9.4* The shaded area of the diagram depicts the consumer surplus. Consumer surplus for water, in this instance, occurs when the price that a consumer pays for this service (water tariff) is less than the price the consumer would be willing to pay. This shaded area is the additional benefit received by a community because they are paying less than what they are willing to pay.

The information received from a WTP analysis allows planners to improve efficiency by knowing the price of water that will maximize the number of households receiving clean and affordable water, while also covering the fixed and variable costs of the water utility.

When done well, the WTP information can be instrumental in the cost/benefit analysis. The WTP survey presumes that those being surveyed can effectively grasp the benefits to be obtained from the new water supply.

Analysts should be concerned about households' responses to hypothetical CVM surveys. Do households answer questions honestly and accurately, and are the responses reliable measures of economic benefits? These questions should be considered carefully, as strategic bias can result when respondents believe they can influence a decision in their favor by not responding honestly. This possibility underscores the importance of engaging people with considerable experience in survey design so that any biases can be minimized.

Whether the project is in water or another sector, the demand assessment is a critical initial step. Planners should be responding to community demand (this is often called taking a demand-responsive approach). When designed well, the demand assessment will provide relatively good estimates of the quantity or level of service that users are willing and able to pay for.

The demand assessment also provides guidance for structuring policies to deliver a cross-subsidy to low-income users and achieve the objective of distributive justice. The survey work should provide different questions for different income levels. In this way, the payment mechanism for poor households can be designed to meet their needs and provide a sustainable payment structure.

### Consumer Surplus

An economist working on the economic appraisal of an impact investment project will want to maximize the net social benefits for certain stakeholders, as well as, for the entire community. The construction of the demand curve will provide not only insight into the demand for a service or product, but also an understanding of the benefits of the project. The economic analysis compares the costs and benefits for the entire project area and beyond. Prices are measured in constant dollars so as to reflect the true cost and value to the economy of goods and services, after the adjustment for effects of government intervention and distortions in the market structure.

Let's go back to our WTP curve. The total gross benefits for a project are made up of two components: the consumer surplus and the WTP for incremental water consumed. Remember, the WTP is an estimate of the demand curve that indicates the different quantities that could be consumed at different price levels. Where inadequate data are available to determine the demand curve, the CVM can be used as an estimate.

The consumer surplus represents the additional benefit that a consumer receives as a result of paying less for a product or service, over what they are willing to pay for it.

The demand curve reflects WTP of consumers for additional units. Figure 9.5 presents an example of gross economic benefit of consumption and the consumer surplus. The consumer surplus, or net benefits, is the difference between the WTP and the actual amount paid to purchase the given quantity. The total consumer surplus is the area between the demand curve and the price line (the price paid by consumers). The gross economic benefit of consumption is equal to the financial value plus the consumer surplus.

Figure 9.6 summarizes the makeup of consumer surplus, producers' surplus, and gross economic costs.

Every project will have economic benefits and costs. Let's continue with the example of drinking water. The preferred method for measuring economic benefits is a cost-benefit analysis (CBA). The CVM and community preferences are core documents for benefits estimation. Within the water sector, time savings for fetching water can be monetized based on the economic and social value of money. In a more general sense, not only should the capital and operational costs of the project and direct beneficiaries be included, but also those external to the project that will maximize economic efficiency, such as public subsidies. Box 9.6 provides an understanding of the difference between the financial and economic appraisals.

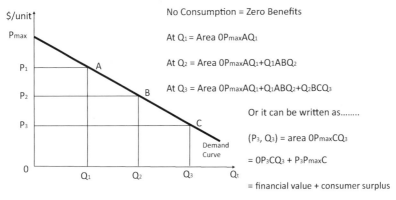

*Figure 9.5* The gross economic benefit of consumption comprises two components - i) financial value and ii) the consumer surplus. This is shown in the figure.

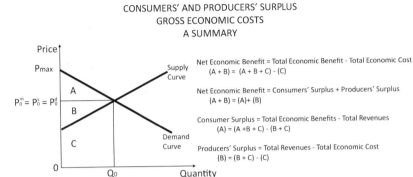

CONSUMERS' AND PRODUCERS' SURPLUS
GROSS ECONOMIC COSTS
A SUMMARY

A = Consumers' Surplus
B = Producers' Surplus
C = Gross Economic Costs

*Figure 9.6* This figure introduces a supply curve and the concept of producer surplus. Producer surplus is the amount a producer benefits from selling a product or service at the market price. The net economic benefits are the producer surplus and the consumer surplus.

---

**BOX 9.6   FINANCIAL AND ECONOMIC APPRAISALS**

The financial appraisal is focused on the project and its financial viability.

The economic appraisal is focused on the effect of the project on the community and the benefits to society, taken as a whole.

---

An alternative approach to economic appraisal when benefits cannot be estimated is a cost-effectiveness analysis (CEA). This would involve comparing the cost of providing a quantity and service delivery to the least costly option. CEA uses the ratio of cost to a nonmonetary input, output, or outcome measure. For instance, in the health sector, one might estimate the cost per life saved. Most sanitation projects are justified based on a CEA since there are no clear measures of economic benefits that result directly from improved sanitation. Water projects also rely often on CEA, especially when the demand assessment studies are not justified. CEA and CBA will be discussed in more detail in Chapter 12.

*Price Elasticity of Demand (ep)*

---

**BOX 9.7   DEMAND ANALYSIS AND THE PRICE ELASTICITY OF DEMAND**

Price elasticity of demand is an important factor in the demand analysis exercise. Without the ability to measure and predict how much people are likely to respond to economic changes, all the economic theory in the world would be of little help to policymakers.

---

Price elasticity of demand is an important concept for understanding the dynamics of changes in quantity demanded as a result of a change in price. Understanding those dynamics is critical to understanding demand, as in some instances the percentage change in quantity

Table 9.1 Price elasticity of demand measures the change in the demand for a product or service in relation to a change in the price. The table shows different types of elasticity - inelastic demand when the percentage change in demand is smaller than the percentage change in price. Similarly, elastic demand would have a greater percentage change in demand than in price.

| TYPE | DESCRIPTION | EXAMPLE |
|---|---|---|
| Perfectly Inelastic | Quantity demanded is constant | Insulin |
| Inelastic | A 1% change in price causes the quantity change by LESS that 1% | Food |
| Unit Elastic | A 1% change in price causes the quantity change by EXACTLY 1% | Necessary goods, but not essential with substitutes—bananas |
| Elastic | A 1% change in price causes the quantity demanded to change by MORE than 1% | Housing |
| Perfectly Elastic | Price is constant | Luxury Products |

demanded will be less than the percentage change in price. The opposite can also be true for some products and services. The Table 9.1 shows the different types of price elasticity and a description and example for each.

For example, in a society with cars, demand doesn't change much when the price of gas increases. We saw this happen in 2022 after the Ukraine-Russia war began and the price of gasoline escalated in most of the world. During this time, the percentage change in the quantity of gasoline used was considerably less than the percentage increase in the price of gasoline. Understanding the elasticity of demand is very important in constructing the demand curve. Box 9.7 describes the importance of understanding price elasticity of demand.

To put it another way, the price elasticity of demand measures how sensitive the quantity demanded is to its price. As we have seen, when prices rise, the quantity demanded falls for almost any good or service, but it will fall more quickly for some items than for others.

The price elasticity of demand can be calculated by using the formula in Figure 9.7, which takes the percentage change in quantity and divides it by the percentage change in price.

In this chapter, our discussion has largely focused on the importance of understanding the demand for a service or product, because understanding demand is critical to the success of a business or of a project. The demand module represents the initial attempt to quantify project benefits. Measuring these benefits is quite complex, but the measurements are all built on this theoretical foundation.

The overall shape of the non-linear demand curve in Figure 9.7 shows the overall decreasing marginal value of water. The initial amount of water received each day has great value, because it is essential to sustaining life. In most communities around the world, the subsequent amounts of water are important—for example, for hygiene, cooking, and washing. But as still more water is provided and the necessities of life are covered, the marginal value of water declines as its use is of lesser importance. The WTP survey will make this clear by means of the individual-level responses, which can then be aggregated at the community level.

A water supply design team will be very interested in understanding the changes in the quantity of water that will occur with a change in the unit price of water. The reason for this interest is to make sure the water system is being operated in an efficient manner. The price elasticity of demand can be used to help the team answer this question.

The demand curve for water is often very inelastic for the initial quantity of daily water supply. As we noted above, this water will be for drinking and sustaining life. Not surprisingly, households are willing to pay a higher amount for the initial supply of water. As the

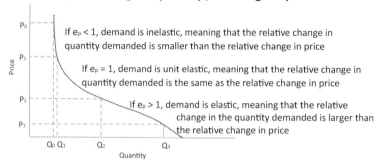

## Price Elasticity of Demand: $E_{(p)}$

**$E_{(p)}$ = % change in quantity / % change in price**

If $e_p < 1$, demand is inelastic, meaning that the relative change in quantity demanded is smaller than the relative change in price

If $e_p = 1$, demand is unit elastic, meaning that the relative change in quantity demanded is the same as the relative change in price

If $e_p > 1$, demand is elastic, meaning that the relative change in the quantity demanded is larger than the relative change in price

*Figure 9.7* The demand curves shown earlier in this chapter were linear, with a slope which remained constant on each point of the curve. The above figure shows a non-linear curve with slopes that are different at each point. At the top of the curve, the price elasticity of demand is inelastic - the quantity demanded for water when used for life-sustaining purposes will remain largely the same regardless of a price increase - whereas, towards the bottom of the curve, the demand is elastic - the quantity of water consumed for drinking and hygiene has been provided, and an additional unit is of less value; therefore, a price increase will have a higher percentage decrease in the consumption of water at this level.

marginal value of water declines along with the household need for water, the demand curve becomes increasingly elastic, meaning that price fluctuations will result in larger changes in the quantity demanded.

Since effective demand is closely related to a certain level of product quality, it should not be surprising that water quality also impacts effective demand. These quality issues include chemical composition, taste, and smell. In a broader sense, water pressure, reliability of supply, accessibility, and convenience are also important factors that will contribute to determining effective demand.

Some communities will have different sources of water depending on the particular use, and a well-designed WTP survey will capture these different sources. An individual or household demand curve will represent the aggregation of the demand curves for these different purposes and sources. The new water supply project will change the range of options available. This is where the broader issues of water quality have a significant role even when the basic quality factors (taste, smell, and chemical composition) are considered to be excellent. The economic value of a water supply will be largely dependent on these broader water quality issues.

Too often, INGOs and governments would deliver water services based on their own experience and what had traditionally been done in that country and area. Sadly, in many cases, the services were either not used at all or used for a short period of time, especially if residents had to pay for the water. Although studies were done and subsequent reports often stated that the tariff was too high and shifted blame to the donor, the real cause of the system's lack of use was usually that the community was not given a genuine voice in deciding on the standard of service. Today, it is widely acknowledged that successful water supply projects must inform communities as to the different service delivery options, including private household connections. The lesson learned is that, in many cases, individuals and families are willing to pay for value. If they know that the water quality is excellent and that it is available 24/7 there is a much higher willingness to pay for the service. Many flagship projects have successfully implemented household connections after doing the proper analysis and then responding to the actual demand (providing the technology requested) of the community.

Demand will always include real and perceived benefits. The most significant perceived benefits are cost and time savings. Unfortunately, many communities have been relatively unconvinced of the anticipated health benefits, although successful and appropriate social[5] marketing has improved the perception of health benefits.

Whether water or other services are involved, individuals and households are often prepared to pay a higher price for higher quality. It's a matter of value for value. What has caught many practitioners by surprise was the importance communities often place on service delivery options—most notably household water connections. While many local utilities learned to listen to communities and to provide the technology that was within the community means, they did not build their own capacity to not only adopt a demand-responsive approach, but to also provide excellent customer service including repair and maintenance to the systems being installed. It's like any business, if the client is provided a good quality product and this is supported through excellent customer service, then clients are willing to use and pay for the services offered.

To pay for higher quality, people need higher income. Not surprisingly, households with higher incomes tend to be willing to pay more for a given quantity of water. However, we must keep in mind that higher-income households generally pay a smaller percentage of total income for water than lower-income households.

## Managing Demand

At times, the quantity of a commodity will have to be managed, and understanding the demand curve will be a prerequisite for this work. For instance, it might be necessary for the water utility team to reduce the demand for water. The most obvious way to do so is to increase the price for a quantity beyond a basic level. As we know, a price adjustment will cause a movement along the demand curve. The price increase will incentivize users to consume less water.

Unfortunately, price changes do not always bring about the desired effect. We know from experience that, when significant price changes occur—whether it is for water, electricity, education, or some other item—users will look for other ways to meet the need. These other sources will often be detrimental to individuals, as well as to public policy objectives. The new piped water system provides high-quality clean water. With the price increase, some people will go back to using the river or other sources of water. Another example is if the cost of electricity from a mini-grid system increases, users will revert to previous energy sources, such as kerosene or diesel generators. Most of these sources will have negative externalities, especially if a major user such as an industry is involved.

In some cases, a combination of interventions will be necessary. For example, a price change might be more effective if combined with the availability of devices to reduce total use, marketing and public education to change user behavior, and regulatory changes.

Demand can also be managed from the supply side. In this regard, water demand could be influenced by improved efficiency on the part of the water utility or by achieving economies of scale through a merger with neighboring utilities.

## Determining the Tariff Structure

Regardless of the service, the price should ideally reflect its full cost, so as to incentivize people to use the commodity in the most efficient manner. Full cost refers to the estimated economic prices, which include the impact on the entire community or entire economy depending on the project size. The economic prices might not equal the financial prices because of subsidies or taxes.

The full cost of a service will include the following:

1. Long-run marginal costs for supply include the costs of expansion for both capital and operational needs.
2. Externalities are costs (or benefits) incurred by the utility or other company but paid for (or accrued) by individuals or society as a whole. These are referred to as negative and positive externalities, respectively. Improving public school education benefits everyone, which is why education costs are usually covered by local taxation. Negative externalities, such as water pollution, are caused by the water utility but paid for by downstream water users.
3. Opportunity costs. Again here, the focus is on the community or the economy at large, but opportunity cost refers to the cost of not using the resources in a certain way because a different use has higher economic benefits. For example, water might be used for household drinking, and the opportunity cost arises if the water is thus unavailable for irrigation and agricultural purposes.

In many countries, the price of water will be determined by the government ministry responsible for water resources. Many water projects have failed to be sustainable because the government set a price for water that was insufficient to sustain the costs of operations and maintenance. In such cases, the community ends up with low-quality water and unreliable service.

Project planners must weigh the viability of public subsidies as a means of paying for capital and for operational and maintenance costs. Subsidies are a legitimate policy option when they are used to achieve distributional justice and are sustainable. But in reality, too often these criteria are not considered; rather, political factors determine the use of subsidies.

Cross-subsidization can be given based on income so that all community members have access to the resource. Cross-subsidization means that the unit amount the utility charges one consumer segment is artificially lower than another group in order to provide the same quality of service to both. The economic benefits for the lower income consumers might be higher than other income segments of the population, but the decision in such a case is based on financial ability to pay and arguably human rights of having access to clean water. In the case of some commodities, such as sanitation, where there is no strong inherent demand, a subsidy might be required to correct this market failure. Such market failures are evident when community members fail to realize that they could significantly improve their own health and welfare by adopting improved hygiene and use of sanitation facilities.

## Project Demand

Once the project demand forecasting has been completed, the project team will want to reconcile these findings to the actual project demand, which in most cases will be the same or very similar, but in some instances might also be quite different.

There are various reasons why the actual project demand might have variances from the forecasted demand. These reasons include the following:

1.  WTP for different service levels was not calculated correctly. This can happen for several reasons, including any bias of the facilitator when community data is collected. The person facilitating a group meeting might have made incorrect assumptions or recorded data incorrectly.
2.  Unaccounted-for usage within the system. These can include both technical and non-technical losses. In many demand-forecasting exercises, the budget does not include pipe leakage, unless it is obvious but in many cases, it can go undetected unless the proper equipment is used.
3.  The price elasticity of demand was not properly calculated, or household estimates from the survey were incorrect. It is not uncommon to calculate the community members' perceived benefits from the project as higher than what they actually experience. When this happens, the project demand has been distorted, and poor residents tend to use other, lower-cost alternatives.
4.  In some instances, the project facility might be perceived as offering free services and products, especially if managed by a non-governmental organization that has a reputation for being wealthy and not charging. In some cases, a community-based management team can be more successful in delivering the message that the product or service must be paid for.
5.  In most instances, community members are willing to pay for value. If the quality of the product or service does not meet expectations, then demand can drop considerably.
6.  The supply network might be unreliable, thereby affecting the product or service's quantity and/or quality.

It is important to ensure optimal use of the project resources. For projects that provide services, such as water or electricity, physical and policy measures may need to be reviewed before a project is implemented. For instance, physical measures for a water or electricity project, might include illegal connections, leakage control, and the need for improved maintenance and operations. Policy measures might include identifying an economically efficient tariff.

The process of ensuring optimal usage of a project or facility will include determining the future requirements based on the effective demand. Effective demand refers to that level of demand that represents an individual or household's real intention to purchase based on their means of doing so. The effective demand will be used to calculate the project output level that can ensure optimal usage.

## Other Modules

In comparison to the demand module, the characteristics of which apply to virtually any project, the other four modules vary in nature depending on the type of project. Each one is important in the investment appraisal process, but these modules have less of an analytical component than the demand module. When we were talking about the demand module, we could use a water supply project as a helpful illustration, because the tools and the analytical process are consistent and transferable to most other projects. This is not the case for the other modules. Since these other four modules, that are part of the feasibility stage, are so much more project-based, we will give only a brief general description of each one.

## Technical Module

The technical module is focused on the quantities of different types of inputs required for the construction of the project. It will be important to include the source of these inputs as it will determine the future real prices if imported into the country. For instance, if water pumps, pipes or specialized filters need to be imported then this will need to be noted as part of the technical analysis. The technical module will provide the analyst with the initial indication of any negative environmental externalities that will need to be taken into consideration.

The technical module allows the analyst to very effectively use secondary data as the costs for the same or similar technology will be available on-line or, if needed, can be purchased from an engineering or technical organization that understands and has experience in the proposed project work. This is a routine means of gathering very accurate cost estimates. Contracts make it clear that firms providing the data will not be eligible to participate in the Request for Proposal or other contracting mechanism, as there would be a conflict of interest.

It is common to retain the consultants used in the feasibility study for review at the (subsequent) detailed design stage. Otherwise, the consultants have an incentive to keep the estimated costs low enough to have the project approved so that they will be selected to do the detailed design work. If the consultants are hired to review the detailed design, then there is a professional integrity incentive to keep the pre-feasibility estimate as close to the amount in the detailed design.

## Budget Module

The budget module integrates the financial and technical variables in order to construct a cash flow profile. As with any cash flow, the budget module will identify the expected receipts and expenditures over the life of the project. During the pre-feasibility study, financial flows will be calculated with the intent of identifying key variables to be used during the economic and stakeholder appraisal.

The financial cash flows are expressed in nominal prices since certain key variables such as taxes and debt repayments are also calculated in nominal values. The real value equivalent can be calculated by simply dividing by the price index. The use of real prices will be important in determining the project's sustainability. The project benefits and costs are expressed in real terms, and the early economic analysis is concerned with taxes, subsidies, and other distortions.

## Human Resources Module

When work is taking place in low- and middle-income countries, putting together a strong project team might be a challenge. Many of these countries will lack management capacity, although an exhaustive search, including looking outside the country, should be undertaken to identify qualified nationals. In some instances, projects will need to recruit expatriates to fill key positions. Making sure the best people are in place is extremely important to the project's success.

The human resource module will be closely linked to the technical module and the overall project management requirements. For modeling purposes, human resource requirements are broken down by occupational and skill groupings. If the project may be unable to fill key positions, then this concern should be flagged prior to the go-ahead to begin the feasibility stage gate approval process that was described in a text box at the beginning of this chapter.

## Stakeholders

Every project will have stakeholders, some of whom will be primary or targeted beneficiaries of the project while others might be secondary. The stakeholder analysis identifies these groups and, if possible, quantifies the project's impact on each of them. We will further discuss the stakeholder analysis and distributional impact assessment at the end of Chapter 11.

## Feasibility Stage Gate Approval

The TOC will have described how the interventions are supposed to deliver the desired results. The causal logic should be clear from the TOC. There might be other projects with similar social objectives. If so, it might be necessary to compare the cost-effectiveness of this project with that of the other project. If the project has the equal or greater cost-effectiveness than that of other projects, then it should be approved as part of the stage-gate process. When using an integrated project analysis, the financial and economic analysis will provide the necessary data for estimating the specific stakeholder impacts. The most important aspects of this analysis are the distribution of benefits and verifying that they reached the targeted group. Similarly, the project wants to make sure there are no groups that unintentionally is subjected to unreasonable burden as a result of the project without receiving compensation.

## Chapter 9 Annex

For those readers that might not have an economics background the following pages have been written to provide important understanding on how the demand curve reacts to the presence of *complementary* goods and *substitute* goods. Complements are goods that are often purchased together, so that a decrease in the price of one good results in an increase in demand for both goods. Similarly, if the price increases, then the demand for both goods will decrease. A substitute good, in a very simple manner, is a good that can replace another good. In economics, a substitute can refer to a product or service that a buyer would see as achieving the same purpose.

In Figure 9.8, consider a school in rural Africa where there is an initial change in the price of school notebooks. We can observe a movement along the demand curve from $Q_0$ to $Q_1$ and because of the decrease in price there is an increase in the quantity purchased.

If more notebooks are purchased, then more pencils may also be purchased, since pencils are a complementary good. Since the pencil market is taken out of equilibrium by a factor other than the price and quantity of pencils, an outward (increasing) shift occurs in the demand for pencils.

The next example in Figure 9.9 shows a contraction in demand (or an inward shift) due to a reduction in demand for a complementary good. If the price of mobile phones increases, we can expect a decrease in demand, or a movement along the demand curve. Since SIM cards are sold with mobile phones, we would expect to see a reduced number of SIM cards sold, but since the price of mobile phones is the factor that caused the SIM card market to move out of equilibrium, there will be an inward shift in the demand curve.

## AN OUTWARD SHIFT IN DEMAND WITH A
## DECREASE IN PRICE OF A COMPLEMENT GOOD

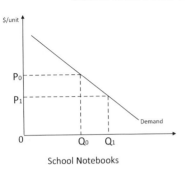

School Notebooks

A decrease in the price of school
notebooks increases the consumption of
school notebooks

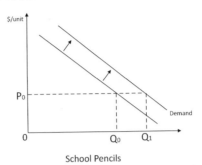

School Pencils

An increase in the use of school notebooks
could mean an increase in the use of
school pencils

*Figure 9.8* An outward shift in the demand curve can occur when the price of a complement good decreases. This shift indicates that consumers are now more willing to purchase the main good because the complement has become cheaper, leading to an increase in the quantity demanded at every price level. As a result, the demand curve shifts to the right, reflecting higher demand for the main good at each price point.

## AN INWARD SHIFT IN DEMAND (CONTRACTION) WITH AN INCREASE IN
## PRICE OF A COMPLEMENT GOOD

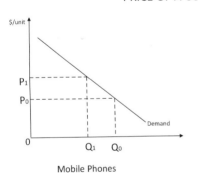

Mobile Phones

An increase in the price of mobile phones
decreases the sales of mobile phones

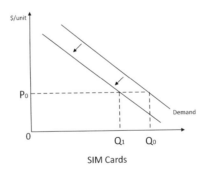

SIM Cards

Less mobile phone purchases could translate into less
purchase of SIM cards at the same price level

*Figure 9.9* An inward shift in the demand curve occurs when the demand for a product decreases at every price level. This can happen when the price of a complement good, which is often used together with the original product, increases. As the price of the complement rises, consumers may buy less of both products, leading to a decrease in demand for the original product.

The Law of Demand states that there is an inverse relationship between price and quantity demanded—i.e., when prices go up, the quantity purchased will usually decrease. Similarly, when there is a price drop, usually there is a quantity increase.

Now we can turn to substitutes, or goods that can serve as replacements for other goods. When the price of one good increases, demand for the substitute good will increase. Consider Figure 9.8 which shows what happens when there is a decrease in the price of notebooks.

## AN INWARD SHIFT IN DEMAND (CONTRACTION)
## WITH A DECREASE IN PRICE OF A SUBSTITUTE GOOD

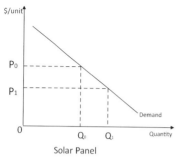

Solar Panel

A decrease in the price of solar panels leads to more household connections to renewable energy source (solar panels)

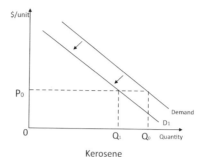

Kerosene

A reduction in the price of solar panels leads to consumers switching from kerosene for solar connection with a decrease in quantity kerosene

*Figure 9.10* An inward shift in the demand curve occurs when the quantity demanded decreases at every price level. When the price of a substitute good decreases, consumers are more likely to choose the now cheaper substitute over the original product, causing a decrease in demand for the original product and leading to an inward shift in its demand curve. This shift signifies a change in consumer preferences away from the original product due to the more attractive pricing of the substitute.

## AN OUTWARD SHIFT IN DEMAND WITH AN INCREASE IN PRICE OF A
## SUBSTITUTE GOOD

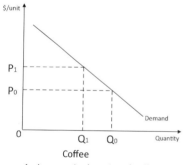

Coffee

An increase in the price of coffee decreases consumption of coffee

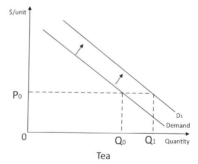

Tea

Some of coffee consumers will shift to tea consumption, hence, increase in demand for tea

*Figure 9.11* An outward shift in the demand curve occurs when the price of a substitute good increases, leading consumers to switch to the original good. This shift reflects an increase in the quantity demanded at every price point due to the substitution effect. As a result, consumers find the original good more attractive relative to the now more expensive substitute.

Since school notebooks and pencils are often purchased together, a decrease in price of notebooks from $P_0$ to $P_1$ will cause a shift in the demand for school pencils from a quantity of $Q_0$ to $Q_1$ while maintaining the price at $P_0$.

Figure 9.9 is a similar situation in that two complementary goods are involved. In this case, an increase in the price of mobile phones causes a reduction in the number of mobile phones purchased. Since SIM cards complement the purchase of mobile phones, there should be a shift in the demand for SIM cards without any change in price.

The next two figures (Figure 9.10 and Figure 9.11) illustrate examples of substitute goods.

In Figure 9.10, a decrease in the price of solar panels (from $P_0$ to $P_1$) enables more people to be able to install them in their homes. This shift in energy sources reduces the amount of kerosene being consumed, because solar energy provides better light than kerosene. As a result, the quantity purchased moves down from $Q_0$ to $Q_1$ even though the price does not change. The shift in the demand curve is inward, as shown by the arrows.

In Figure 9.11 there is an increase in the price of a substitute good. As coffee prices increase, some consumers will instead drink tea as a substitute, leading to a growing demand for tea.

### Market Demand Curve – Horizontal Summation of Individual Demand Curves

Figure 9.12 shows three individual demand curves. In this example, the market demand curve for electricity is the horizontal summation of the individual demand curves. The individual demand curve is the quantity of a good that an individual consumer will buy at a given price, all other things being equal. (The Latin phrase *ceteris paribus*—or 'all other things being equal'—is commonly used in economics to highlight the effect of one economic variable on another, provided that all other variables remain constant.) The concept of *aggregate demand* represents the total demand for all goods and services produced in an economy. Aggregate demand is expressed as the total amount of money exchanged for goods and services at a specific time and price.

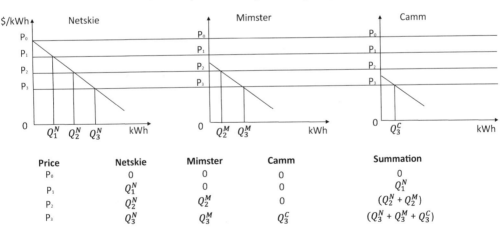

THE MARKET DEMAND CURVE
THE HORIZONTAL SUMMATION OF INDIVIDUAL DEMAND CURVES
An Example of Monthly Electricity Usage (kWh)

| Price | Netskie | Mimster | Camm | Summation |
|---|---|---|---|---|
| $P_0$ | 0 | 0 | 0 | 0 |
| $P_1$ | $Q_1^N$ | 0 | 0 | $Q_1^N$ |
| $P_2$ | $Q_2^N$ | $Q_2^M$ | 0 | $(Q_2^N + Q_2^M)$ |
| $P_3$ | $Q_3^N$ | $Q_3^M$ | $Q_3^C$ | $(Q_3^N + Q_3^M + Q_3^C)$ |

*Figure 9.12* The market demand curve is the horizontal summation of individual demand curves because it represents the total quantity of a good or service that all consumers are willing to buy at different prices. Each individual demand curve shows the quantity of the good a single consumer is willing to buy at various prices. By adding up the quantities demanded by all consumers at each price level, we can derive the market demand curve, which shows the total demand for the product across the entire market. This aggregation of individual demand curves illustrates how the total demand in the market changes with price.

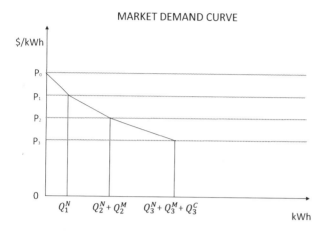

MARKET DEMAND CURVE

*Figure 9.13* Figure 9.12 shows the individual demand curves. In this figure the horizontal summation of these individual demand curves is now presented as the community demand curve for electricity.

The individual demand curves of Netskie, Mimster, and Camm are each influenced by their age, sex, income, habits, and other competing goods. The market demand curve is also influenced by these factors, but at a community level. In Figure 9.13 we see the horizontal summation of the individual demand curves that were shown in Figure 9.12.

When doing a feasibility study for an impact investment, the analyst will want to determine the demand for the product or service within a specific community. A survey will be used to gather household information, from which the market demand curve will be constructed and used in the financial and economic modeling. Box 9.8 describes the relationship between marginal benefits and the demand curve.

---

**BOX 9.8  UNDERSTANDING MARGINAL BENEFIT AND MAXIMIZING BENEFITS IN ECONOMICS**

The value of one more unit on the WTP is considered the marginal benefit and since it represents the demand curve it is often the case that the demand curve is referred to as the marginal benefit curve. When marginal benefits are equal to marginal costs the project will have maximized the benefits.

---

To know whether there will be a shift in the demand curve or movement along the demand curve, one must determine whether, at a given price, consumers will want to buy more if various other factors change. The price for a certain commodity might increase and will cause a movement along the demand curve, or incomes might rise, allowing for the purchase of more of a certain commodity at the same price. In this latter case, the demand curve would shift outward.

Keep in mind that a consumer market demand curve is the horizontal summation of individual demand curves. For example, the demand for a toll highway could be calculated by asking a sample of people to indicate their willingness to pay at different toll rates. This could be further broken down by the type of vehicle they are driving. If we have to consider trucks, buses, motorcycles, and passenger vehicles, then we might have a total demand curve for the use of the toll road, as well as separate demand curves for each type of vehicle using the toll road (since charges are usually set separately for each type of vehicle).

## Notes

1 In this chapter, the author drew inspiration from Glenn P. Jenkins's work and expertise, with whom he had the pleasure of having professional learning and collaboration opportunities. The chapter also draws heavily from the valuable insights shared by Glenn P. Jenkins, Chun-Yan Kuo, and Arnold C. Harberger in their seminal work, "Cost-Benefit Analysis for Investment Decisions," published in June 2012.

2 A value is considered to be deterministic when the analyst has all of the data required to 'determine' the outcome with 100% certainty.

3 This general rule will not hold in those cases where there are market failures and distortions.

4 A water tariff price is the price assigned, usually by government, to water supplied by a public utility.

5 Social marketing refers to activities aimed at changing or maintaining people's behavior for the benefit of society.

# Chapter 10

# Cash Flow, Environmental, and Gender Assessments

## Introduction

Cash flow[1] has always been a focus of the financial appraisal. This is not surprising since the cash flow statement provides all the sources and uses of cash over the project lifespan. For all investments, the cash flow is an important area of analysis. In impact investing, two foundational analyses feed into the cash flow: environmental assessment and gender assessment. In Figure 10.1 we see how the environmental and gender assessments feed into the cash flow in addition to modules that were discussed in Chapter 9. This chapter discusses the importance of having both of these embedded within the project, along with the challenges when doing an investment appraisal using a monetization methodology. Figure 10.2 shows how the cash flow is an integral part of the modules and the primary gender and environmental analysis.

At this phase of the investment appraisal, data collection or the use of data collected from a reliable source will often be required for both the environmental and gender assessments. The pre-feasibility study will have used estimates, but these are now replaced by data collected from primary sources. Primary data, in this context, do not necessarily have to be collected by the project itself, although that might be required if there is no reputable source available. Figure 10.2 shows how the cash flow is an integral part of the modules and the primary gender and environmental analysis.

The analyst often obtains primary data from multiple sources. In identifying these sources, it will also be important to know how the data or other types of information were compiled.

Reliability must be demonstrated when collecting or using other data for analysis purposes. Data reliability will be largely dependent on data collection methods and having confidence that if the process were replicated, it would get the same results. The analyst must state the reasons that the primary source is reliable and explain how it is significant. A reliable source will help stakeholders understand specific environmental and gender issues.

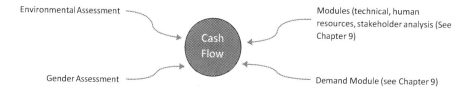

Environmental Assessment

Cash Flow

Modules (technical, human resources, stakeholder analysis (See Chapter 9)

Gender Assessment

Demand Module (see Chapter 9)

*Figure 10.1* Traditionally, a feasibility study would not include a gender analysis. During the past three decades, development organizations have increasingly recognized the importance of gender analysis to the improvement and sustainability of financial, economic, and social benefits. (European Institute for Gender Equality (EIGE).

DOI: 10.4324/9781003276920-11

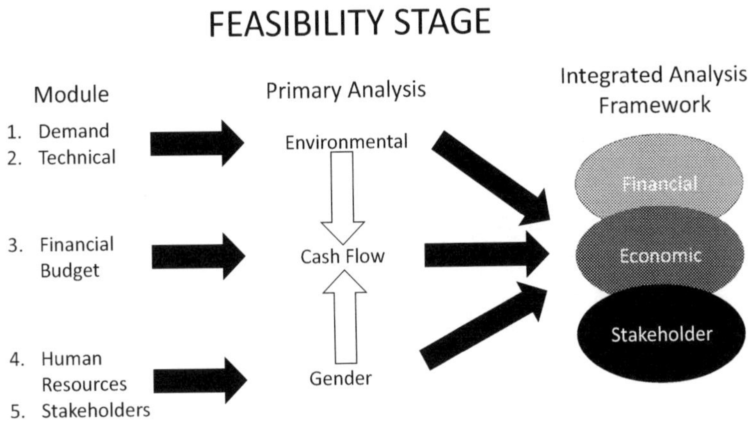

## FEASIBILITY STAGE

Figure 10.2 There has been strong recognition for the need to include environmental mitigation costs identified during an environmental impact assessment. Although gender analysis has been used for many years, the associated costs for the possible redesign of interventions has not always been included in the feasibility study.

A primary source might be reliable but still not provide statistically significant evidence to inform specific project initiatives. In these cases, the primary source should be reconsidered.

Perhaps the most important question is whether the primary sources make sense. In some cases, there might be good insights, but additional evidence is required and might involve data collection. Regardless, the analyst must question everything so that verifiable insights can strengthen the overall project design.

In this chapter we highlight some of the challenges associated with gender and environmental analysis within the project investment appraisal process. This chapter is meant to bring to the attention of the reader the types of challenges that will be experienced and that social scientists and others are working on to find adequate solutions. The overriding challenge that is brought out in this chapter is the difficulty or perhaps inability to monetize certain impacts. In Chapter 12 we discuss monetization and the increasingly important role it has in impact investing. Gender impacts and certain environmental impacts, such as carbon emissions are two hotly debated subjects in project appraisal work.

### Environment

The environment is featured prominently in the Sustainable Development Goals (SDG) and is commonly known as SDG15. Sustainable development aims to promote the kind of development that minimizes environmental problems and meets the needs of the present generation without compromising the ability of the future generation to meet their own needs.

The environmental assessment is a process of identifying and then evaluating the various project impacts in order to develop a mitigation plan. The main starting point is to bring together the team(s) that worked on the demand module as well as the technical module.

This new cross-functional team will be responsible for assessing the expected environmental impacts and making recommendations on the most cost-effective means of mitigation.

These types of cross-functional teams will, in most cases, be taking on a well-established systematic process for calculating the project benefits and costs. The actual steps taken in an environmental impact assessment tend to be similar regardless of the amount of diligence and the types of tools used in the analysis. The following chart highlights these major steps in the EIA process.

**Typical Key Steps In an Environmental Impact Assessment (EIA) Process**

| Steps | Step Description |
| --- | --- |
| Screening | The regulatory environment differs across countries, and in less developed countries it might not be fully developed. In many of these cases, the investors or project financiers (foreign government donor, regional bank, etc.) will insist upon either their own EIA standards or those of another internationally recognized institution. Still, even within these contexts there is a need to determine whether the environmental impacts of the proposed project would justify the development of a full EIA. |
| Community Consultation | Community consultations will be required to understand the project and its potential impact. They also provide insights into the design of the EIA and the type of analysis that will be required at each stage. Community consultations provide valuable insight into project alternative approaches. |
| Impact Assessment and Mitigation | Although the entire EIA process requires experienced professionals, the impact assessment requires expertise in evaluating the socioeconomic and environmental impacts of the proposed development project, as well as its alternatives. In addition, the evaluation will take into consideration the mitigation measures that can be implemented to reduce the impacts. The tools used during this step will be determined by the required rigor and diligence of the EIA. |
| Mitigation and Risk Management | Plans must be prepared to address the mitigation measures and other identified project risks. The use of sensitivity analysis would be appropriate when identifying risk variables. This analysis tests how sensitive the project's outcomes are to changes in the value of one parameter at a time. |
| EIA Report | The EIA Report is the compilation of the research and analysis that have been done on the project. It is structured so that it clearly responds to all of the required report components. |
| Regulatory Review and Appraisal | The regulatory review and appraisal might involve not only the host government's environmental officials, but also those of the lending institution or donor. The responsibility of those conducting the regulatory review is to determine whether the EIA plans are sufficient to protect the community and the environment. Based on this determination, a decision is made as to whether an operational permit will be provided to the project. If the project is permitted to begin an implementation phase, it will then begin to engage with authorities on the monitoring of this phase, followed by the operational and close-down phases. This work will be ongoing throughout the project lifetime and will focus on ensuring that mitigation strategies are fully adhered to and are effectively addressing negative environmental externalities. |

In our discussion of the EIA, our emphasis is not so much on the process, but on the current economic and social challenges resulting from certain phenomena such as climate change. Analysts are not only requiring new tools to achieve environmental improvements, but are also being forced to reconsider the assumptions of some well-established tools.

Within economics, the social discount rate is considered an important calculation, as small changes in this rate can reveal, in certain instances, large present values that are a major determinant in deciding whether a project or component will proceed. While working on the impact assessment and mitigation step of the EIA, the cross-functional team will be responsible for determining whether mitigation strategies can be effectively deployed to reduce negative externalities. Although these measurements have been done for years and on many different projects, the calculations become more complex when consideration is given to environmental implications for generations of people to come.

The social cost of carbon (SCC) is an important concept in the discussion of costs associated with climate change and making decisions on whether to proceed with a project. The SCC is an estimate of the economic costs of emitting one additional ton of carbon dioxide. It measures the present value of this additional tonne of carbon dioxide into the atmosphere.

Estimating the price of carbon, or anything that is not sold directly in the market for an identifiable price, can be very difficult. That's because there is no precise connection between the carbon emissions and the resulting costs—such as healthcare needs, alterations in weather patterns, or the eventual need to relocate homes because the sea level has risen—that may occur. In economics, we call these costs 'shadow prices' because they are hidden and uncertain. But in assessing costs and benefits, we cannot leave these impacts out. As a result, project developers usually include some 'shadow price' of carbon emissions in its investment appraisal analysis. The practical impact of this analysis often takes the form of a surcharge on goods and services that create significant carbon emissions within the project lifecycle.

The calculations used in determining a shadow price are beyond the scope of this book, but they can be best described as the real economic prices (nominal prices adjusted for inflation) assigned to goods and services once an adjustment has been made to remove distortionary market instruments that interfere with the maximizing of social benefits and welfare.

## Gender

The environment and gender are highlighted in the analysis because of their importance in sustainable development. Gender equality is known as SDG5. These goals have independent objectives and strategies, but they are also very much interrelated. For instance, the UN and others are interested in determining the cost-effectiveness of investing in gender programming as a way to achieve climate change adaptation objectives. Climate change can exacerbate gender inequalities. In many countries, women are unable to own land and therefore have control over how it is used. These cultural and legal limitations lead to a lack of capacity to address climate change impacts either through mitigation efforts and/or adaptation action. The literature has clearly demonstrated that women have significantly contributed to safeguarding the environment as agents of change. In many instances, women have provided leadership to the adoption of clean energy technologies, climate-smart agricultural practices, and taking measures to reduce climate-related disasters. A focus within the development community is to make climate finance gender-responsive.

It is important to better understand the role of gender in the theory of change and how it is contributing to sustainable outcomes. There is mounting evidence of the benefits of gender equality in all programs, but there are still often gaps in the logic models, making the net benefits of these projects less than optimal. This should no longer be acceptable as it is a poor use of limited resources.

The lack of a proper gender analysis has resulted in ineffectiveness and inefficiencies that can have extreme implications, including economies that are not as robust as might be possible, ongoing violence against women and girls, and communities that are less safe and healthy. There are significant gaps in understanding with regard to how specific projects can best integrate gender.

Gender analysis is an important component in the project appraisal process. It recognizes the relationship with important social variables such as ethnicity, age, culture and social class. These variables can enhance the impact of projects through an understanding of how they interact and contribute to achieving project objectives.

Many practitioners downplay the use of cost-benefit analysis on gender issues because of its apparent inability to quantify and place a dollar value on most gender impacts. A common argument is that cost-benefit analyses contain a bias towards quantifiable indicators and are better suited for efficiency rather than equity objectives. Similar arguments are made with regard to $CO_2$ emissions. This theoretical debate will continue, but the more important takeaway is that different analytical and measurement techniques will evolve with experience and time. It is important to recognize limitations, but also to foresee the possibilities and uses of different techniques.

## Cash Flow

The financial cash flow is a central focus of an investment appraisal and will encapsulate the essence of the project. In addition to revenue sources, it will show how the investment resources will be used over the life of the project, including addressing important environmental and gender equality priorities. Box 10.1 provides an understanding of the difference between cash flow and revenue and expenses.

---

### BOX 10.1   CASH FLOW VS. REVENUE AND EXPENSES

It's important to recognize the difference between cash flow and revenue and expenses.

For instance, revenue refers to the income earned by a business or project by selling goods and services. A sale can be done on a credit or payment plan and will not provide immediate cash. This is why the accounts receivable and the accounts payable (expenditures) are important in a cash flow forecast as they tell the analyst when actual cash should become available. Until that time, these amounts do not represent actual cash flows although they will be recorded as revenue.

---

Although there are differing formats, it is important that sufficient data be included so that the economic and stakeholder analysis can be undertaken with confidence. The analysis is concerned about money that goes into the project and money that leaves the project. Although this concept is relatively straightforward, it is important to provide the necessary detail. For instance, purchases of equipment and inputs need to be broken down between local and imported items, so as to the calculate the amount to be paid in tariffs and VAT. This information can then be used in the economic and distributional analysis.

The financial appraisal of the business or project will focus on the cash flows. The construction of financial cash flows involves a complete and sufficient listing of expected sources of cash and the expected uses of cash over the duration of the project. In addition to having sufficient detail for economic and distributional analysis, the primary reason for the cash flow forecast is to understand the timing of money coming in and going out of the project or business. Many businesses and projects that fail do so out of poor cash flow—more specifically, not anticipating when there will be a need for investment or loan capital.

The cash flow forecast of the inputs and outputs is done for the life of the project. Over time, the prices are influenced by changes in the real price of a good and the effect of inflation. The real price is determined by the market demand for a good or service, whereas inflation is often a combination of money supply and the production of goods and services along with monetary and fiscal policies. Since inflation is difficult for a project to forecast, it is most often treated as a risk variable, and a sensitivity analysis can be used to identify the impact over a range of inflation rates.

The cash flow forecast will be developed so that the projections over the life of the project are done using nominal (also referred to as current) prices.[2] These prices should be consistent with the projected inflation rates over the same time period.

## Notes

1  Acknowledgement is extended to the economists at Limestone Analytics and other individuals who have graciously contributed their knowledge and expertise in analyzing the economic ramifications of conservation efforts, ecological enhancements, and the incorporation of gender considerations.
2  To construct the cash flow forecast in nominal or current prices, consideration must be given to the movement of both real prices and the general price level. A full discussion of this topic can be found in an introductory finance book.

# Chapter 11

# Integrated Analysis Framework – Investment Criteria and Risk Management

## Integrated Analysis Framework

For the investment appraisal,[1] we suggest an integrated approach, which means measuring the benefits and costs of the project over its lifespan for both the financial and economic appraisals. This is not unique to impact investing, but traditionally investment appraisal work was often done in silos where the financial analysis would be completed. Then, the economic evaluation would occur separately. As part of this process, the analyst will convert all future cash flows to their present value through discounting. The analyst can generate financial NPV and IRR, economic NPV (ENPV), and economic IRR (EIRR). In Figure 11.1 we see that the integrated analysis includes the financial and economic analysis. It also includes the stakeholder analysis to make sure the benefits are reaching the intended stakeholders.

A financial evaluation and an economic evaluation have different objectives and perspectives. The financial evaluation assesses the project's ability to generate adequate cash flows to cover the financial costs over a specific time-period of the project. An economic evaluation considers the project's impact on the entire community and country. The economic evaluation assesses the impact on the welfare of all citizens, but it can segregate the population to determine the impact on key stakeholders. The project must be financially, economically, and socially viable for impact investing.

## FEASIBILITY STAGE

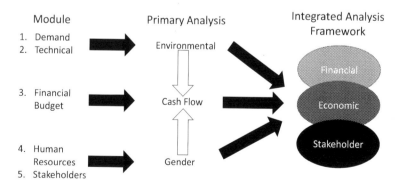

Figure 11.1 A distinctive feature of the investment appraisal process for impact investing is that a social enterprise or project must be financially, economically, and socially viable.

DOI: 10.4324/9781003276920-12

Understanding the investment criteria used to determine whether a project is financially and economically viable is important. In the following paragraphs, we provide detailed explanations of NPV and IRR. At the end of this section, a more modest explanation is provided for the Debt Service Coverage Ratio (DSCR) and Benefit Cost Ratio (BCR).

## Investment Criteria

### Net Present Value

Discounting is the inverse of compounding.[2] Discounting is the essence of net present value in that benefits and costs occur at different times throughout the project. In other words, all future cash flows are discounted to determine their present value. For the current year, a dollar would be worth a dollar; at the end of year 1 (t=1), that dollar will have an NPV of $0.95 if the discount rate r is 5%, using the formula $\frac{1}{(1+r)^2}$.

Consider the net benefits for the next several years. They could be represented as

$$(B_0 - C_0), \ (B_1 - C_1), \ \ldots\ldots \ (B_n - C_n)$$

The NPV of this stream of net benefits can be expressed algebraically:

$$NPV^0 = \frac{B_0 - C_0}{(1+r)^0} + \frac{B_1 - C_1}{(1+r)^1} \ldots\ldots + \frac{B_n - C_n}{(1+r)^n}$$

$$NPV^0 = \sum_{t=0}^{n} \frac{(B_t - C_t)}{(1+r)^t}$$

In this formula, $n$ is representative of the life of the project.

$\frac{1}{(1+r)^t}$ is commonly referred to as the discount factor for year t.

A positive NPV project will provide impact investors with a return on their investment greater than would have been received from the best alternative investment (opportunity cost). Since the opportunity cost is the same as the discount rate, all positive NPV projects should be selected; a zero-NPV project and the best alternative will provide equal returns on investment.

NPV is often a preferred investment criterion because it has hard-and-fast rules that apply to all situations. This is not the same as other investment criteria discussed later in this chapter. Under no circumstances should a project with a negative NPV be considered for financing when discounted by the opportunity cost of funds. Similarly, when working with a fixed budget, the project with the highest NPV should be selected.

### Internal Rate of Return

When calculating the IRR of an investment, the analyst is looking to see whether it is higher than the opportunity cost of capital. If so, it will have a positive NPV and will create additional impact or value. If the IRR of the investment is less than the opportunity cost of capital, the NPV would be negative, and the project should not be considered.

While the IRR of a project is often referred to in impact investing, an analyst must consider how calculations were done when considering certain types of projects. The IRR criterion is unreliable as several problems are inherent in its calculation. Unlike the rules for NPV, which were presented in the previous section above, the IRR rules have shortcomings that the analyst must be aware of. The IRR equation is based on incremental net cash flows. Determining the IRR may be impossible if these cash flows have multiple positive and negative cash flows over a project period. Moreover, selecting between two or more mutually exclusive projects of different scales is not uncommon. NPV takes the project scale into account explicitly, whereas the IRR ignores the differences in scale, possibly leading to an incorrect investment choice. Another concern when using IRR is that different project life spans and similar projects with different implementation time frames can lead to incorrect analysis.

Our intent is not to give an exhaustive list of problems with IRR but to provide the reader with an understanding of why impact investing prefers NPV as a primary investment criterion. An experienced analyst can use IRR very effectively. In our experience, IRR is valuable in communicating to prospective investors. We find that IRR is useful when multiple projects are being compared or when there might be difficulty in determining the opportunity cost or discount rate. NPV tends to be used as a primary investment criterion in situations where there are positive and negative cash flows for a period of time and, perhaps, also a need to use multiple discount rates.

It's essential to understand how IRR and NPV relate to each other and the pros and cons of using them as investment criteria. In the next section, we formally compare NPV and IRR investment criteria.

### Net Present Value (NPV) and Internal Rate of Return (IRR)

A positive NPV provides a more significant project surplus than the best alternative project. In contrast, IRR is focused on a project's breakeven cash flow level compared to the best alternative project investment.

The IRR is considered helpful in evaluating a project when it must be compared to a discount rate. The IRR is of limited value if a discount rate is unknown or cannot be applied to a specific project. In such cases, the NPV method is superior. The discount rate is critical in applying investment criteria for project selection. A slight variation in its value can alter the analysis results and affect the final choice of a project.

In summary, the discount rate ($\rho$) is the internal rate of return and can be obtained from this formula:

$$\sum_{j=}^{n} \left[ \left( B_j - C_j \right) / \left( 1 + \rho \gamma \right) \right] = 0$$

The net benefit flow is calculated from B and C in year j. As discussed earlier, the NPV is zero, and investors will earn a return equal to the IRR.

### Debt Service Coverage Ratio

The debt-service coverage ratio (DSCR) is increasingly used in impact investing to measure a project's available cash flow and ability to pay its operating expenses and current debt obligations. The DSCR is an easy way for investors to know that the social enterprise or project has enough income to pay its ongoing debts.

Investors will want to know a project's debt service capacity ratio year-to-year. Many also want a loan life cover ratio (LLCR) summary. A DSCR is the ratio of the project's net cash flow or net operating income over the amount of debt service due.

$$ADSCR_t = [ANCF_t / (Annual\ Debt\ Repayment_t)]$$

The LLCR allows the lenders to determine confidence in the project's ability to service its debt. It gives the lender an indication of the number of times the outstanding debt on a project can be repaid through the project Cash Flow Available for Debt Service (CFADS) over the life of the loan.

$$LLCRt = PV\ (ANCFt\ to\ end\ year\ of\ debt\ )\ /\ PV\ (Annual\ Debt\ Repayment\ )$$

Within impact investing, the DSCR is commonly used to calculate debt coverage service-ability at a point in time. In contrast, the LLCR is longer-term and used with the break-even analysis.

Taken from the work of Glenn Jenkins, Chun-Yan Kuo, and Arnold Harberger on Discounting and Alternative Investment Criteria, the following are a few ways in which the DSCR can be improved:

1  Increase your net operating income
2  Decrease the interest rate on the loan
3  Decrease your operating expenses
4  Decrease the amount of debt financing
5  Pay off some of your existing debt
6  Increase the duration of the loan repayment

To help understand a debt service ratio, let's suppose that the DSCR is > 1. This would indicate that the project is generating sufficient income to cover its annual debt and interest obligations. Within the impact investing sector, an ideal ratio is greater than 2. This would indicate that the project can take on additional debt if needed.

### Benefit-Cost Ratio

A Benefit-Cost Ratio (BCR) expresses the ratio of present-value project benefits to the costs in monetary terms. It is sometimes referred to as the profitability index. Using this criterion, the BCR must have a value greater than 1 for a project to be acceptable.

The BCR is the ratio of the present value of cash inflows (benefits) to the present value of the cash outflows (or costs) using the opportunity cost of funds as the discount rate:

$$BCR = \frac{\text{PV of Cash Inflows (Benefits)}}{\text{PV of Cash Outflows (Costs)}}$$

The BCR may yield an incorrect ranking of projects and an incorrect investment decision. This tends to happen when there are different project sizes and may have more severe consequences when costs are not clearly defined and adequately included in the cash flow.

## Uncertainty and Risk

---

### BOX 11.1   KEY RISK VARIABLES

Key variables might include rate of inflation, the market exchange rate, the prices and quantities of inputs and outputs.

---

In the financial analysis for a project or business, project variables are based on fixed or deterministic values, which the analyst sets as a projection covering the years throughout the investment lifespan. A deterministic model does not include randomness, providing single values with 100% certainty. The analyst can run the model with the same initial conditions and get the same result.

Of course, the reality in which projects and businesses operate is different. Since randomness does happen, it is highly unlikely that all the project's key variables that have been projected into the future will prove to have 100% certainty throughout the project life span, which might be five or ten years.

To project any uncertain outcome into the future, the analyst introduces a predictive model, which uses statistics to indicate the predicted outcome given a set amount of input data.

Since key variables will inevitably change throughout the project's life, the NPV will also change. Box 11.1 provides examples of common key risk variables. Project risk becomes the deviation from the projected outcome. The risk analysis identifies the project's risk variables and the extent of uncertainty. The analyst moves from a deterministic to a dynamic and probabilistic reality to deal with uncertainty and risk in the investment appraisal.

In this reality, uncertainty and risk in outcomes are considered through a predictive model that allows the analyst to provide more objective and realistic results. A predictive model frames risk as the possible deviation from the projected outcome. Project risk also comes from the market and is managed by reallocating it to stakeholders who are best positioned to manage it.

At this point, the focus becomes more on NPV with an expected value range and less on a single number. The analyst has moved from forecasting the outcome of a future event based on a single-value estimate (deterministic) to a frequency and probability distribution (predictive).

For most investments, including impact investing, there are three methods for dealing with risk. These are highlighted below:

1. Sensitivity analysis

   As a part of risk management, the analyst needs to identify the critical risk variables, which will be done by using sensitivity and scenario analysis. To test the sensitivity of a project's outcome (NPV or the key variable) to changes in value, the analyst will need to consider one parameter at a time. The sensitivity analysis is often dubbed the 'what if' analysis. In selecting the uncertain variables, the analyst will choose those that can potentially have a significant influence on the project benefits and costs and can cause serious variation in terms of the final outcome.

   A sensitivity analysis is conducted on the deterministic financial cash flow model. The base case analysis model[3] will include the NPV and DSCRs. The sensitivity analysis is done by altering the values of the project input variables. It can also be done by changing the assumptions underpinning the estimated values. The values of other variables are held constant. This one-at-a-time testing is often seen as not realistic because of the correlations among variables. The analyst can sometimes deal with these correlated effects using scenario analysis, but limitations exist.

   Sensitivity analysis and scenario analysis are analytical methods that help determine the amount of risk and its effect on economic benefits. In most cases, a sensitivity analysis is undertaken to understand better the effect of changing a single variable at a time. In contrast, a scenario analysis allows the analyst to simultaneously assess the effect of changing all the variables.

2. Scenario Analysis

   Scenario analysis is best used by experienced analysts with strong modelling experience; otherwise, the process can be time-consuming and may have questionable results, especially if probabilities are not calculated correctly (which can be a challenge for the best analyst). Box 11.2 provides a short list of reasons that a scenario analysis might be required for a project.

   As mentioned above, scenario analysis recognises that certain variables are interrelated, and a small number of variables can be altered consistently simultaneously. There are cases when the NPV is positive and others where it is negative. The results are inconclusive and it might be necessary to examine the range of possible outcomes using a Monte Carlo analysis. The scenario analysis can be a good way to communicate the results of a Monte Carlo analysis.

3. Monte Carlo

   A Monte Carlo simulation is a natural extension after the sensitivity and scenario analyses are conducted. It is a broad class of computational algorithms that involve repeated random sampling to approximate the expected values and variability based on the assumptions. The results are probability distributions for the most uncertain risk variables or parameters. A Monte Carlo simulation is helpful when the outcomes cannot be easily predicted because of the many random variables.

---

**BOX 11.2 WHY USE A SCENARIO ANALYSIS?**

- Risk management can be proactive
- Specific scenario concerns of management can be analyzed
- Improved understanding of the variables at play in achieving benefits and mitigating risk

Investors are often keen to use Monte Carlo to generate a probability distribution of NPV at a certain level. The probability distribution of project outcomes can influence an investor's decision whether to proceed with the investment.

The usefulness of a Monte Carlo simulation is mainly based on the analyst's experience and expertise in financial modelling. The adage 'garbage in, garbage out' pertains to financial modelling; if poor parameters are inputted into the model, poor results will be given as outputs. A Monte Carlo simulation will require a lot of time to find a solution when many variables are used, as the simulation will entail many computations, which can be very inefficient.

### Risk Analysis and Risk Management

Risk analysis and risk management should work seamlessly in a project appraisal. We have explored the three most popular risk analysis tools; now, we will look at an overview of risk management.

Risk management has been less of an issue with impact investors than investors involved in infrastructure projects with significant investment outlays. Most impact investing projects have been relatively small in total investment amount. As investors gain experience with impact investing, larger projects will be demanded. Risk management will become necessary because of uncertainties about sharing risks and returns. Some problem areas include extended periods of project payout, unstable contracts (especially when the government is involved), and some parties (especially the NGO sector) inability to bear risks. Experience has shown that the keys to sound risk management are to ensure that contracted parties have proper incentives to perform in those areas that will influence outcomes and to avoid actions that undermine the terms of the contract. The use of incentives is foundational to economics. In our discussion on demand, we saw how people are incentivized by price and other factors. When monetary and nonmonetary incentives are used well, they can sway human behavior. A specialization within economics called behavioural economics uses insights from psychology related to economic decision-making processes. This will be discussed in Chapter 12.

### Blended Financing and Risk

One primary purpose of blended financing is to reduce risk. Blended finance is meant to support developing countries in pursuing the SDGs. It relies on concessional investments that will absorb much of the project risk. This philanthropic financing most often comes from a government or quasi-government entity.

The premise behind blended finance is that the private sector will meaningfully participate in impact investing only if the perceived and real risks are mitigated. The best means of doing so is through financing, which takes on the role of first loss. In essence, blended finance is a strategy that uses philanthropic capital with different levels of risk to catalyze risk-adjusted investments.

Although blended financing can reduce risk and might increase commercial investing and help bridge the financing gap (estimated at $2.5 trillion) for achieving the SDGs, using blended finance has not been a strong incentive for the private sector. Between 2016 and 2022, blended projects and funds have not been able to achieve more than about $20 billion. The goal for 2015 had been $100 billion. Institutional investors have not been involved, mainly because of the small deal sizes. Instead, NGO-created financing institutions have become involved and, while helping to achieve the NGOs' objectives, have added little to the overall sustainability of the model.

Further complicating matters, low- and medium-income countries struggle to make projects investment-ready as they lack the expertise to do feasibility studies. In Africa, Rwanda has shown signs of prioritising investment appraisal, which has made this country attractive for investment, among other reasons.

### Stakeholder Analysis (Distributional Impact Assessment)

Technically, the stakeholder analysis is part of the economic analysis. Because of its importance in impact investing, a separate section is given to this component of the integrated analysis framework. Often, a project will be targeted toward a particular social group, so it is essential to assess the actual amount of the total project benefits enjoyed by this group. If there are losers, then the project developers must assess whether this burden is too much or whether there can be appropriate compensation for their loss. Knowing who bears the project cost is essential as part of the analysis.

A stakeholder analysis can provide a transparent and evidence-based approach to affecting policy and policymakers. The evidence is in the financial and economic analysis and the detailed design, which should include structuring the project and using incentives to target a particular subset of society, such as the most vulnerable.

Most government offices use stakeholder analysis during the budgetary process and are thus familiar with the tool. Governments, at different levels, are much more likely to support a social impact initiative if they know that thorough due diligence has been completed.

Similarly, potential investors will have confidence in the projected project impacts and, based on this experience, will become more demanding of others that they, too, raise the bar on investment appraisal. Stakeholder analysis is also valuable for investors (especially institutional investors) tracking their progress toward achieving the SDG 2030 goals.

## Notes

1 In some instances, the work of Glenn Jenkins, Chun-Yan Kuo and Arnold Harberger has been used (see my earlier comment in this chapter on the DSCR) from their book on Cost-Benefit Analysis for Investment Decisions, June 2012.

2 To compute the future value, an analyst will use the compounding of interest rates. If $100 were invested at a market interest rate of 5.0%, we would expect that at the end of year 1, the investment would be worth $105, and after year 2, the investment would be worth $110.25 ($105 x 1.05). The calculation applies compound interest, or paying interest, on the principal and the cumulative interest to date. In this example, interest is paid annually, whereas in some cases, it is paid monthly or even daily. The number of compounding intervals will affect the future value of the amount invested today.

3 A base case analysis refers to the results obtained from doing the analysis of the financial model with the most likely set of assumptions and outcomes.

# Chapter 12

# Measurement, Management, and Appraisal

Impact investing relies heavily on impact measurement as a means for continual learning and identifying new insights on how corrective measures can be made to further improve the effectiveness and efficiency of a project. Impact measurement is critical to some impact investing instruments, such as conditional contracts where payment is 'conditional' on the project achieving a certain level of performance. To verify the performance, some measurement methods will need to be used.

Impact investing is about improving development outcomes and using the markets to provide financing that historically was not available. In order to be competitive, managers are finding innovative means to gain insights on how to improve projects and businesses. Project management teams are using behavioral science to properly incentivize their teams to use appropriate measures to better understand how an initiative, or a combination of initiatives, works to improve outcome results. In other words, understanding the causal logic. Both the incentives used and the initiatives being implemented need to be evaluated and this is often through the use of both qualitative and quantitative impact measurement methods.

Although impact measurement methods provide valuable information at a moment in time, it is the performance management system that provides near real-time managerial insights so that project management can make dynamic adjustments throughout the project to improve outcomes. Impact measurement brings insights into whether the theory of change worked properly; whereas performance management brings insights on whether the project is on track and how it can further improve. Both are important.

As an impact investment, there is the need for investors to have confidence that a project or small and growing business (SGB) can achieve the intended outcomes and repay the investment capital with a return. To do so, will require an investment appraisal which is another measurement method. In the investment context, it is specifically answering the question of whether the project or business is feasible and, if so, how best to structure the financing and governance. Depending on the structure of the investment the use of either qualitative, quantitative, causal, or a combination of impact measurement methods might be required. In this chapter, we will also discuss the increasing demand for the use of monetization methods for investment appraisal.

This chapter is divided into three main sections—i) impact measurement; ii) performance management; and iii) investment appraisal and conditional contracts. All three require specific measurement methods and techniques which will be discussed.

DOI: 10.4324/9781003276920-13

## Impact Measurement

There are many impact measurement methods, and an experienced practitioner will know which are the most important for the project type and its current phase. For those organizations interested in impact investing and wanting to improve outcome level results, the process of making them investment-ready begins with strengthening the theory of change and the logic model.

The theory of change should be supported by evidence, often initially from a literature review and then supported with both qualitative and quantitative data. Before looking at these two impact measurement methods, it is worthwhile to emphasize the approach required to undertake such work.

When developing the metrics and indicators, team members must understand the process so that they can be fully engaged as active stakeholders. Metrics and indicators are not meant to be developed in isolation by some expert. The development process should engage all stakeholders. For this to happen, there must be a willingness to invest time, significant energy, and other resources toward gathering and analyzing data. For many organizations, collecting data is a tedious chore because there is no clear purpose for using the information obtained. When this is the case, the organization often stops collecting data after a short period of time, or it is used only for secondary purposes.

The project's theory of change and results chain are living documents that can and should be revised as new insights are identified. The management focus should be on improving outcomes and giving project staff the freedom to 'experiment' on the basis of the data gathered. Trying new things should be encouraged as long as the new approach is set up as an experiment, the hypothesis is based on evidence, and the right metrics and indicators will be available to provide vital insights into whether the changes are producing improved results.

The Role of Incentives

As a means to improve results, organizations using impact investing have begun to incorporate psychology and behavioral science to design incentives that will improve project results. Because of the important role they have in motivating project staff and targeted groups, these incentives should be evaluated in order to better understand their effectiveness.

Everyone needs to be motivated to track and analyze data that can lead to solutions during project implementation and later with project management challenges. This motivation can often come in the form of purposefully placed incentives. A strong incentive will motivate a project team to find suitable solutions to problems. Impact investing often uses financial incentives as motivation, especially for senior project staff and others to take certain actions. For instance, the diagrams in Figure 12.1 in the Annex of this chapter, demonstrate how a financial incentive might be used to improve results. To have incentives that improve results there will need to be an evaluation done on their effectiveness. A properly designed program will combine different types of incentives that can achieve strong outcomes.

Behavioral economics has been a discipline since the 1980s (Richard Thaler would argue that some important ideas in behavioral economics date back to economist Adam Smith in the 18th century), but it became more popular recently when Thaler and Cass Sunstein published *Nudge*. Their book combined the principles of economics and psychology to better understand how people behave and why. Behavioral economics has aroused some controversy, but it has given practitioners further insight into how preferred outcomes can be achieved. It has also challenged neoclassical economics, which assumed that all community members make informed decisions based on their self-interest.

A nudge is a type of incentive in that it helps someone make a choice. It can alter stakeholders' behavior so that it becomes more predictable, but it does not take away other options and should never be mandated. A hallmark of a responsible nudge is that it can be avoided easily and at negligible cost. Like all interventions, nudges should be evaluated by gathering evidence on whether they are producing the expected results.

Types of Impact Measurement

Impact investing can use a broad spectrum of evaluation methods. The choice of methods will largely depend on the reason for the evaluation, as well as the type of impact investment. It is important to understand the trade-offs of the various methods. Evaluation approaches can be characterized into two broad categories: observational and quantitative. In Table 12.1, we highlight these two broad categories and then further break them down into four methods that we explore in this chapter. It should be noted, we do provide a brief explanation of a development evaluation, but do not go into detail as this evaluation method is most often used for pre-impact investing purposes.

Development evaluation will be important for an organization when it is introducing a new product or service. The evaluation involves gathering data that can be assessed and used in making adaptations to the interventions that can then be further tested. Evaluators assess how the interventions have improved outcomes. The focus is on identifying the right interventions and beginning to refine them through testing. At the same time, a theory of change and logic model are being developed or updated along with indicators.

---

**BOX 12.1   PRE-POST ANALYSIS**

Impact investing will often use a pre-post analysis as an observational evaluation method. This method allows the evaluator to quantify how participants' outcomes change over the project lifespan. It will often compare how stakeholders' outcomes change from when the project began (baseline/pre) and the end of the project (final evaluation/post).

The difference in outcomes from baseline/pre to final evaluation/post represents the change. When aggregating this difference for all targeted stakeholders the analyst can quantify how outcomes changed on average for two assessment points, for example.

The average change provides the analyst with an understanding of the change of direct stakeholders during the project. It is important to note that the average change does not imply the impact of the project. The methodology does not use a counterfactual and, as such, cannot attribute the change in outcomes caused by the project from other occurring outcomes that might be natural or from another project. An analyst can use these findings and combine them with analytical analysis for more robust findings, but cannot provide attribution to the project.

---

Observational methods can indicate the change in outcomes over a period of time, but they cannot prove that the change is attributable to the interventions. There might be external factors that contributed to the results. For instance, a gender education project might be able to say that schoolgirls' test scores have improved by 30% from the previous year.

Table 12.1 There is a diverse range of impact measurement approaches available, each offering unique insights into the effects of actions and projects. A robust measurement system effectively connects these actions to their resulting impacts, enabling a deeper understanding of outcomes. Identifying the intended impacts of a business or project is crucial for choosing the most appropriate impact measurement method to accurately gauge success and progress

**IMPACT MEASUREMENT**

| Types | Observational | | Quantitative | |
|---|---|---|---|---|
| Subsets | Investigation | | Causal | |
| Methods | Qualitative | Analytics | Quasi-experimental | Experimental |
| Rationale | To improve the implementation of the theory of change Improve the use of project incentives Learning about values, causes, and effects | | To provide evidence that is attributable to project interventions Focus on proving more so than on improving Identifying effective and efficient programs | |
| Strengths | Understand target project stakeholders and required behavior change | Understand relationships among interventions | Validating stable, well-defined relationships and causal logic from the theory of change and logic model Conditional payment based on project results | |
| Approach | Use of structured and informal interviews and observations. How to optimize inputs, activities, and outputs to achieve the best outcomes? | Used to understand interventions through exploring patterns in data. Data collection dependent on impact goals and logic model | Estimate of Counterfactual with baseline data (Difference-in-Differences) and without baseline data (Regression Discontinuity Design) | Counterfactual by randomization—use of a treatment group (receiving project interventions) and a control group (similar characteristics as treatment, but no project interventions) |

While this calculation might be correct, the result can't be attributed to the project; perhaps a new Science, Technology, Engineering, Math (STEM) program was also introduced at the beginning of the school year and might be partially or totally responsible for the change in test scores.

Regardless of the measurement requirements, evaluation tools should be using evidence-based approaches. In the case of observational methods, in some instances this might include professional observations and judgement. In such situations, the initial observations can be validated through similar independent observations. In other instances, it might not be possible to measure social impacts other than through trained judgement. For instance, applicants for medical school and other medical education professions have historically been selected solely on test and exam scores. Observations have led researchers to question this approach because many students with high exam scores who performed well in training did not perform well in postgraduate clinical practice. In this case, an actual Situational Judgement Test (SJT) was set up by experts to assess individual reactions to different situations. These scenarios were based on a detailed analysis of the actual role. They were developed in collaboration with subject matter experts so that they could accurately assess the key attributes associated with competent performance.

Investigation methods are designed to provide the project team with an in-depth and integrated qualitative and analytical understanding of a situation. The combination of qualitative and quantitative/analytics is part of the evaluation design so that the strengths of both are integrated into the findings and learning.

Qualitative methods focus on understanding and making sense of things within their natural settings. Researchers use empirical methods, which means that the results are verifiable. The methods might include structured interviews, personal experiences, field visits, and observations. In other words, qualitative research is an inquiry process that explores a social problem using interpretive and naturalistic approaches.

Often qualitative methods are used to investigate certain elements of the theory of change or logic model that have the potential to improve the program's impact. In other instances, the research is intended to provide overall confidence in the program design. Doing qualitative research well requires a systematic research design and testing of the hypothesis as it relates to the theory of change and logic model. Qualitative research is demanding, especially in its commitment to extensive time in the field collecting data and gaining access to a community perspective on issues. The data analysis requires sorting through large amounts of data and categorizing them in a manner that is consistent with the objectives of the research. It is not uncommon to use analytics in combination with qualitative methods.

In Box 12.1, we describe the use of pre-post analysis which is a good example of a useful impact methodology, but that has limitations. The pre-post findings can provide an analyst with a very good understanding as to whether the project is on the trajectory towards achieving its objectives. The data gathered during the evaluation can be used to test the hypothesis that was put forward in the theory of change and logic model. Certain outcomes will change naturally with time and the analyst must take this into consideration, but with the use of statistical techniques can draw conclusions as to whether the project has been effective in achieving intended results. The major limitation is not being able to attribute the estimated effects to the project. The importance of attribution will depend on the objectives of the evaluation. This will be discussed later in the chapter.

It is not uncommon for potential investors and practitioners to use quantitative/analytic methods alongside qualitative or trained judgement methods. Quantitative methods use a data collection and data analysis process that can be used to test causal relationships and make predictions. As the Impact Measurement diagram shows, quantitative methods include analytical and causal methods. These latter methods (we discuss these later) can claim attribution to the project; whereas, the former is not able to do so.

Analytical methods are often used to identify patterns in data in order to better understand how outcomes are achieved. A major issue in these methods is the quality of data that is available for analysis. Data quality simply refers to how suitable the available data is for providing insight to the research question. Data quality might refer to the accuracy in collection, as well as completeness and timeliness.

It is important to make sure that the survey sample size is representative of the project area. An experienced surveyor will make sure the survey sample is done randomly and includes a large enough sample so that the analysis will not be affected by an unknown variable. There are cases when it is not possible to get a random sample. In such cases, the use of matching, a quasi-experimental method, can be used if the data sets are large. Matching does require an analyst with experience in statistical techniques to construct a comparison group for a given treatment group.

---

**BOX 12.2   COST-EFFECTIVENESS ANALYSIS (CEA)—AN APPRAISAL TECHNIQUE IN THE ANALYSIS OF SOCIAL PROGRAMS**

CEA can help in identifying opportunities that are of very low cost but have high benefits. A great example is the use of oral rehydration therapy. It became a standard component of early Child Survival programs and resulted in saving the lives of millions of young children who otherwise would have died from dehydration brought about by diarrhea.

---

Statistical techniques are also used in analyzing data, outside of the use of matching, to determine the strength of relationships. Impact investing uses correlation and linear regression along with statistical techniques to determine the strength of the relationship between two quantitative variables. Regression analysis expresses the relationship as an equation; whereas correlation quantifies the strength of the linear relationship between the two variables.

When mentioning quantitative techniques, it is important to recognize the role of decision analysis and cost-effectiveness analysis (CEA). Both of these approaches provide a systematic evidence base for making an optimal choice under conditions of uncertainty. Decision analysis and cost-benefit analysis are often used in the health sector. In Box 12.2 there is an example of when CEA is very appropriate for social programs.

Using the health sector as an example, decision analysis would allow an analyst to use a model that includes costs, probabilities, and health-related quality-of-life values. It can also include other inputs that would provide further insights to the program.

There have been a substantial number of impact investments made in global 'reproductive, maternal, newborn, and child health' (RMNCH) over the past three decades. Many international organizations—the Global Alliance for Vaccines and Immunization (GAVI); Clinton Health Access Initiative; Children's Investment Fund Foundation; and the Bill & Melinda Gates Foundation—have used CEA to introduce cost-effective means of addressing RMNCH challenges. Because of the ability to examine one or more interventions and then to identify those with low cost/high benefit there has been an increased interest in conducting CEA and other analyses of maternal and child health interventions.

## Performance Management System

This section on performance management systems has been significantly influenced by our (primarily Terry's) work with Instiglio and their contribution to this body of knowledge.[1] Instiglio is committed to working with government and organizations to accomplish greater social outcomes, and one tool for making this happen is the performance management system.

Instiglio's mission is to "transform global development effectiveness by using results-based approaches to incentivize impact, redirect large-scale funding towards innovation, accelerate the uptake of evidence, and strengthen delivery systems."

The section on the Performance Management System very closely follows the Instiglio approach.

A performance management system is structured to provide insights on how to improve outcomes. This is in contrast with a monitoring system, which primarily provides insights on whether the project implementation is going according to plan. Although the monitoring system lends itself to reporting to donors, it does little to support continuing improvement. A performance management system can also be used for reporting, but its main purpose is for learning new information and ultimately improving project outcomes.

As discussed earlier in the chapter, impact evaluations have an important role in determining whether the project theory of change was correct. An impact evaluation provides insight into whether the intended outcomes were achieved. This is important, especially for transparency and accountability, but is limited to providing applications of meaningful learning to the next phase of programming.

Unlike the impact evaluation which provides insights at a moment in time, the performance management system provides ongoing insights and understanding of whether the project is on track to achieve expected outcomes and learning on how to improve the project outcomes. The following are key steps taken towards implementing a performance management system.

### Identifying Key Metrics and Indicators

Chapter 7 discussed the importance of selecting indicators all along the results chain: activities, outputs, and outcomes. The reason is to allow the project team to track the causal logic at different levels of the logic model. A performance management system is meant to shift the measurement focus towards gaining insights on how to make dynamic adjustments to improve outcomes. To do so requires an understanding of how interventions work towards achieving outcomes, and having good metrics and indicators is critical to making this happen. A project manager wants to know not only whether outcomes are achieved, but also the cause-effect logic behind making it happen. It is important to identify those project interventions where there are risk factors to the project. The data on these risk factors will be important in the analysis to make sure that intended results are not jeopardized. Table 12.2 highlights the two sets of indicators - i) project performance, and ii) external factors

*Table 12.2* Project performance indicators should be identified across the logic model so that the causal logic can be tracked and understood. Indicators for external factors are important as they potentially have a high risk to the project achieving intended outcomes

**SELECTION OF INDICATORS**

| Indicators | Description |
|---|---|
| Project Performance (across the logic model) | • Aligned with expected outcome results<br>• Include 'risk' factors that need to be monitored<br>• Under the project's control – otherwise, include in External Factors |
| External Factors | • Not related to project implementation, BUT<br>• Potential implications on project outcomes |

The indicators used for project performance should all be within the control of the project team. Otherwise, the project team will not be able to make changes to activities that will affect meaningful change.

While it is important to select performance indicators that are under the control of the project team, it is also important to have indicators for external factors unrelated to the project implementation, but that might have a substantial impact on project outcome results.

### Information System

To analyze data and make decisions in real time there needs to be an information system that effectively collects data, often through the use of mobile devices. It is important that data is collected in a timely and reliable manner. The collection of data on mobile devices is considered very efficient because it dramatically reduces manual data entry errors. When the mobile devices are synchronized with the data storage location it provides for simultaneous collection and entry of data.

Data management is essential for aggregating and making sense of data coming from multiple sources into a single database. When a database can automate the data aggregation and cleaning it allows for near-real time analysis. This data can be effectively used to construct or update performance indicators.

At this point, the data needs to be transformed into information that reflects the project context. This process allows for this information to be used for actionable insights. Performance insights allow the project team to aggregate the metrics into a simple, but powerful dashboard. Data visualization is a very effective means of analyzing information. Depending on the project, data visualization might use charts, graphics, and maps. The importance of these tools is to allow the project analysts to see patterns based on time or under different scenarios or assumptions. Visualization is considered to be a very effective means of developing a deeper understanding of performance issues.

It should be noted that, in some cases, a project analyst might require additional data to make informed insights. This might require additional work to diagnose the cause of certain problems that the project is experiencing. This additional work might require digging deeper into existing information and data or collecting additional quantitative and qualitative data.

The final step for the project analyst is to take the relevant and specific insights and use them to make meaningful recommendations to the project team that will improve project results. These recommendations will have taken project insights and formulated actions that can be used to make adjustments to the project implementation design. In our experience, the project team will need to take into consideration the cost of making changes. In most instances, the additional cost will be either minimal or non-existent. In other cases, it might be significant and the project team will want to make sure the benefits outweigh the costs. In situations where the actual outcome is in question, it would be prudent to implement the changes in a phased approach to make sure all assumptions around the insights are correct.

### The Performance Management Team and Organizational Culture

As with any professional team, there need to be well-qualified people in key positions. The information system needs to be managed by a person with experience in data entry and data management. The data analyst will require data management skills but will also have a versatile skill set that includes experience with databases and data analysis tools. Quantitative statistical techniques will have often been learned through formal education training as part of a degree in mathematics or statistics. Other team members will have experience and expertise in qualitative and quantitative data collection.

In our experience, the most challenging part of implementing a performance management system is to transform information into insights and then take clear action by making adjustments to the project activities. Often, the problem is that there is not an adequate performance culture to support this work. Many organizations have become masters at solving technical problems within their area of expertise, but they still struggle to be a learning organization that is focused on performance. Making changes is difficult, often due to senior leadership priorities and beliefs.

It can be very easy for an organization to fool themselves about their effectiveness. Some assume that raising more money automatically translates to greater impact. These are often revenue-first organizations that have placed much of their organizational self-worth on hitting revenue targets. Some of these larger organizations may have set up a performance management system, but the organizational culture will often deteriorate performance. An example, a large International Non-Governmental Organization (INGO) realized the need for capacity development of key project partners to ensure sustainability. After successful implementation, the leadership insisted that the project team revert to direct implementation as the capacity development initiatives were too slow and income targets were being affected.

In our experience, a high-performance culture can be built within a project team, but it can be quickly eroded if this same culture is not throughout the organization. An organization culture is a set of values, beliefs, and behaviors. We have seen INGOs that emphasize strong leadership, but are unable to make meaningful difference. In part, this is often because there is not a strong alignment between high-performance and their values, beliefs, and behaviors. Of course, everyone wants high-performance, but the culture will dictate how possible this will be within the organization. The example above provides an understanding of how organizational culture can undermine the best-designed projects if the leadership is not committed to changing the organizational values, beliefs and behaviors.

Most high-performance culture organizations will make sure that employees are able to access tools and information that helps them make informed project management decisions. This whole concept of continuous learning is critical for employees as well as at the project level.

High-performing INGOs are focused on outcome results. This is characterized, for example, by the professional conversations during meetings and even the content of the annual report. Unlike the organization that mentions the 500 boreholes that have been drilled, the high-performance INGO will be talking about the learning that led them to implement an innovative, evidence-based initiative to further reduce water-borne diseases in children under five years of age.

## Project Investment Appraisal and Conditional Contracts

In this section of the chapter, we are focused on specific measurement methods that are often required in impact investing during the project investment appraisal and then when structuring the measurement design for results-based financing instruments.

Within the impact investing industry there is an increasing use of monetization methods for investment appraisals. Cost-benefit Analysis (CBA) uses monetary values for both market and nonmarket impacts. This impact measurement has been used extensively within governments and the private sector. In addition to CBA, Cost-Effectiveness Analysis (CEA) and Social Return on Investment (SROI) are also used in appraising impact investments. These will be discussed later in this section.

For some impact investments, the attribution of development results is important because the payment is conditional on achieving a predefined level of performance. As such, the measurement method must be able to provide confidence to the investor that the project is responsible for the improved results. Social Impact Bonds (SIB) and Development Impact Bonds (DIB) are classic examples of when a randomized selection method or a quasi-experimental method would be used to validate the results.

Impact bonds are part of the family of results-based financing (RBF) contracts. RBF is also referred to as Payment by Results (PBR). Investor funding provides the working capital for the project. The service provider is working on a conditional contract where payment is based on the results achieved. There is an outcome payer (government, foreign government donor, foundation, other) who pays a predetermined amount based on the results achieved once validated by an independent body. The investor is only repaid once the outcome is successfully achieved and it triggers payment from the outcome payer. If the project does not achieve the agreed-upon results, the investor either does not receive a repayment or it is done on a sliding scale as detailed in the conditional contract.

The difference between a SIB and a DIB is who the outcome payer is for the conditional contract. For an SIB, the government; whereas, for a DIB it is a third party, such as a government donor or foundation.

The Impact Measurement diagram, from earlier in this chapter, shows that causal evaluations can be sub-divided into two further categories: experimental and quasi-experimental. A causal evaluation will include a measurement of the outcome changes but can also provide analysis of how an intervention produced these changes. An experimental evaluation involves comparing the intervention group to a control or comparison group, that uses a randomized selection method. This type of impact evaluation methodology is referred to as a randomized control trial (RCT) and is considered the 'gold standard' of evaluations. A quasi-experimental evaluation does not use randomization. Still, quasi-experimental methodologies can also demonstrate causality between an intervention and an outcome. This will be explained later in the chapter.

An impact evaluation is intended to answer cause-and-effect or impact questions. This differs from other evaluations which might be designed to answer other types of questions. The theory of change lays out the project's understanding of how outcomes will be achieved. This proposed causal relationship must be understood and examined so as to further improve outcomes that are directly attributable to the project. Table 12.3 provides examples of measurement methods for investment appraisals and conditional contracts.

Later in this chapter, we will be discussing different methodologies (experimental, quasi-experimental) that can be used to determine a program's impact (causal effect) on outcomes.

*Table 12.3* Impact measurement methods for investment appraisals and conditional contracts focus on evaluating the social and environmental implications of investments. These methods assess the broader impact of projects or businesses beyond financial returns, considering factors like sustainability, social responsibility, and community impact. By incorporating impact measurement into evaluation processes, investors and businesses can make more informed decisions aligned with their values and long-term goals

**MEASUREMENT METHOD FOR INVESTMENT APPRAISAL AND CONDITIONAL CONTRACTS**

| Situation | Impact Measurement | Characteristics |
|---|---|---|
| Project Investment Appraisal | Cost-Benefit Analysis (CBA) Cost-Effectiveness Analysis (CEA) Social Return on Investment (SROI) | Monetization technique Monetization technique Monetization technique |
| Conditional Contract | Experimental <br> • Randomized Selection Methods <br><br> Quasi-Experimental Methods <br> • Regression Discontinuity Design <br> • Difference-in-Differences | Use of treatment and control group Estimate counterfactual (no baseline) Estimate counterfactual (require baseline) |

The one common feature among all these methodologies is identifying a comparison group, which allows researchers to compare the outcomes of the intervention with the outcomes that would have occurred had the intervention not taken place. It is obviously impossible for a researcher to observe the same group simultaneously in a scenario where they are receiving and not receiving the project intervention. To make a credible comparison, the comparison group must have the same characteristics as the group receiving the intervention (treatment group). The only difference between the comparison and treatment group is that the comparison group does not immediately benefit from the project intervention. Box 12.3 describes the need for a counterfactual analysis for when attribution is important to project stakeholders.

---

**BOX 12.3   THE COUNTERFACTUAL AND ATTRIBUTION**

A counterfactual analysis allows evaluators to attribute cause and effect between interventions and outcomes. A 'counterfactual' measures what would have happened to targeted groups if the intervention did not take place – Impact is measured by comparing counterfactual outcome to the treatment group.

---

### Casual Methods

A randomized selection method simply means that the program participants are equally selected using a lottery from a large eligible population. When this is done, a robust estimate of the counterfactual can be determined. Every eligible person must have an equal chance of being selected for the program. The selection method is random and does not use any arbitrary or subjective criteria. The proper use of randomized selection ensures that the treatment and comparison groups are statistically equivalent—i.e., that they have the same characteristics. Since the two groups are identical, any differences in outcomes between the two groups can be explained only by the program interventions.

## Experimental Method

As discussed above, randomized controlled trials (RCTs) are the most rigorous way to determine the causal relationship between an intervention and outcome. A well-administered RCT can reduce bias through randomization. Nevertheless, an RCT is not the only means or necessarily the best evaluation method for impact investing, especially because of the cost and complexity of implementation. Observational results are often preferred when a program is only partially funded through an impact investment. In such cases, the risk of a biased estimate does not justify the expense of an RCT or other causal method.

## Quasi-Experimental Methods

A quasi-experimental method evaluates interventions but without the use of randomization. They can work in a similar manner to randomized trials in that they can show causality between a program intervention and the outcome. A couple of quasi-experimental methods that are often used in impact investing include regression discontinuity design (RDD) and difference-in-differences (DD). The following is an overview of these two quasi-experimental methodologies.

**Regression Discontinuity Design** can be used with social programs when there is a continuous eligibility index. For instance, a poverty program may be targeted at poor households as defined by their income level, with a cut-off point to determine who can participate. Although we use a poverty index, in this example, other evaluations might have a cut-off using test scores, age, or other.

Using our example of a poverty index, the program can measure the difference in an outcome between households that are near the eligibility cut-off. The households that were not eligible but were close to the cut-off would constitute the comparison group, allowing for an estimate of the counterfactual outcome.

**Difference-in-Differences** unlike the RDD method, which has estimates of the counterfactual based on explicit program rules, that are well understood by the evaluator, the difference-in-differences (DD) method has less clear program assignment rules. The DD and other similar methods, such as matching methods, are unique in that they can evaluate the impact in situations where RCT and RDD are not feasible.

Another distinctive feature of DD is that it requires the existence of baseline data. The DD method compares the changes in outcomes over a period of time for both a group that is part of the program (treatment group) and a group that is not receiving any program interventions (comparison group). The before-and-after differences are observational and by themselves cannot provide a causal impact, as there can be other contributing factors. However, if the before-and-after changes in an outcome are measured for both the treatment and comparison groups, then a DD method can evaluate the program's impact.

The initial step is to calculate the before-and-after outcome difference for the program or treatment group. This difference will control for factors that are constant within the treatment group, since the group is being compared to itself. These calculations by themselves are very limited as external factors are at play, but we can overcome this hurdle if we also measure the before-and-after change in the comparison group and make sure that all other factors are similar to those of the treatment group.

If we do the same calculation for the comparison group and subtract it from the change for the treatment group, we will in essence have eliminated the bias that is inherent in comparing before-and-after data. Stated differently, the DD method combines the 'before-and-after' calculations for the treatment group and the 'before-and-after' calculations for the comparison group to achieve a better estimate of the counterfactual. This estimated counterfactual is the change in outcomes for the comparison group. In summary, DD requires researchers to measure outcomes in the treatment group (part of the program) and the comparison group (not part of the program) both before and after the program.

In concluding this section on quasi-experimental methods, it is worthwhile to emphasize, once again, that when evaluation methods are being considered for impact investing it is important to understand the trade-offs of the different evaluation methods.

### Monetization Methods and the Future of Impact Investing Appraisals

#### Monetization

Governments and the private sector use cost-benefit analysis (CBA) to make investment decisions on highways, bridges, and social programs. Although NGOs and especially INGOs have often been leaders in adopting measurement approaches, CBA has not been commonly used. The Global Impact Investing Network (GIIN) and other networks have been instrumental in facilitating a dialogue on the use of monetization methods for impact investing. For some impact investors, the use of SROI has become popular, in part, because of there being more rigor and addressing their concerns on what should be included in an investment appraisal.

Of the different monetization approaches, CBA has increasingly become a subject for debate. While most NGOs are not using CBA, many institutional investors still expect it to be used in investment appraisals, maintaining that it exhibits professionalism and a well-accepted approach. Those in the social sector are often opposed, stating that such economic frameworks are unreliable and do not meet the requirements for evaluating social programs.

In our experience, there is truth in both arguments, but one of the more serious obstacles has been an unwillingness or inability to pay for a project investment appraisal using CBA. The confusion and ongoing discussion on CBA within the impact investing industry is partially to blame, but the more likely reason is that no one wants to finance the appraisal or due diligence in the social sector. At the moment, there is a growing impact investing sector that requires that these investments be appraised, and there is no consensus on how this should be done.

During the late 1980s, many institutional donors were introducing results-based management (RBM), and during the past 40 years, INGOs and their associated networks have done remarkable work in mainstreaming this accountability framework within programs. Non-profits and particularly INGOs have an important role in testing and selecting the most appropriate tools and frameworks for impact measurement in the impact investing sector.

There is a general acknowledgement that the use of economic frameworks can be a challenge for social enterprises, non-profits, and others who are entering the impact investing market. Still, this is not in itself a reason to eschew such impact evaluation frameworks. What is apparent is the need to adapt CBA and other similar appraisal methods for the needs of impact investing.

It seems reasonable that these economic frameworks should be appropriately adapted for the social sector. Frameworks that have been used successfully in infrastructure projects and policy analysis are not necessarily ready to be taken off the shelf and applied to social impact investing. Key areas of focus need to be on the use of monetization of key metrics. The framework adaptations need to provide increased confidence in the analytical conclusions. This might mean that not all impacts should be monetized. The tool must serve the needs of the various stakeholders—investors, service providers, and the community. Overall, the use of an economic tool must maintain its primary purpose—namely, making decisions on what projects should be financed or declined.

The following section provides an overview of the three monetization methods highlighted:

## COST-BENEFIT ANALYSIS (CBA)

The underlying purpose of CBA is to allow decision makers to stop bad projects or bad policies, and to prevent good projects from not being implemented. Many people have opinions and anecdotal evidence as to what is a good or bad project, but CBA is meant to eliminate speculation and provide evidence on what projects should be advanced or prioritized.

A CBA analyst will calculate the total benefits of a project and then subtract the associated project costs to determine the net benefits or costs. The project costs and benefits are monetized, including those that are intangible. For instance, we are working with a project partner on a homelessness project. As with every project there are operational costs, as well as benefits that are directly related to the project. The expected direct benefits will be a reduction of homelessness because of the project activities, but it might also have other less tangible benefits that can be monetized, such as a decrease in crime and healthcare expense. A CBA that results in more benefits than costs will be approved as an investment. This definition is simplified as the major steps in doing a CBA have been largely discussed in earlier chapters.

## COST-EFFECTIVENESS ANALYSIS (CEA)

CEA is considered a quantitative impact evaluation approach and was discussed briefly earlier in this chapter. CEA is also an economic analysis framework. It compares the benefits and costs of projects in relative terms. CEA is very useful in resource allocation decisions. Using a healthcare example, the economic evaluation of a healthcare program compares the resources consumed in monetary values with the health benefits or project outcomes that are not expressed in monetary terms, but in physical units such as life expectancy. CEA is very helpful in comparing alternative programs, the effects of which are measured in the same physical units.

With continual technology improvements, CEA analysis often shows that new interventions have, in many instances, much improved outcomes but that they also come with extra costs. In such circumstances, a cost-effectiveness cut-off level is required. If a new intervention improves outcomes and benefits and actually lowers costs at the same time, it is referred to as a dominant strategy.

## SOCIAL RETURN ON INVESTMENT (SROI)

SROI is a monetization technique increasingly used by investors, philanthropists, foundations, and non-profits. Although there are common features between SROI and the return on investment (ROI) used in traditional business applications, the social component has implications for what is considered in the analysis. As with CBA (see Chapter 11), a stakeholder distributional analysis is done to see whether the benefits of the project will actually go to the targeted groups.

SROI is meant to evaluate the returns on a social investment. It monetizes the social benefits and costs relative to the financial costs. The SROI is then calculated by dividing the social impact of the project by the amount invested. The larger the ROI, the bigger the social benefits for the investment dollar. The SROI techniques are similar to CBA in that it can use similar levels of rigor. CBA tends to hold to a high level of rigor (which is attractive to some investors); whereas SROI can adapt more easily to different scenarios requiring various levels of rigor while maintaining integrity in its approach.

## Annex to Chapter 12

Over the years, we have enjoyed working with many well-recognized people and organizations who have been pioneers in impact investing. One of these organizations is Instiglio who we have had the pleasure of traveling together, working on different initiatives, and presenting a conferences. We have used a lot of the learning from our Instiglio colleagues and particularly in the structuring of well-designed incentives. Although the examples provided are from our projects, the learning was from spending time and working closely with these well-respected colleagues. In this Annex we provide additional information on incentives and measurement that were discussed earlier in the chapter, and we use an example from our work in housing veterans. There are a couple of common question that we are often asked with regards to incentives and then on the frequency of payments and the need for measurement with respect to results-based financing contracts.

### *Incentives*

During the feasibility study phase, the intermediary will work with the project stakeholders to determine the best financing instrument to use to achieve the intended results. Once the financing instrument has been selected, the intermediary will work with stakeholder to structure appropriate incentivizes that will contribute towards maximizing the net social benefits. These incentives will need to be taken into consideration when doing impact measurement.

The project financial modeling and the risk analysis will also need to take into consideration the types of incentives that are being utilized. In Figure 12.1 there are several incentive scenarios each of which will influence the measurement methodology and analysis.

The following table highlights several payment incentives that can be used to improve performance using results-based financing.

### *Payment Timing and Measurement*

Many projects will have payments aligned with the frequency of the measurement of payment metrics. Minimally, measurement takes place at the end of the project, but to a large extent this can be determined by the investment team during the detailed design phase.

During the detailed design phase, the investment team will include a payment schedule that will have taken into consideration the pros and cons of having more frequent payments. The following are the main considerations given by the investment team while structuring the payment schedule and, of course, when updating the financial model and cash flow projections.

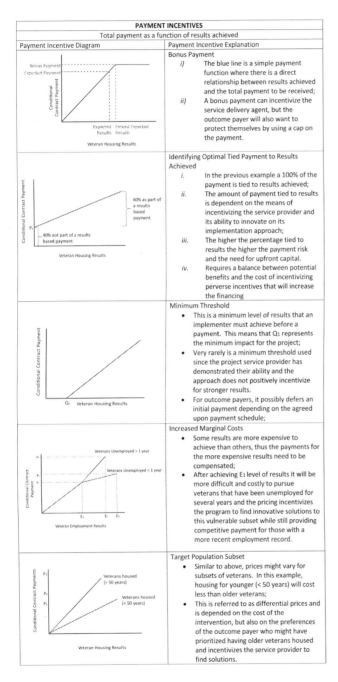

| PAYMENT INCENTIVES | |
|---|---|
| Total payment as a function of results achieved | |
| Payment Incentive Diagram | Payment Incentive Explanation |
|  | **Bonus Payment**<br>i) The blue line is a simple payment function where there is a direct relationship between results achieved and the total payment to be received;<br>ii) A bonus payment can incentivize the service delivery agent, but the outcome payer will also want to protect themselves by using a cap on the payment. |
|  | **Identifying Optimal Tied Payment to Results Achieved**<br>i. In the previous example a 100% of the payment is tied to results achieved;<br>ii. The amount of payment tied to results is dependent on the means of incentivizing the service provider and its ability to innovate on its implementation approach;<br>iii. The higher the percentage tied to results the higher the payment risk and the need for upfront capital.<br>iv. Requires a balance between potential benefits and the cost of incentivizing perverse incentives that will increase the financing |
|  | **Minimum Threshold**<br>• This is a minimum level of results that an implementer must achieve before a payment. This means that $Q_1$ represents the minimum impact for the project;<br>• Very rarely is a minimum threshold used since the project service provider has demonstrated their ability and the approach does not positively incentivize for stronger results.<br>• For outcome payers, it possibly defers an initial payment depending on the agreed upon payment schedule; |
|  | **Increased Marginal Costs**<br>• Some results are more expensive to achieve than others, thus the payments for the more expensive results need to be compensated;<br>• After achieving $E_1$ level of results it will be more difficult and costly to pursue veterans that have been unemployed for several years and the pricing incentivizes the program to find innovative solutions to this vulnerable subset while still providing competitive payment for those with a more recent employment record. |
|  | **Target Population Subset**<br>• Similar to above, prices might vary for subsets of veterans. In this example, housing for younger (< 50 years) will cost less than older veterans;<br>• This is referred to as differential prices and is depended on the cost of the intervention, but also on the preferences of the outcome payer who might have prioritized having older veterans housed and incentivizes the service provider to find solutions. |

*Figure 12.1* In impact investing, incentives play a pivotal role in maximizing the net social benefits of a project by encouraging service providers to make the most of every dollar invested. Through well-designed incentive structures, investors are motivated to allocate resources towards initiatives that generate positive social and environmental impacts. By aligning financial incentives with social objectives, impact investing can effectively drive positive change while ensuring sustainable financial returns for investors.

I. **Pros—more frequent payments and measurement**
   i. Reduce Financing Costs—with more frequent payments the same money can be reinvested and this will lower the cost of financing the project
   ii. Improved Outcomes—in the absence of a performance management system, there will likely be improved learning that will lead to improved outcomes
II. **Cons—more frequent payments and measurement**
   i. Transactional and Measurement Costs—increased costs associated with more frequent payment and measurement (collection of data and its analysis)
   ii. Agreement among Actors—the ideal payment schedule might not benefit all actors—service providers possibly benefit from reduced financing costs outcome payer has increased administrative challenges

When structuring the payment schedule consideration should be given to the overall impact of the project. If more frequent payments and measurement are expected to provide substantial insights into improving development outcomes then these benefits need to be weighed against the transactional and measurement costs.

## Note

1 We gratefully acknowledge Instiglio's substantial influence on the development of the performance management system. Terry Gray had the pleasure of working closely with several members of Instiglio and learning from their experiences. We deeply appreciate the valuable insights shared during those opportunities for collaboration. Instiglio, with its commitment to partnering with governments and organizations to achieve impactful social outcomes, exemplifies the transformative power of the performance management system.

# Chapter 13

# Creating A Nurturing I3 Ecosystem

Impact investing has been embraced by institutions across the public, private, and non-profit sectors, but the environment has not been very nurturing. This is one of the many reasons why I2, as practiced up to this point, has underperformed and presents a low ceiling for future potential. If I3 is to achieve a far greater influence on the finance sector and accomplish the transformational effects we desire for it, stakeholders in the I3 ecosystem must become true partners and collaborate to make I3 the best it can be. To accomplish that goal, I3 stakeholders must be convinced that they have better prospects for achieving their own personal and/or organizational missions and goals by using the I3 approach than through whatever other approaches they are employing now.

It is easy to see why impact investing caught on so quickly. It didn't take long for institutions in the I2 ecosystem to endorse the idea and incorporate it into their strategies and operations and, more importantly, into their messaging. But too often, I2 has become simply the packaging that these organizations use to advance programs, funding, and investments they were already providing. It is not uncommon to hear impact investing enthusiasts say that someday all investments should be impact investments. If they mean that we should adopt the I3 approach for all investments, we support that! But usually, this comment reflects a failure to grasp how radically different investing becomes when you are fully committed to achieving social benefits.

It didn't take long for investors to recognize the value of branding investments as 'impact investing'. I2 has proven to be a wonderfully reputation-enhancing brand. It is difficult to complain about financing projects that achieve important social goals and make some money as well. That sounds like an easy win-win. But most of the institutions supporting the I2 approach have taken an interest in its integrity and authenticity only because it helps them attract new investments and investors. This view may sound cynical, but it is grounded in extensive experience.

As we have mentioned before, by all accounts, Green Bonds—where the funds are to be used for an environmental or climate change initiative—continue to attract a premium from investors of a few basis points and often are oversubscribed, even when there is no clear evidence that the investments made by such Green Bonds are different from those financed by other financial instruments. These observations are not intended as a criticism of the current I2 ecosystem, but as a recognition that for most organizations, I2 is only a convenient means to achieve their own ends. If another approach came along that appears to help these organizations even more, they would quickly abandon their fealty to I2 and switch to the new financial instrument.

DOI: 10.4324/9781003276920-14

At the same time, the appetite for impact investments that investors have demonstrated is a very encouraging sign for the I3 approach. It means that investors are seeking out investments that have a reputation as being impactful. And even though the impact investment product does not have to be of such high assurance regarding its social impacts to draw investor interest, it reveals a market opportunity for the I3 approach to distinguish itself in the market and raise awareness of investors. There is no doubt that many investors have limits on how meaningful or reliable the impacts of their 'impact investments' need to be. But this 'market gap' creates an opportunity for I3s to compete with I2s based on their genuineness and the delivery of Holy Grail of impact investing. That also means that the I3 approach could have a bright future if institutions participating in the impact investing ecosystem decide that it is preferable to I2.

The future success of I3 relies on a strong ecosystem whose participants understand the conditions that help make I3s successful and provide support for a new enabling I3 ecosystem. That will be no easy task. We have seen that many participants in the I2 ecosystem are big on talking the talk but less engaged in knowing if they are walking the walk. Accordingly, I3 must make the case that successfully adopting this approach will require significant changes in how people do business. A nurturing I3 ecosystem will not appear automatically. Just as we propose I3s as a new way to think about and make truly impactful investments, institutions in the I3 ecosystem will need to think through their own interest in I3 and modify many of their tenets, practices, and expectations to engage effectively.

The conceptualization of what we mean by an 'ecosystem' in the I3 context was developed for the BWLC project with Ford Motor Co. and is shown is Figure 13.1. The ecosystem for the BWLC project is not as expansive as we describe below for the I3 Approach, but it illustrates the central importance of the project ecosystem—comprised of governments, NGOs, private investors, and social entrepreneurs—in achieving the outcomes of the project.

I3 cannot thrive unless it is nestled within a welcoming ecosystem whose stakeholders are willing to make efforts to ensure its success. If stakeholders believe that I3s can help their organizations succeed, they will have a built-in incentive to support the approach. We will now discuss how several stakeholder groups can change their manner of engagement to better nurture I3 investments.

## Government Agencies

Government agencies are typically restricted (by authorizing legislation, executive decisions, and/or funding limits) regarding the types of goods and services they provide and the terms under which those services are provided. Furthermore, bureaucracies organized in the conventional public management paradigm are intentionally designed to be accountable through hierarchical layers. For this reason, innovative approaches, out-of-the-box thinking, and 'seeing around corners'—all hallmarks of I3—are not incentivized or are even discouraged. But that doesn't mean government agencies cannot play an important role in the I3 ecosystem.

First, government agencies can help to identify the gaps that their programs and services are not addressing. They may be short on funds or face limits on what they are authorized to do, or there may be a difference of opinion about the nature of the problem or the best

# THE ECOSYSTEM DEVELOPS ALONG WITH THE PROJECT

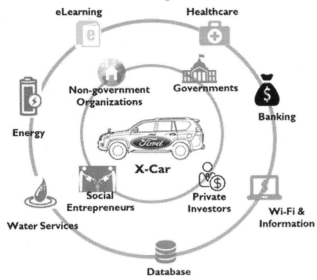

*Figure 13.1* Example of a potential I3 ecosystem.

way to organize and fund a solution. Often, government agencies have employees who have worked on an issue for many years and know what has been tried in the past. They can see like everyone else that the current efforts may not be effective, and although they are powerless to reform their own agency's approach, they know where the gaps are in government programs and where action is needed.

Government agencies may also be able to provide very specific support and resources, even if that does not address the entire need. For example, in Trinidad, some farms lack access to good roads. We learned in our discussions that a loan program for agriculture could include financing for road improvements and expansions, as long as the money was applied to public lands. The road access problem involved both public and private land, but at least the public piece of the puzzle was resolved.

Government involvement in I3s, even if on a limited scale, can demonstrate a program's importance. In Trinidad, in addition to improving farmers' access to roads, government agencies connected with our C3 project in other ways that addressed their policy issues as well: pest control on cocoa farms, ecotourism linked to chocolate (or 'choco-tourism'), the exporting of beans and chocolate products, and carbon reduction. By shaping our C3 model to address the issues of interest to government agencies, we became a vehicle promoting their efforts and in return gained access to expertise (and potentially funding support) for activities that strengthened the overall project. Moreover, the partnership with government agencies provided some assurance to other stakeholders that public interests and policies would be given consideration in the project.

## Foundations

Public foundations such as the Rockefeller Foundation have been strong champions of impact investing. One of their preferred strategies has been to introduce concessionary financing into potential deals. The idea is to shift some risk onto the foundations, who are in a position to have more patient capital, and thus make the project more attractive to impact investors.

'Buying down' risk is a critical role for public foundations. The proponents of catalytic capital want to lower the risks associated with potential impact investments, thereby increasing the prospects for achieving project financial returns. But what I3s need is support for buying down the risks associated with providing social impacts that push the boundaries of comfort as to what is doable.

One way to do this is to focus on bundling social benefits, but that can raise the risks of a project as it requires collaboration among partners and stakeholders. And it introduces greater uncertainty because of its innovative nature. Recall that I3 projects start with developing an I3 solution. We identify the needs in underserved communities; working with local stakeholders, we introduce innovations designed to provide those needed services; and then we use a value creation model to identify ways to create a business value and financial returns sufficient to attract impact investors.

Building a strong theory of change for I3 projects requires more resources than conventional impact investing. Foundations could be a powerful driver of I3s by providing technical assistance to people constructing I3 projects, particularly in underserved communities. Risk reduction is needed in the design and development of social impacts in communities with otherwise poor prospects—the high-hanging fruit. We want foundations to commit to participating in the reversal of misfortune.

Foundations could support the establishment of I3 Centers of Excellence (COEs) where institutions and individuals could obtain training on I3 tools and techniques. They could also become repositories of I3 project models that could be studied and made available to the public. Past I3 project models could be replicated and adapted in other communities. This would reduce the cost of project development and help to disseminate knowledge of how to design I3s. The I3 COEs could also study past projects, document their successes and shortcomings, and identify alternative approaches to design, financing, and operation that would provide a roadmap for future I3s.

## Development Finance Institutions

This group of stakeholders has the mission of making investments in communities of need so as to stimulate economic growth. They also have funds that can be used for technical assistance, which can make a project more attractive to impact investors.

I3s are compatible with development finance institutions' (DFIs) *inclusive* development as it is built around stakeholders' priorities and preferences. Supporting the development of models that include new or previously unfunded projects and benefits takes time, expertise, and engagement to assess what is possible and to develop the investment opportunity and implement the plan. But these do not need to be one-time undertakings; they can be funded as replicable models.

DFIs could harness the advantages that come from using the I3 approach to support I3 projects that are linked to their development goals and mission. They could provide grants for organizations to develop I3s with specific and combined social impacts that are aligned with the DFI's mission, such as climate change mitigation and adaptation, gender-sensitive activities, or re-aligning value chains. It must be anticipated that efforts to develop I3 projects with these social outcomes and reasonable financial returns may not always succeed. People may not know how to develop an impact investment solution that meets the specifications set out by a DFI. But these efforts will add to the overall knowledge of where I3s can make a significant contribution and where they cannot.

## Corporate Foundations and CSR Programs

The level of funding that corporations direct to projects creating positive benefits for their stakeholders is enormous. One report estimates that Fortune Global firms spend around $20 billion a year on CSR activities (Briscese 2021). Common activities include reducing carbon footprint, engaging in charity work, purchasing fair-trade products, investing in environmentally conscious businesses, becoming involved in volunteer work, improving labor policies, and supporting human rights (Victoria University 2023).

Corporations could play a major role in promoting I3 projects by transitioning away from their current funding for CSR programs and corporate foundation gifts and toward financing such activities by the I3 approach. One enduring challenge in impact investing is to develop high-quality projects, but corporations are funding thousands of such projects each year. And the design and operations are closely monitored by the corporation to ensure that the funding is accomplishing the anticipated outcomes. In addition to having the capacity to develop new I3 projects from scratch, corporate CSR functions offer an invaluable inventory of projects that are creating positive social benefits and that could be converted into I3 projects.

In essence, many CSR projects have already developed the core of an impact investment solution, because they are funding innovative approaches to addressing a problem identified as a priority in a local community. In our experience, many of these CSR programs are of high quality—impactful, well-managed, and responsive to local conditions. One example is Unilever's Water fir All is Everyone's Business, described in Box 13.1.

---

### BOX 13.1   CSR PROGRAM BY UNILEVER

*Why Water is All of Our Business*

Water is critical to both mitigating and adapting to the effects of climate change, and access to safe water sources is essential to reduce the spread of disease and provide opportunities for women and girls. It's also critical for businesses like ours, from helping our crops to grow and being a vital ingredient in our foods and manufacturing to enabling people to use our products.

To this end, Unilever committed to the following by 2030:

- To make 100% of its product formulations biodegradable
- To implement water stewardship programs around 100 Unilever manufacturing sites in water-stressed locations
- To empower farmers and smallholders to protect and regenerate farm environments, including introducing a pioneering regenerative agriculture (Unilever 2023) code for all suppliers

- To take action through Unilever brands, such as Lifebuoy and Domestos, to improve health and well-being and advance equity and inclusion (including hand hygiene and sanitation), to reach 1 billion people per year
- To work with the 2030 Water Resources Group (WRG) to contribute to transformative change and build water management resilience in key water-stressed countries

To achieve these goals collaboration and innovation are critical.

With those projects in place, I3 tools and techniques can be used to identify revenue streams that could help to provide a reasonable return to the impact investor(s). The advantages of funding CSR programs through I3 financing is obvious. I3 financing provides a more stable source of funding. Corporate funding levels for CSR projects are particularly vulnerable during economic recessions. I3 financing could enable corporations to reduce their expenditures in CSR, or (preferably) they could continue to develop partnerships and innovative CSR programs, knowing that at some future point impact investors would take over the project funding and the corporation could move on to develop new projects. Conceivably, some corporations might decide to create their own impact investment fund to invest in the I3 projects they helped to develop.

Adopting an I3 approach to funding corporate CSR activities is consistent with recent industry trends in what is called 'New Corporate Philanthropy'. The idea is that corporations will give gifts and grants to support stakeholders' interests and strengthen communities, and that these efforts are of benefit to the giver as well as to the receiver. The notion that corporate philanthropy should be leveraged to benefit the corporation is consistent with the I3 approach of leveraging resources to produce both social benefits and business value. In the Unilever CSR example, the company's CSR funding for greater access to clean water is seeking a balance between supporting an important SDG and efforts to grow and expand Unilever's own markets.

We understand that corporations might resist this idea. Swapping out their CSR funding for impact investments could make them feel they have lost their connection with the project, but they could finance or co-finance it and still maintain a role in technical assistance. The branding of their role in the project could be altered, but the reputational value they acquire need not be diminished.

Corporations might have to respond to criticisms, in policy, advocacy, academic, or other circles, about actually making money from what is considered CSR. But if it meant greater funding stability, long-term support that makes a project's financial situation recession-proof, leveraging corporate CSR funds to expand impact, and reaching high-hanging fruit, they could make a strong case that both beneficiaries and the corporation are gaining by applying the I3 approach.

## IDAHOs

International Development and Humanitarian Organizations (IDAHOs) are often the lead organizations in efforts to bring greater investments to underserved communities but this arrangement presents a paradox that we have witnessed and contended with firsthand. The funding from governments, corporations, and foundations to advance development around the world is managed predominantly by large global not-for-profit entities. Box 13.2 lists the top 5 IDAHOs

---

**BOX 13.2   FIVE LARGEST GLOBAL IDAHOS**

#1. Save the Children
  Established in: 1919
  Global presence: 120 countries
#2. Oxfam International
  Established in: 1942
  Global presence: 90+ countries
#3. Doctors without Borders
  Established in: 1971
  Global presence: 70+ countries
#4. BRAC
  Established in: 1972
  Global presence: 11 countries
#5. World Vision
  Established in: 1950
  Global presence: 100+ countries
  https://www.humanrightscareers.com/issues/biggest-ngos-in-the-world/.

---

In our experience, IDAHOs embody a paradox that poses a significant difficulty to the I3 approach. In many ways, they promote and implement the cutting edge of innovations when designing and delivering desperately needed goods and services.

The most significant effort underway to have impact investors support the work of IDAHOs has been in the use of development impact bonds. Very few of the larger IDAHOs have considered being involved with a DIB. In our experience, much of the reason has been the organizational culture and the adaptive challenges that come from decades of using marketing and other fundraising techniques. There is a crisis in leadership in many IDAHOs as the challenges on becoming involved in impact investing can only be addressed through a change in belief and priorities. For organizations that have built large marketing departments it is going to involve courageous leadership to forge new revenue streams even when they show a much stronger likelihood of substantially improving development impact.

For those IDAHOs that have shifted from solely working with donors to becoming involved in impact investing, there has been a strategy that enables the organization to fully embrace the impact investing ecosystem. Most of these organizations have been small and medium in size, and it has required them to strengthen their programming team, so that an adopted evidence-based approach creates an environment for dynamic decision-making that leads to improved outcomes.

Some of the larger IDAHOs have initiated impact investment funds to raise investor capital for loans and equity investments for social enterprises. This work with social entrepreneurs and enterprises should be supported but it is not innovative in that it is a natural extension of work many organizations have been doing for the past several decades with microenterprises, and more recently with small and growing businesses.

Some IDAHOs can be very rigid and inflexible in their own operations. Sometimes, they exhibit the 'not invented here' problem. If a new approach is adopted by the IDAHO, they can become its strongest advocate, but when they are offered a new way to deliver services—such as the I3 approach—there is often limited enthusiasm.

Some years ago, The Coca-Cola Company developed the idea of EkoCenter Kiosks (note the use of Coke spelled backwards) as described in Box 13.3.

---

**BOX 13.3   EKOCENTER**

To help provide communities in need with access to safe drinking water and other basic necessities, The Coca-Cola company, together with DEKA Research and Development Corp have launched 'EKOCENTER'—a modularly designed kiosk, which has been transformed from a 20-foot shipping container—with the 'slingshot' water purification system housed within a community center. The initiative aims to improve the holistic well-being of developing communities around the world, focusing on those within the 'bottom of the pyramid', the largest, poorest socioeconomic group—representing nearly 4 billion people who live on less than $2 USD per day. (Caula 2014)

---

The project was an innovative approach to combining greater access to commerce and public goods in remote locations. It proposed to address numerous SDGs while providing an enterprise model for long-term funding support. We know that one major IDAHO was approached as a partner but declined because the IDAHO leadership was uncomfortable with the commercial affiliation. Many people will undoubtedly sympathize with those sentiments. But the success of I3 is grounded in private investment, taking a firm stand against affiliations with businesses denies millions of disadvantaged communities an opportunity to receive investment and solve problems. And there just aren't enough public and foundation funds available.

I3 success will require IDAHOs to embrace private-sector investments and learn how to manage the use and application of those funds so as to fulfill public-sector values and accountability, while fully respecting the local community's priorities and preferences. IDAHOs will also have to respect the fact that private-sector funds will be managed with private-sector values and interests. This requires full participation in collaborations across many sectors and embracing governance networks as the form of global governance in the future.

IDAHOs can be powerful I3 partners with their knowledge of best development practices and community engagements that build trust. Adopting the I3 approach could reduce the constant demand for fundraising from public foundations, family funds, generous individuals, and government grants by making funding available from impact investors

## Universities

'There is no reason that someone can't make the world a better place and make money at the same time'. We have emphasized this point consistently in our teaching, our research and our work. It is the fulcrum on which our development of the I3 approach rests. But in our experience, a serious knowledge gap remains among students interested in development and making a social impact through the efforts of the private sector and impact investments.

We know that university programs offering degrees and courses on impact investing have expanded recently. Some are more grounded in traditional finance while others are more rooted in inclusive development. Two good examples are the Oxford MSc in Sustainability, Enterprise and the Environment and the Queen's University Certified Professional Impact Analyst program that is made up of three courses.

But overall, we sense a cultural divide between the business and finance students, on the one hand, and the development students on the other hand. Or more precisely, there is a divide in their biases. Students majoring in business but aspiring to use their business skills to solve problems and create benefits for people can earn a degree without studying about development, the role of governments or NGOs, issues involving equity, government grants, or multisector collaborations. Similarly, students studying public policy or development may be interested in public-private partnerships but may earn their degree and still know nothing about businesses or corporations, the role of risk in investing decisions, what a discounted cash flow (DCF) means, or the difference between EBIT and EBITDA.

Most importantly, graduates often have limited understanding of the norms of different organizations—private, public, non-profit. They do not grasp why people in those organizations make decisions as they do, what the driving institutional incentives are, how success is conceptualized, measured, and valued, and how employees are valued and rewarded. The clash of cultures is readily evident.

To help bridge these gaps and support a multidisciplinary approach to learning about the I3 approach, we suggest a set of skills students could consider focusing on in their studies in Box 13.4.

---

### BOX 13.4    I3 APPROACH SKILL SET

The following is an indicative list of some core skills required in social impact investing. Social impact investing combines skills from several disciplines.

Personal/sector/organizational values (skills in self-awareness and facilitation)

- Impact investing is value-driven
  - All social investment decisions are driven and sustained by values that will differ between individuals, sectors (private, public, social), and organizations (based on internal culture—beliefs, priorities, obligations, etc.)
  - Values should be aligned between investors, entrepreneurs, and project managers—those initiatives based on common values benefit the most from impact investing

Proper motivation for continual improvement (skills in psychology, economics)

- Combining extrinsic and psychological incentives for improving team performance
  - Extrinsic incentives come from the outside environment
  - Intrinsic incentives are psychological and come from within

- Outcomes are almost always achieved as a result of behavioral change
  - Combination of values and incentives to achieve what needs to be done
  - Evidence-based Theory of Change in knowing what to do to change behavior

Maximizing net social benefits (business analysis and development sector skills)

- Understanding the major components of the financial and economic investment appraisal
  - Feasibility study (cash flow, investment criteria, uncertainty, and risk)
  - Detailed design—structuring financing, governance, legal)
- Understanding the causal relationships and design to the desired social impact
  - Theory of Change based on evidence and a learning hypothesis (use of impact measurement methods (experimental, quasi-experimental, qualitative/observational, and others) and logic models to better understand how social impacts are created)
  - Integration of key cross-cutting sectors (environment, gender)

Project and business governance structuring (skills in partnering and brokering, policy, human resources, financial, legal)

- Understanding the governance implications of different project partnerships
  - Public-private partnerships for social sector (for example, Build-Operate-Transfer BOT)
  - Reporting relationships—accountability to investors, relationships between the board and executive management, appointment and assessment of the board of directors, board membership criteria)
  - Criteria for the selection of the project team members (inclusiveness, experience, team structure)
- Understanding of financial and data governance
  - Project and organization internal controls, policies, security
  - Systems for collecting and validating information and data
  - Internal and external audit systems

Aligning investment stakeholders (skills for investment instruments and data management systems)

- Understanding the different types of impact investors
  - Equity investing with a focus on high growth potential (venture capitalist VC)
  - Trade-offs between safety, income, and growth
  - Personal debt investing for a passionate cause (angel)
  - Equity investing with a focus on high impact potential (angel and VC)
  - Investment instruments to help further a specific social cause
- Use of an evidence-based approach for dynamic decision-making
  - Data collection
  - Data management
  - Data analysis to identify insights
  - Implementation of insights

We have seen too many times when international affairs students had no interest in learning about business or investing, as well as business students who could care less about NGOs and IDAHOs. In contrast, once they are exposed to the idea of impact investing, their interest in expanding their knowledge across sectors is sparked. Yet most universities find it difficult to provide students with the knowledge they need for their major or degree while also allowing additional coursework in other areas. additional coursework in other areas.

---

**BOX 13.5   COMPASS: IMPACT INVESTING ADVISORY GROUP**

Compass: Impact Investing Advisory Group consists of George Washington University students who serve as advisors to social enterprises and non-profits seeking funding from impact investors. Impact investing is a rapidly growing field in which investors deploy capital investments to secure financial and social returns. A common challenge facing the impact investing space is the gap between investment capital and investment-ready projects. Compass' mission is to advance and maximize social impact through the development of partnerships, collaboration, and accountability and measurement frameworks. The organization will function as an advisory service for projects that were unable to receive government funding and will undergo a capacity and proposal building process in order to attain capital from an impact investor.

---

For I3s to grow, a cadre of experts is needed who not only grasp the approach but also understand and appreciate the government, business, and non-profit sectors. At the George Washington, a student group has been established and is dedicated to learning about impact investing and the I3 approach. The students for teams and work on different impact investment projects at different stages of their development.

The I3 approach is more complex, resource-intensive, and challenging than I2. Accordingly, it requires a stronger ecosystem within which stakeholders can support and contribute to the prospects for a successful investment. But a new I3 ecosystem will also require current I2 stakeholders to alter their expectations as to what I3 projects require for success, and to modify their current practices so that they can contribute powerfully to the future success of the I3 approach.

## References

Briscese, G. (2021, February 24). 'Who really benefits from corporate social responsibility?'. *ProMarket (blog)*. https://www.promarket.org/2021/02/24/corporate-social-responsibility-employees-salary -cost-donations/.

Caula, R. I. (2014, July 29). 'Coca-Cola EKOCENTER: Water purifying shipping container unit'. *designboom*. https://www.designboom.com/architecture/coca-cola-ekocenter-water-purification -shipping-container-10-9-2013/.

'Understanding Corporate Social Responsibility (CSR) | Victoria university online'. (2023, July 26). https://online.vu.edu.au/blog/what-is-corporate-social-responsibility.

Unilever PLC. (2023, September 7). 'Regenerative agriculture and farming practices'. *Unilever*. https:// www.unilever.com/planet-and-society/protect-and-regenerate-nature/regenerating-nature/.

# Index

Printed in the United States
by Baker & Taylor Publisher Services